WESTMAR COLLEGE LIBRARY

Kierkegaard's "Fragments" and "Postscript"

Kierkegaard's "Fragments" and "Postscript"
The Religious Philosophy of Johannes Climacus

by

C. STEPHEN EVANS

HUMANITIES PRESS
Atlantic Highlands, N.J.

B
4378
.R44
E83
1983

© Copyright 1983 by Humanities Press Inc.

First published in 1983 in the United States of America by Humanities Press Inc., Atlantic Highlands, N.J. 07716

Library of Congress Cataloging in Publication Data

Evans, C. Stephen.
  Kierkegaard's "Fragments" and "Postscript."

  Bibliography: p.
  Includes index.
  1. Kierkegaard, Søren, 1813-1855—Religion.
  2. Religion—Philosophy—History—19th century.
  I. Title.
B4378.R44E83   1983   200'.1   82-23329
ISBN 0-391-02737-9

All rights reserved. No part of this publication may be reproduced or transmitted in any form or by any means, electronic or mechanical, including photocopy, recording, or any information storage and retrieval system, without permission in writing from the publisher.

Manufactured in the United States of America

102965

To Lise
who, like this book, began in Denmark

Table of Contents

EXPLANATION OF
PRIMARY SOURCE CITATIONS

All quotations from Kierkegaard's published writings are taken directly from the first edition of *Søren Kierkegaard's Samlede Værker,* edited by A. B. Drachman, J. L. Heiberg, and H. O. Lange (Copenhagen: Gyldendals Publishing House, 1901-1906). Responsibility for the translations belongs to me, though I have occasionally used the existing translation where I preferred it. The pagination of the Danish edition of Kierkegaard's works is included in the margins of the new English edition of *Kierkegaard's Writings* being published by Princeton University Press. Readers who wish to consult that edition can therefore do so easily.

The citation scheme is as follows: Page references will be given in parentheses following quotations or paraphrases. The first reference given will be the volume and page number of the Danish edition (example: VII, 231). The *Concluding Unscientific Postscript* is volume VII in that edition, and the *Philosophical Fragments* is in volume IV. The overwhelming majority of citations will be from those two works. Quotations from other works of Kierkegaard will be identified by the English title prior to citing the Danish volume and page reference.

The second reference given in parentheses (example: p. 243) is to the old English translation of Kierkegaard. A list of these translations for books cited appears in the bibliography. A typical reference will therefore appear as follows: (VII, 142; p. 148). This reference is to the *Concluding Unscientific Postscript,* page 142 of volume VII of the first Danish edition of Kierkegaard's *Collected Works;* page 148 of the old English translation by Swenson and Lowrie.

Quotations from Kierkegaard's journals are taken from *Søren Kierkegaard's Journals and Papers,* edited and translated by Howard J. Hong and Edna H. Hong (Bloomington: Indiana University Press, 1967-68), identified as *J. and P.* Volume number and the Hongs' citation number will be given. The Hong edition includes for each entry the appropriate citation to the Danish edition of the *Papirer* for readers who wish to consult that edition. References to untranslated sections are taken directly from the second edition of *Søren Kierkegaard's Papirer,* vol. I-XI³, edited by P. A. Heiberg, V. Kuhr, and E. Torsting, and vol. XII-XVI, edited by Niels Thulstrup (Copenhagen: Gyldendals Publishing House, 1968-78).

Preface

It is a venturesome thing to write a book about Kierkegaard. His humorous jibes at "the professor" cannot but be noticed by the professors who continue to write about him, unless those professors are as absent-minded as the "systematic thinker" caricatured in the *Concluding Unscientific Postscript*. While I am hardly oblivious to the irony of writing a scholarly work on Kierkegaard, and doubtless deserve to be the object of some of S. K.'s humor, I hope this is a book that Kierkegaard could appreciate.

This book embodies a strenuous attempt to respect Kierkegaard's wish to attribute to the pseudonyms the contents of his pseudonymous authorship. It attempts to take seriously the literary form of the works discussed and the underlying irony and humor. However, it is *not* assumed that these characteristics empty the works of serious philosophical content. My major purpose has been to shed some light on the *Philosophical Fragments* and *Concluding Unscientific Postscript* by elucidating the key categories the books embody. I hope my discussions will be illuminating to anyone interested in reading these or any works of Kierkegaard's authorship, to which the two works discussed are certainly central. Along the way I have discussed a large number of important philosophical and religious issues, and some of my discussions may have interest in their own right. My hope is that this book will show the relevance of Kierkegaard's thought to some contemporary debates in philosophy. I have tried to adopt the standpoint of an appreciative, empathetic reader of Kierkegaard and his pseudonyms, making the most possible sense of the text and the best possible case for the plausibility of the way of thinking found there, but not afraid to disagree in the end.

There are a number of people to whom I am indebted in connection with this book. The original research and thought were done at the University of Copenhagen in 1977-78. That year of study was made possible by grants from the George Marshall Fund of Denmark and the Wheaton College Alumni Association. While in Copenhagen I was assisted in a number of scholarly and nonscholarly ways by Paul Müller and Julia Watkins. Niels Thulstrup kindly provided an office at the Kierkegaard library. The late Gregor Malantschuk graciously allowed me to sit in on a series of lectures he was giving at the time, an opportunity for which I will always be grateful. I would also like to mention Poul Madsen and Leif and Nancy Pedersen, who really made me feel a part of Danish life and culture. I could not possibly convey how much I owe to my wife, who learned Danish with me, typed the first draft of this book, and generally supported my vision in countless ways.

Thanks are also due to my colleagues at Wheaton College, to David Schlafer of Trinity College, and to Bob Roberts of Western Kentucky University for giving the manuscript a close and critical reading and for making many helpful suggestions for changes. Finally, I am grateful to the Aldeen Fund, whose assistance played a key role in bringing the manuscript to publication. At this Thanksgiving period I would like to say a hearty "thank you" to all of those people, and especially to the Providence that brought their lives into touch with mine.

November 25, 1981

Chapter I

READING KIERKEGAARD'S
PSEUDONYMOUS LITERATURE

1. *Writing About Kierkegaard*

Søren Kierkegaard continues to enchant, provoke, frustrate, and anger the twentieth century. On the whole he would probably not find this situation too distasteful. Now that Kierkegaard is no longer a "fad", there is perhaps a better chance that he will be read in the way he would have wished, both by serious scholars and ordinary human beings. But even when read seriously, he remains elusive and enigmatic. A steady stream of wildly divergent interpretations and criticisms continue to appear.

Despite this situation I am convinced that Kierkegaard is one of the few great thinkers in the history of Western thought who can be read with profit by ordinary human beings. Many readers are overawed by the historical and linguistic experts. They despair of reading Kierkegaard for themselves and choose to rely on these scholars. Such readers might perhaps glean some comfort from the fact that Kierkegaard himself did not pretend to be a learned scholar, yet he dared to write in a helpful way about some issues that are discussed by scholars, but are not their exclusive property. I think that Kierkegaard could have said about his whole authorship what his most significant pseudonym, Johannes Climacus, said about a section of that authorship.

> Honor be to learning and scholarship, praise be to he, who with the certainty of knowledge and the dependability of a first-hand acquaintance can control the material detail. But the life of the problem still lies in the dialectical. (VII, 3; p. 15)[1]

By "the dialectical" in this context Climacus means simply "conceptual relationships." In other words, an understanding of basic concepts and their relationships is his fundamental task, and he does not see this task as an essentially learned affair. It is at least one helpful way of reading Kierkegaard to view him as doing just what Climacus describes here; Kierkegaard was a "dialectician," what today we would call a conceptual analyst, who saw it as his task to sort out a confused tangle of concepts to enable ordinary human beings to understand their beliefs, their actions, and their lives better. (Of course Kierkegaard does many other things as well.) The reader of Kierkegaard (and this book) may then take comfort in the fact that what is essentially needed to understand Kierkegaard's works is not vast learning, but the ability to think clearly and consistently. Since Kierkegaard is a thinker who focused his attention more than any other on "the individual" and the problems connected with "existing," it would be tragic if he became the special property of a band of scholars.

The present book is not a speculative attempt to uncover some hidden "philosophy" in Kierkegaard's writings. It is not an attempt to give an esoteric interpretation of what is regarded as essentially esoteric literature. It is an attempt to make the reader's task easier rather than more difficult. Johannes Climacus is fond of saying that his task is to make things difficult, yet not more difficult than they actually are. I might say it is my task to make things easy, yet no easier than they actually are.

Climacus and Kierkegaard succeeded sufficiently well in making themselves difficult to read and understand. Reading Kierkegaard will never be a substitute for soap operas and grade-B novels. But the difficulty should be such as to discourage lazy and merely curious readers, not to stifle the serious searcher. Though I cannot and do not wish to make Kierkegaard easier than he is, I can perhaps remove some of the obstacles that bar the way for contemporary readers, mainly by attempting to clarify a forbidding array of strange and unfamiliar terms, and some familiar terms used in unfamiliar ways.

As will become apparent when Kierkegaard's views on communication are discussed, it is a venturesome thing to write a book on Kierkegaard. In many ways the ideal situation would be simply to give him to "the individual" who would be his reader and let come what may. (I used to tell my students I would gladly agree to a pact among all students of Kierkegaard to cease all publication concerning him.) However ideal, this does not seem realistic. For one thing, a tremendous amount of confusing secondary literature already exists and continues to appear, some of it very misleading. The existence of this literature clearly shows the need and demand for help in understanding Kierkegaard; the disagreements among scholars are ample proof of how confusing Kierkegaard's authorship can be and are a further proof of this need. Thus although vast learning is not essential to understanding Kierkegaard, it is helpful—for many readers essential—to have certain puzzling features of Kierkegaard's works illuminated. For English-speaking readers today Kierkegaard lived in another age and another culture. While most of his problems remain alive today, the particular terminology that shaped his intellectual world is foreign. And there is good reason to think that he at times succeeded too well in making things "difficult" for his reader and thereby mystifying him.

  2. *The Specific Character of this Book: How It Differs from Some Others.*

  Though I will of course be delighted if this book should be of aid to a serious scholar, it is primarily intended as an aid to readers who wish to study Kierkegaard for themselves or who have done so; it is certainly not a substitute for that study. Readers will not find here any attempt at a "plot summary." It is an attempt to clarify a number of key concepts that are basic to one section of Kierkegaard's authorship. In this process of clarification, a number of significant philosophical and religious issues are considered. My primary purpose has been to get clear as to what Kierkegaard (or rather, in most cases, his pseudonym) has said on these issues. To a much lesser extent I have offered some critical reflections and questions, particularly in the final chapter, which I hope will stimulate readers to further reflection on their own. As much as possible, I have resisted the temptation to engage in polemics with other authors. It was in many cases a hard temptation to resist, but I have tried to mention other secondary authors only when helpful to illuminate my own views and approach either through agreement or contrast. I have polemicized only against views I thought readers would be likely to have already encountered and that are likely to lead them badly astray.

  This book differs from many on Kierkegaard in several respects. First, I have tried to limit its scope. Here I deal only with a relatively small but significant portion of Kierkegaard's total authorship—the two books ascribed to the Johannes Climacus pseudonym, *Philosophical Fragments* and *Concluding Unscientific Postscript to the Philosophical Fragments.* Many books on Kierkegaard in English are introductions to his thought that attempt to survey or summarize his whole literature. Many others are thematic studies that draw from the authorship as a whole or from the pseudonymous part of it. There is certainly justification for this procedure in that Kierkegaard's "authorship," as he calls it, does indeed form a unity and is intended to be read in that way. But it is my hope that by limiting the present study to just two books, it will be possible to consider certain key themes in more depth. The remainder of Kierkegaard's literature, including even his *Journals and Papers,* is referred to at times, but only to illuminate the ideas that are the chief focus. I believe that readers who understand the *Fragments* and *Postscript* will have found a key by which they can enter the authorship as a whole, or at least the pseudonymous portion of it. Also, many of the philosophical issues discussed in these works can be discussed and debated independently of the merits of other sections of Kierkegaard's writings.

The second way in which this book differs from many is that its focus is on the *content* of the books considered. I am a philosopher by training, and the Climacus section of Kierkegaard's authorship is generally regarded as the most philosophical part of that literature. My purpose then is to examine, clarify, and critically reflect on the ideas and arguments themselves. I believe that much of what Johannes Climacus is doing would be recognizable as philosophy today and that much of it is good philosophy. I shall therefore ignore as irrelevant the relationship between Kierkegaard's personal life and the content of the books, rejecting (by ignoring them) attempts to explain away the content of the books through psychoanalytic interpretations (which are plenteous here).

This book also differs from a third kind of book. There have been of late interpretations of the Climacus literature that take seriously its ironical, humorous, and poetic character, but understand these characteristics as making it impossible to read the books as serious philosophy. For example, Josiah Thompson tells us with regard to all of Kierkegaard's pseudonymous books that "to paraphrase them, to earnestly elucidate the philosophy expounded or the metaphysics presupposed in this or that work, is to miss the point that ultimately they seek to show the vanity of all philosophy and metaphysics."[2] Louis Mackey, who views Kierkegaard as "a kind of poet," says of Climacus with respect to the *Philosophical Fragments* that "by making light of everything he says, by accusing himself of plagiarizing God, he reneges the conclusions he implies and comes up with no results at all."[3] Mackey adds of the *Postscript* that "read as a philosophical treatise it is nonsense."[4]

Johannes Climacus is certainly humorous and ironical, and Kierkegaard himself is really "a kind of poet." However, we shall see that these characteristics by no means rule out a serious consideration of the intellectual content. Kierkegaard is also a "dialectician." As Climacus himself says, it is only assistant professors who assume that when irony is present seriousness must be excluded (VII, 236n; p. 246n). That Kierkegaard personally did not think that all philosophy and metaphysics is vanity can be shown by an examination of his *Journals and Papers*, which show a great familiarity with, and an appreciation for, Greek philosophy. The best way of showing that Kierkegaard's *Fragments* and *Postscript* are not nonsense when read as philosophical treatises, however, seems to me to be simply to read them as philosophical treatises. For when they are read in this way, "nonsense" is the last word I should choose to apply to them. On the contrary, they are a passionate attempt to do away with certain kinds of nonsense by sharpening our tools of thought—clarifying the concepts we employ in thinking about existential questions.

This book is also different, however, from certain other books that have dealt with the intellectual content of Kierkegaard's work. Many books on Kierkegaard which do take the content seriously more or less ignore the literary form by straightforwardly attributing to Kierkegaard himself the views of the pseudonym. This is in plain contradiction to Kierkegaard's own request in the "First and Last Declaration," printed at the end of the *Postscript*, that citations from the pseudonymous books be attributed to the pseudonyms themselves and not to himself (VII, 547; p. 552). I shall follow S.K.'s wishes in this respect, because, as will become apparent, the literary form of his authorship has an essential relation to its content. I will therefore try to pay special attention to that form, and to the use of humor and irony, so as to see how the content is related to, and reflected in, the form.

In this work I have chosen to discuss groups of concepts centered around paired key categories and to introduce these pairs in what seemed to me to be a logical order. No attempt is made to follow the order of the books being discussed. This book is therefore not a commentary in any ordinary sense, but it may be viewed as a companion to Kierkegaard's *Fragments* and *Postscripts* in the sense that it is intended to elucidate these works. Alternatively, if the reader wishes, it could be viewed as an essentially independent philosophical study that takes the *Fragments* and the *Postscript* as the "occasion" for discussing a number of key issues, which still are of concern to philosophers, psychologists, theologians, and most importantly, human beings interested in understanding what it means to exist.

3. Getting Started: The Problem of Pseudonymity

One of the major difficulties one encounters in discussing Kierkegaard is the intricate way his basic concepts are interrelated. One of the first things one notices about Kierkegaard's pseudonymous literature is precisely its pseudonymity. What is the purpose of the pseudonyms? How are they to be approached? It is impossible to answer these questions without an understanding of "indirect communication," which is itself expounded at greatest length by one of the pseudonyms. Indirect communication is in turn closely connected to the concepts of "existence" and "subjectivity" or "inwardness," which in turn can only b ∶ understood in connection with the concept of the "spheres" or "stages" of existence. A single one of these concepts is unintelligible apart from the others. (It is for this reason that the discussions of these concepts in the following chapters overlap, and therefore are to some extent repetitive.) Yet one must begin somewhere, and one cannot do everything at once.

We begin by tackling the question of pseudonymity because, until this is clarified, we shall not even know how to approach a large section of Kierkegaard's writings. Kierkegaard of course began his pseudonymous authorship with *Either-Or* in 1843, a book that purports to be edited by Victor Eremita and contains the papers of two other men. This was followed by a long series of pseudonymous books by a variety of interesting authors, culminating in the *Concluding Unscientific Postscript* by Johannes Climacus in 1846 (also the author of the earlier *Philosophical Fragments*). Throughout this period Kierkegaard also published a series of "edifying" or "upbuilding" discourses under his own name. After the *Postscript* Kierkegaard wrote several more works under his own name and published two works under a new pseudonym, Anti-Climacus, who is distinctively different from the earlier pseudonyms and must be considered separately.

A good starting place to understand this literature is Kierkegaard's own "First and Last Declaration," which was attached to the *Postscript*. There Kierkegaard affirms that his pseudonymity was not grounded in any personal quirk but was rooted in the essential character of the books themselves. These works required "that heedlessness in good and evil, in broken-heartedness and hilarity, in despair and arrogance, in suffering and jubilation, and so on, only ideally limited by psychological consistency, which no factually real person within the moral limitations of reality dares permit himself or can want to permit himself" (VII, 545; p. 551). For the sake of achieving his goals, whatever those may be, Kierkegaard found it necessary to invent characters, namely the pseudonyms, who could say things that he as actual person did not dare to say. The pseudonyms are not then merely pen names but independent (though fictitious) characters, with the possibility of holding views and convictions, moods and attitudes, that Kierkegaard did not personally share. This makes it obvious why Kierkegaard requested anyone who wished to cite a quotation from the pseudonymous books to attribute the quotation to the pseudonymous author rather than to himself.

What is the actual relation between Kierkegaard and his pseudonymous authors? Many writers on Kierkegaard have simply ignored the pseudonyms and cheerfully written long expositions of "Kierkegaard's" thought, gathered almost wholly from the pseudonymous works. Others have taken with great literalness Kierkegaard's assertion in the "First and Last Declaration:"

> There is therefore in the pseudonymous books not a single word of my own; I have no opinion about them except as a third party, no knowledge of their meaning except as reader, not the slightest private relation to them...(VII, 546; p. 551).

Some have taken this as implying that nothing in the pseudonymous books represents Kierkegaard's opinions. For example, Johannes Climacus gives a thorough discussion of the necessity for "indirect communication" when discussing existential truth. Indirect communication is necessary where the truth is the type that must be personally appropriated and cannot be merely objectively passed to another as a "result."[5] This concept of indirect communication greatly illuminates the pseudonymous books (including Climacus' own book). However, isn't Johannes Climacus himself one of the pseudonyms, and would it not be a mistake then to think that his theory of indirect communication can illuminate Kierkegaard's purposes?[6]

There is an elementary logical mistake being made here. Kierkegaard tells us we are to regard the pseudonymous authors as independent beings whose views are their own. However, it by no means follows from this that Kierkegaard does not hold some of their views, still less that he *rejects* their views. For suppose the pseudonyms were genuine human beings who actually existed. In such a case their views would certainly be completely their own. But Kierkegaard could still agree with some of their views and disagree with others.

As a matter of fact, it is not hard to show that a good many of the opinions expressed by the pseudonyms were held by Kierkegaard himself. The method whereby this can be done is simply to compare the pseudonymous works with works that Kierkegaard wrote under his own name and with his opinions as expressed in his *Journals and Papers*. No doubt it is these similarities that have led many authors (including this one at times) to regard the pseudonymous writings as Kierkegaard's.

This identification is particularly tempting in the case of Johannes Climacus, who more than any other pseudonym (except Anti-Climacus), seems to express views that lie at the core of Kierkegaard's own thought. The theory of indirect communication alluded to earlier, the notion of the "three stages of life's way," the special understanding of "existence," the connection between religiousness and suffering, the understanding of Christianity as a mode of existence centered around the "absolute paradox" that God became man, the contempt for rationalistic apologetics, both historical and speculative—all these Climacus and Kierkegaard share. The closeness of their connection is shown by the fact that Kierkegaard originally intended to publish *Philosophical Fragments* in his own name; the pseudonym was basically attached after the book was written, with only minor rewriting after the decision for a pseudonymous author.[7]

Does this mean that we must disregard Kierkegaard's request and simply take Climacus' work as Kierkegaard's? By no means. Kierkegaard's statement in the "First and Last Declaration" does not concern the extent to which his views do or do not converge with the pseudonyms. It is advice to us as to how best to read the books. And we are perfectly free to follow that advice regardless of the extent to which the pseudonyms may resemble him or fail to resemble him. That is, we simply read the books quite straightforwardly and take their authors and their contents at face value, without thereby presupposing or implying anything about Kierkegaard personally.

There are in fact some very good reasons for doing this. For one, it immediately helps clarify the purpose of reading Kierkegaard. If our purpose is historical, we might no doubt take a different attitude. That is, biographers and intellectual historians have a right to examine the pseudonymous literature and use it as best they can to fulfill their goals of understanding Kierkegaard's life and thought. (Though in view of Kierkegaard's warnings they should employ extreme caution in doing so.) But if our purposes are essentially personal and philosophical—if we are interested in the truth of the views presented, in understanding more profoundly some basic existential concepts, and thereby understanding ourselves and our existence more deeply—then it really does not matter very much whether Kierkegaard personally held these views. For from the fact that he held a view, nothing follows as to the truth, profundity, or value of the view. If we accepted a view simply on the basis of our respect for Kierkegaard's authority, we would be deceiving ourselves and would certainly have missed the point he was trying to make. Thus there is great value in taking his advice and simply thinking of the *Fragments* and *Postscript* as the work of Johannes Climacus. In so doing our admiration for S.K. (or our distaste for him) will not get in the way of our understanding.

4. *Indirect Communication and Subjective Understanding: A First Look*

This conclusion is further confirmed and illuminated by Kierkegaard's notion of indirect communication. This theory is propounded by Johannes Climacus, and we will give it much more careful examination later on as part of our consideration of his thought. It is not Climacus' personal property, however, as Kierkegaard employs the concept in his own writings and in his *Journals and Papers,* not only to expound the idea itself, but to understand his pseudonymous authorship.[8] At least a preliminary understanding of this concept is essential to understanding the Kierkegaard corpus as a whole and the pseudonymous section of it in particular.

The basic idea is that a distinction can be drawn between objective knowledge, which can be communicated directly from one person to another as a "result," and a type of self-knowledge that can only be communicated "artfully."[9] The former type of knowledge is primarily what we would term information. For example, it is possible for an historian to communicate directly to me some historical facts I can peruse, employ, laugh about, or whatever. A mathematician or engineer can tell me how I should build a bridge by providing the solution to an equation. In such cases I can know and usefully employ the result without reproducing the perhaps strenuous exertions of the historian and mathematician in discovering this result.

There is a type of self-knowledge, however, that cannot be communicated merely as a "result." This self-knowledge is not acquired simply through gaining more information about oneself, particularly not more information in which the self is viewed from an objective, "third-person" perspective. This self-knowledge is closer to what has traditionally been termed wisdom. It involves self-understanding, which can be possessed by uneducated people and can be lacking in people who know a great deal of information. As Kierkegaard sees it, self-understanding in this sense must be acquired by individuals for themselves. No mere human being can helpfully communicate his achievements as a "result" that another human being can straightforwardly appropriate. The reason for this is that the understanding and the process whereby it is acquired are essentially linked; the self-understanding is acquired as "a way," not as "result." The "what" is tied to the "how."

There is an analogy to this even within the "objective" sphere of knowledge which can be communicated directly. There is a sense in which a non-historian or non-mathematician does not really understand the "result" she appropriates if she has not reproduced the process whereby the result was acquired. A person who cannot herself solve an equation does not really understand the result; to acquire a deeper understanding she must herself go through the process whereby the result was acquired.

The analogy is not perfect because the lack of mathematical understanding does not prevent the result from being profitably communicated and employed. In the case of self-understanding, however, this is unlikely to happen because the object of self-understanding is existence, and existence is itself a process. Just as in the case of mathematical truth, to fail to understand the process by which a truth is acquired is to fail to understand the truth. But in this case the process of understanding cannot be separated from the use of what is understood.

In the case of mathematical truth the relationship between mathematical understanding and the use to which mathematical understanding is put is external. One can be had without the other, and an impersonal sort of knowledge is possible. But where the truth essentially concerns understanding oneself, an impersonal sort of knowledge is impossible. Someone who fails *personally* to understand the truth automatically fails to understand *himself*. In not understanding the process by which he can personally acquire the truth, he fails to understand his own existence. The "what" is essentially bound up with the "how."

Essentially, Kierkegaard's point is not difficult. It is in fact widely acknowledged, at least verbally. He is simply saying that when one is dealing with what has traditionally been termed moral and religious knowledge, it is essential for each person to be able to grasp the truth for himself, and that the truth he must understand is essentially related to his own existence. The major difference is that Kierkegaard takes this much more seriously than most writers and attempts to take it into account in the very form of his literature.

Socrates is the person Kierkegaard thought had most consistently and beautifully realized this truth. Socrates practiced indirect communication through his use of "the maieutic method," rather like the method of a midwife, who does not give birth herself but assists another to do so. Socrates, with his claim to be ignorant, did not claim to offer any positive truth of his own. He rather attempted to help others "give birth" to their ideas by his use of critical questioning. Socrates, as Kierkegaard sees him, wanted no disciples. His ignorance pushes away every would-be follower, forcing the learner to discover the truth for himself.

It is clear that Kierkegaard's pseudonymous writings are an attempt to follow this Socratic "maieutic ideal." The pseudonyms are Kierkegaard's attempt to "withdraw" Socratically from readers, leaving them to interact with the fictitious pseudonym and discover the truth for themselves. The pseudonymous works do not contain Kierkegaard's final thoughts about communication, at least not as far as the communication of Christianity is concerned. He later becomes suspicious that his pseudonymous authorship is a "mystification" rather than a maieutic help. (It is this mystification that makes it necessary for the reader to have help in reading Kierkegaard.) He later comes to the conclusion that for the communication of Christianity "bearing witness" in a more direct way is necessary.[10] But even here the essential ideal embodied in the maieutic method remains valid: There is no understanding of existential truth apart from the process of personal appropriation. And Kierkegaard thought that a great deal of existential understanding must be presupposed before Christianity can be profitably communicated. This preliminary understanding must be communicated maieutically if at all, and Kierkegaard's pseudonymous writings are an attempt to do this.

5. Existence-Spheres and Pseudonymity

The other concept that is essential to fully understand Kierkegaard's employment of the pseudonyms is that of the "stages" or "spheres" of existence. This again is a theme found in Climacus' writing (as well as that of other pseudonyms), and we will therefore give it fuller treatment later on. But, like indirect communication, it is a concept that is held not only by pseudonyms, but by Kierkegaard himself.[11] This concept of the stages is the most popular and well-known aspect of Kierkegaard's writings, but a brief account of the concept is indispensable here.

At first glance the number of possible ways human beings can exist seems incredibly numerous. The variety of lifestyles, moods, occupations, customs, games, ceremonies, and so on seems infinitely varied. It was Kierkegaard's belief that despite this tremendous variety (which he in no way denied or minimized) the number of possible ways of existing can be profitably classified under a relatively small set of categories. Thus, upon reflection, one finds that there are only a few ways of existing that differ essentially from each other. This scheme of categories is not absolutized. He does not deny the possibility of other helpful ways of categorizing existence. As we shall see later, the scheme is not a "system" but a conceptual tool that is treated differently in different contexts. Nevertheless, S.K. sees his stages as both helpful and in some sense fundamental.

This view of Kierkegaard's is expressed in the very title of one of his pseudonymous books, *Stages on Life's Way*. The three "stages" presented there (and many other places in Kierkegaard's authorship) are the aesthetic, ethical, and religious lives, respectively. In actual fact the term "existence-spheres" is more helpful than the term "stages on life's way," and is used frequently by Kierkegaard, both in his own writings and in the pseudonymous writings. Also, Kierkegaard discusses more than three existence-spheres; there are two patterns of life that are regarded as boundary zones or transitional spheres. These are *irony*, which lies between the aesthetic and the ethical, and *humor*, which lies between the ethical and the religious spheres. In addition, the religious sphere comes in two forms which must be clearly distinguished. A religious life that remains within "immanence" (human consciousness and experience apart from supernatural revelation) differs sharply from the "paradoxical" type of religious life, which supposes that God does not merely relate to mankind through man's natural moral and religious consciousness, but that God has broken into history in a "transcendent" way.

What do these concepts mean? Johannes Climacus gives them all a rather thorough discussion, which we will encounter and discuss in a number of contexts. But a preliminary, rough-and-ready description could go like this.[12] The aesthetic life is life as it is "immediately" lived; it is the lifestyle in which people are absorbed in satisfying their "natural" desires and impulses. The aesthetic life is a life lived for "the moment," and it is life understood in terms of concepts like fortune/misfortune, happiness/un-happiness. The aesthetic life is one in which people simply are what they are, instead of assuming the responsibility to become what they shall become.

The ethical life is precisely the recognition of the significance of choice. The ethicist recognizes that existence is a process in which a person becomes what she becomes through her choices. In its true form the ethical life involves a recognition that the significance and dignity of human life depend upon a person's ability to recognize and actualize eternal values. These eternal values do not destroy the aesthetic; they transform and relativize the natural desires and impulses of the aesthete.

The religious life arises as a possibility when the ethical project of actualizing oneself through choice suffers shipwreck. While the ethical life is essentially self-sufficient, the religious life has an essentially dependent element. No longer convinced of individual self-sufficiency, the religious exister strives to allow himself to be transformed by God. The process of recognizing one's true condition and allowing God to transform one in this way is a painful one, and the individual is thus a "sufferer." Achieving this sort of God-relationship, in which a person becomes the recipient of God's action, is nonetheless an activity—in fact, the most strenuous activity imaginable.

As noted earlier, the religious life can perfectly well be carried on without any special "revelation" or religious authority, and it does not depend upon some particular historical religion being true. It is possible, however, to conceive of a "transcendent" type of religiousness in which one's own "immanent" eternal ideas about God are not the final norm of truth. Instead the individual builds his life around his faith that God has revealed himself to him in history. This is the sort of thing Kierkegaard called "the paradoxical" type of religiousness, and he believed that Christianity was this type of religion.

Leaving irony and humor to be dealt with later, we can now see more clearly the function of Kierkegaard's pseudonyms. In his *Journal* Kierkegaard comments on what he hoped to accomplish in his authorship.

> Even though I achieve nothing else, I nevertheless hope to leave very accurate and experientially based observations concerning the conditions of existence. . .

> Using my diagram, a young person should be able to see very accurately beforehand, just as on a price-list if you venture this far out, the conditions are thus and so, this is to win, and that to lose; and if you venture out this far these are the conditions, etc. (*J. and P.* I, 1046).

Thus he thought that the descriptions of the existence-spheres possessed real value for the individual. But since the understanding that is to be sought concerns existence, it is of no value for the individual simply to be given this understanding as a "result." He must be brought to see the truth for himself.

Take, for example, the aesthetic stage. Kierkegaard personally saw the aesthetic life, if it remains purely within that sphere, as perdition and despair. But it would do no good simply to tell the individual that. After all, if a person rejected this lifestyle merely on the advice of one person, why should she not adopt it on the advice of another? Besides this, Kierkegaard saw very clearly that the decision to live an aesthetic or an ethical life is never a purely intellectual one. Such decisions must be ultimately rooted in what a person cares about and deeply values—what Kierkegaard referred to as "the passions." These sorts of enduring emotional attachments can never be simply "transferred" from one person to another; they are personal achievements. Yet without such achievements it is not possible really to understand the aesthetic life as perdition and resolutely to will the ethical. Such achievements are therefore the precondition for existential self-understanding or wisdom and make it clearer why such understanding cannot be directly communicated.

Therefore, Kierkegaard does not give his reader results. He rather attempts in the pseudonymous literature to embody these existential viewpoints or "spheres." Readers are not simply given information, they are imaginatively presented with existential possibilities which they must reflect on and interact with. We can now understand why Kierkegaard says that his pseudonymous literature required a "heedlessness in the direction of good and evil" that a real person whose life is limited by ethics dare not permit himself. The pseudonymous characters do not merely tell us about the existence-spheres: They live out those spheres, within the realm of imagination, naturally, not as actual fact. The aesthete who reads the first volume of *Either-Or*, for example, finds himself looking into a mirror, and this provides the occasion, if he so wills it, for a new self-understanding and possible resolution. There is therefore an intimate coherence between the concepts of indirect communication, the spheres of existence, and Kierkegaard's employment of the pseudonyms.

Is it a contradiction on my part to write a book about Johannes Climacus, one of these pseudonyms, which employs direct communication? I do not think so. The fact that another person (i.e., Kierkegaard) employs indirect communication is a fact that can be communicated directly, and one can well write directly about the content of that indirect communication. What is the value of doing so? It depends upon the purposes of the reader. I have not directly attempted to accomplish what Kierkegaard (or Climacus) tried to accomplish. That is, I have not by the literary form of this work attempted to engage in indirect communication. I have not made use of pseudonymity, nor am I capable of the humor and irony employed so brilliantly by Kierkegaard. I have tried to write a book that will help readers gain the ability to read and understand

Kierkegaard, and in doing so, I have discussed the content of some of his pseudonymous works.

It is of course always possible that such a "direct" work as this will nevertheless communicate "indirectly." That is, though I do not employ the literary artistry of a Kierkegaard to facilitate this result, it is possible that this book could nonetheless serve as the occasion for some individuals to gain the increased subjective self-understanding Kierkegaard attempted to make possible. That depends upon who reads and why and how they read. My hope is that the direct communication about Kierkegaard's work will at least make it more possible for the individual who wishes to encounter Kierkegaard subjectively to do so. In that way this work might make possible in a somewhat indirect way the indirect communication Kierkegaard aimed at. Of course such a book as this may also have value to historians interested in evaluating Kierkegaard's greatness or insignificance relative to other thinkers, or who wish to classify him or assign him a position in the history of philosophy, theology, or culture in general. And I hope it will have even more value to a thinker who simply has an interest in the ideas and arguments discussed and analyzed.

Having discussed the function of the pseudonyms in general, what about Johannes Climacus, the author of the two books we wish to consider? Who is he? What is his relation to the other pseudonyms? Fortunately, Johannes Climacus has to a great extent answered these questions for himself. As Kierkegaard says that even the names of the pseudonyms are their own, we are well advised to take Johannes' self-understanding seriously.

If anyone is interested in the historical question of Kierkegaard's opinion of Johannes Climacus and his writings, there is evidence that that opinion is not so different from Climacus' own self-assessment. Kierkegaard clearly regarded the *Postscript* at the time he wrote it as the culmination of his pseudonymous writings. In both the *Fragments* and the *Postscripts* the significance of the material presented is signaled by the fact that Kierkegaard's own name is put on the title page as "responsible for publication." Some portions of both works can be found almost verbatim in Kierkegaard's *Papirer*. We have already noted the extent to which Climacus' and Kierkegaard's views overlap. But such questions are essentially historical and are best left to the historians. Johannes Climacus exists as a character in his own right; his statements about himself, particularly in the *Postscript*, are by no means necessarily Kierkegaard's. When Climacus tells us how he became an author, that he is not a Christian, etc., there is no reason to think that he is necessarily giving us

Kierkegaard's autobiography. And even where he expresses views that are essentially Kierkegaard, we have seen that there are valid reasons for honoring Kierkegaard's request to let the pseudonyms stand on their own feet. In addition to these general reasons there are particular reasons for taking the Climacus pseudonym as a genuine character. These have to do with the particular themes and polemics found in the books. Let us turn then to the analysis of Johannes Climacus' thought.

[1] See the Explanation of Primary Source Citations.

[2] Josiah Thompson, *Kierkegaard* (New York: Alfred Knopf, 1973) p. 146.

[3] Louis Mackey, *Kierkegaard: A Kind of Poet* (Philadelphia: University of Pennsylvania Press, 1971), p. 168.

[4] *Ibid,.*p. 192.

[5] This concept is discussed at more length on pp. 9-11 and in Chapter 6.

[6] Josiah Thompson, for example, tells us that Climacus' discussion of indirect communication is only part of the "charade" that he feels the whole book consists of. (See his *Kierkegaard,* p. 185.)

[7] See Niels Thulstrup's "Introduction" and "Commentary" on the *Philosophical Fragments* (Princeton: Princeton University Press, 1962), pp. lxxxv-lxxxvii and 146-154, for an account of the changes made after the decision to make the book pseudonymous. The evidence for this is in the B section of *Papirer V.*

[8] For a listing of significant passages in Kierkegaard's writings, pseudonymous and non-pseudonymous, which deal with indirect communication, see the note on p. 597 in *J. and P.* II.

[9] This is only a preliminary discussion. The concepts here are treated at greater length in Chapter 5.

[10] See *J. and P.*II, 1957.

[11] See for example *J. and P.* IV, 4454, 4467, 4474, and 4476.

[12] None of these descriptions is completely accurate, but they cannot be made so at this point without complicated discussions of "immediacy" and "reflection."

Chapter II

READING JOHANNES CLIMACUS

1. *Hegel and Christianity*

Before attempting a detailed consideration of Climacus' key concepts, it would seem advisable to give some sort of general overview of the *Fragments* and *Postscript*, as well as a more careful look at their pseudonymous author. *Philosophical Fragments or a Fragment of Philosophy* appeared in 1844, *Concluding Unscientific Postscript to the Philosophical Fragments* in 1846. The two books are thus connected not only by the common author but by their very titles. That their pseudonymous author is, as he gives himself out to be, a humorist may also be inferred from the titles. For one thing the *"Postscript,"* which Climacus attached to his relatively brief *Fragments*, is many times as long as the first book!

The titles of the books are not only humorous but revealing. They clearly indicate that both books are polemically directed toward the speculative philosophy of Hegel and even more specifically at the Danish followers of Hegel, particularly H. L. Martensen. Hegel's philosophy was characterized by the claim to have raised philosophy to the level of "science" by making it "systematic." Hence in the universe of Hegelian discourse "philosophy," "system," and "science" were practically synonyms. By designating one of his books as "fragments" and the other as "unscientific," Climacus made his attitude toward this movement and this usage perfectly plain. This also helps us understand what Climacus meant by "unscientific." The term does not indicate any special reference to the natural or physical sciences, as English readers today might naturally tend to assume, but primarily signifies that the contents are unsystematic. The title *Philosophical Fragments* connotes a similar idea. The Danish term for fragment here (*smule*) is a very common word. It could just as correctly be translated by "bit," as it is the word a person would use at a meal to ask for "a little bit more" of this or that. Given the prevailing view of philosophy in Kierkegaard's day, "philosophical bits" had a humorous and almost contradictory ring about it. For it was precisely philosophy's systematic character that was supposed to make it philosophical.

To understand Johannes Climacus it is important to have some understanding of Hegelian philosophy, at least as it was understood in Denmark in the 1840s. It is especially important to understand Hegel's treatment of religion in general and Christianity in particular, as it is this aspect of Hegelianism that aroused Climacus' ire. It is by no means the case that Climacus' thought has no relevance except in relation to Hegelianism. It is rather exceptionally pertinent and fresh. But to understand that pertinence and freshness one must understand the text, which does indeed require some understanding of Hegelianism.

Hegel's view of Christianity is sufficiently complex (or ambiguous) to have given rise, even during his lifetime, to two schools of almost opposite viewpoints. The learned controversy over how Hegel's thought is to be interpreted continues, and obviously cannot be resolved here. However, the following two points would seem to be fairly non-controversial.

First, Hegel claimed that his philosophy was Christian.[1] That is, he regarded his speculative system as a friend and bulwark of the Christian faith, and he attempted to distinguish his view from the growing chorus of critics, who regarded traditional Christianity as requiring beliefs that were superstitious.[2]

Secondly, Hegel's own understanding of Christianity was significantly different from traditional orthodoxy. For example, Hegel seems to rule out the possibility of miracles.[3] His understanding of Jesus is again quite complicated, but it seems rather unorthodox. Hegel accepted the claim that Jesus was divine, but he did not seem to understand this as implying that Jesus was uniquely divine. For Hegel mankind *per se* is divine, at least potentially. Jesus' uniqueness is merely that he was the first person in history to recognize man's true identity and destiny.[4]

The two points we have made about Hegel seem contradictory. How can Hegel maintain he is a friend of traditional Christianity and at the same time offer a radically nontraditional understanding of Christianity as the truth? The answer to this question lies in Hegel's understanding of truth and how the truth is achieved.

Hegel is opposed to the idea that truth can be expressed in straightforward propositions that must either be true or false. For Hegel truth is much more complicated than this. When a person tries to express some truth about ultimate reality in a proposition, he inevitably fails adequately to express the truth he aims at. For example, if someone affirms that "God is a person," a good Hegelian response would be "yes and no." To a certain extent the proposition expresses a truth, but in other ways it expresses something false. It is therefore really a one-sided expression of the truth. Being one-sided inevitably, as Hegel would say, it calls forth its opposite. That is, if one group of people maintain that God is a person, another group, sensitive to the ways that this expression fails to describe God adequately, will maintain that God is not a person. Out of the clash of these two opposing views a more adequate statement of the truth about God can emerge — for example, the assertion that "God is supra-personal." This more adequate expression of the truth in a sense both "annuls" and "preserves" the opposing statements. (Hegel uses the German verb *aufheben,* which has these contradictory meanings, to express this.) It annuls their one-sided, fragmentary character but preserves the truth contained in each. Johannes Climacus often refers to this function as "mediation."

The new "truth," if taken as the final truth, will also inevitably have a one-sided, fragmentary character. Hence the critical process may begin again as the new truth also calls forth a reaction. This process can obviously repeat itself again and again.

This example is only an illustration. It is not intended to correspond with the content of any section of Hegel's philosophy. Rather, it is an attempt to make Hegel's conception of truth clearer or, rather, to make clearer how the truth is attained. For Hegel the truth is not grasped simply by affirming or denying propositions, but through a process. This process we have just illustrated is generally called Hegel's dialectical method, but Climacus generally refers to it simply as "the method." (Climacus uses the term "dialectic" in a different sense.) The totally adequate truth, according to Hegel, emerges only through the dialectical process as a whole

Philosophical thinking is dialectical thinking, and the whole process through which the truth emerges, when understood philosophically, constitutes "the system." Truth then lies "in the whole" and requires systematic thinking.

Given this understanding of truth, we can now see why Hegel can offer a nonorthodox interpretation of Christianity and at the same time claim to have vindicated the truth of orthodoxy. To put it as simply as possible, Hegel regards traditional orthodox Christianity as one stage in the total process that constitutes the truth. Christianity can then truly be said to be "true." But since traditional orthodoxy is not the final step in the process, it is proper for the speculative philosopher to seek a more adequate expression of the truth. Climacus understood this as implying that the simple faith of an ordinary believer is not straightforwardly denied; it is rather treated as a nonultimate statement of the truth that is grasped more adequately by the philosopher. Faith is a "superseded moment" in the philosophical system. But since the "truth" of a superseded moment is supposed to be preserved in the system, the philosopher is justified in regarding his system as "Christian."

For Hegel the ultimate content of all philosophy is what he terms "the Absolute" or God. The Absolute for Hegel is understood most adequately as "Spirit," which has the same dynamic structure as the dialectical method itself. God then is not understood by Hegel as a static "substance" but as a "subject" who is engaged in the process of becoming what he truly is. Spirit as it comes to full self-consciousness requires an object to be conscious of. Spirit inevitably externalizes itself; it demands an "other" in relation to which it can define itself, just as in the dialectical process a proposition engenders its own negation so as to realize the truth more adequately. But this "alienation" of Spirit must be ultimately overcome; the "other" must be reunited with Spirit in a unity that preserves the differences. Thus, for Hegel the whole of the universe is an expression or manifestation of God; however, it is for the most part a manifestation of God in his "otherness." Only in man has this otherness been overcome. Man is the highest expression of Spirit; human history is the history of spirit becoming aware of itself as *Spirit*.

The highest expressions of Spirit for Hegel are man's cultural activities, particularly art, religion, and philosophy. These three spheres together form the philosophy of "Absolute Spirit." The essential objects of art, religion, and philosophy are the same — namely, God or the Absolute itself. These three spiritual activities are differentiated by their mode of presentation.

In art we become aware of the Absolute sensuously or, as Hegel would say, "immediately."[5] In religion the Absolute is grasped through historical or imaginative representations, "picture-thinking" that contains some intellectual content.[6] Still more reflective, however, is philosophy, which conceives the Absolute purely conceptually.[7]

This terminology of "immediacy" is rather important. As we shall see, one of the things Climacus objects to in Hegel is the consignment of religion in general, and particularly Christian faith, to the sphere of (relative) immediacy. Immediacy connotes spontaneity but also something elementary, unreflective, destined to be superseded. Climacus uses the term "immediacy" to refer to the natural attitude of children toward life, or the attitude of an unreflective, uneducated person. In this sense to say of religion or, more particularly, Christianity that it is "immediate" implies that it is something childlike, destined to be superseded in the life of a mature, educated person, but suitable perhaps for children and rustics. This condescending attitude toward faith is not perhaps exactly what Hegel had in mind, but it seems to have been present in popular Hegelianism. And, indeed, this view of faith is still present today in many people, including many who have never heard of Hegel! Climacus thought this view of Christian faith was the worst possible error, and he combats it vehemently. It is certainly true that the Christian life is characterized by spontaneity and newness; it is in that sense "immediate." But Climacus stressed that this Christian immediacy was a "higher" immediacy, an *acquired* immediacy that is far from easy to attain.

2. Climacus' Personal Characteristics; A "Humoristic, Experimental Psychologist"

One might think from this that Climacus is himself a Christian believer and a zealous defender of the faith to boot. This is however, far from the case. Climacus tells us in many places quite explicitly that he is not a Christian. He makes no claim to know whether Christianity is true or false. He describes himself as a "humoristic, experimental psychologist" (VII, 419; p. 431). The concept of humor is actually one of the most significant concepts in the *Postscript*. It does not *merely* mean "funny," though readers will not be harmed if they initially take the word "humorist" in its ordinary sense, waiting for Climacus' own discussion of the concept to see what deeper meaning it may have.

"Experimental psychologist," however, needs some comment. Even the most casual reader will swiftly recognize that Climacus hardly resembles a contemporary experimental psychologist at all. While both Climacus and a modern psychologist may be loosely described as employing observations to study man, the similarity ends there. Contemporary experimental psychologists pride themselves on the use of objective methods; their observations are essentially of humans as "objects." (Which is why they may legitimately employ studies of animals, which as physical organisms resemble man.) Contemporary experimental psychologists take an essentially "third-person" point of view. Johannes Climacus, on the other hand, is interested in what it means to be a *subject*. He tries to focus in on human existence from the perspective of the exister.

In what sense is Climacus an "experimenter"? Fortunately, this is a term that he himself comments on at some length. In one section of the *Postscript* Climacus attempts to analyze the significance of "the pseudonymous authorship." In the course of this he discusses *Repetition* by Constantine Constantius, a book designated "a psychological experiment" on its title page. The significance of this experimental form is that by this means the communication "itself forms an opposition (to itself), and the experiment establishes a yawning chasm between reader and author, puts the separation of inwardness between them, so that direct understanding is made impossible" (VII, 223; p. 235). We can gather from this that the purpose of the "experimental" form is related to indirect communication. Not only does Kierkegaard attempt to distance himself from the reader via the pseudonyms; some of the pseudonyms attempt to do the same thing by writing in the form of an experiment. "The experiment is the conscious, teasing, recall[8] [of the communication], which always is of importance for an exister who writes for existers, so that the relationship is not changed to that of a rote-reciter writing for rote-reciters" (VII, 223; p. 235).

The experimentalist is a hypothetical thinker. He imaginatively constructs and describes existential possibilities, but in the last analysis he does not commit himself. The judgments he seems to make in his presentation are to be regarded as "recalled." Thus Climacus himself issues such a "recall" at the end of the *Postscript* (VII, 539; p. 547). He "has no opinion and wishes to have none." Climacus resists "disciples" as strenuously as Kierkegaard himself. If any readers think that the content of the book is true, they must be prepared to stake themselves to that truth and take responsibility for it. No refuge can be found, at least, in Climacus' authority. "So then the book is superfluous: therefore let no one take the trouble to appeal to it; for he who appeals to it has *eo ipso* misunderstood it" (VII, 538; p. 546).

This distance from the reader is also secured by a jesting, teasing form that pervades all of Climacus' writing. The point is not that the books are not to be taken seriously, as one author has suggested.[9] Climacus tells us many times that "the positive is recognizable by the negative" and that the jest can contain the deepest earnestness. The point is that it is up to the readers how they will take the books. A reader who wishes to dismiss them as foolishness is given ample reason to do so. A reader who sees them as serious will do so because he perceives the seriousness *for himself*.

As for Climacus personally, he is intentionally elusive. It is impossible for the reader to judge as to his personal beliefs or his purposes in writing. He characterizes himself as an "indolent" person who spends his time "idling and thinking" (VII, 154; p. 165). His writing is an "innocent pastime and diversion" (VII, 539; p. 547). Climacus' famous account of "how he decided to become an author" is one of the most humorous and well-known sections in all of Kierkegaard's writings.[10] It must be read as is; it would be a crime to paraphrase it. As a contrast, Climacus' account of how he chose his particular subject matter is one of the most moving sections of Kierkegaard's writings.[11] In both cases the effect is Climacus' withdrawal from the reader. Even though his thought "sounds almost like seriousness" (VII, 152; p. 163), the reader is immediately affronted by Climacus' frivolous motives. Bored with life and with nothing better to do, Climacus conceives the idea of becoming an author to "create difficulties" for people under the plausible assumption that modern life with its manifold conveniences has created "too much ease" (VII, 155; p. 166). The decision to investigate the relationship between the Hegelian philosophy and Christianity is precipitated by a chance meeting with a sorrowing grandfather and grandson in a cemetery, where Climacus overhears the godly old man's grief over his now deceased son's rejection of his childhood faith to embrace "the newer philosophy." It happened that Climacus' studies had led him to the conclusion that there was confusion lurking in the relation between Christianity and Hegelianism, so he felt somewhat competent to pursue a matter that appealed to him "as a complicated criminal-case" (VII, 202; p. 216). He tackles the problem in the same spirit as would a dedicated follower of Agatha Christie!

Climacus is by no means then to be regarded as a Christian or as a zealous defender of Christianity. His standpoint is that of a person who knows what Christianity is but does not necessarily understand what it is to be a Christian. It is a mistake, then, to look to Climacus for an account of what the Christian life is like; his knowledge of Christianity is an intellectual sort of knowledge. This intellectual clarity, incidentally, is something Kierkegaard himself prized highly and respected. But it is of course in no way identical with *being* a Christian.

That it is perfectly possible to know what Christianity is without being a Christian Climacus expressly affirms, since otherwise it would be impossible for someone who is not a Christian to choose to become one (VII, 321-322; p. 332). Climacus understands what Christianity is, and he certainly has a great respect for Christianity, which comes through in many ways. This respect might tempt a person to conclude that Climacus is a believer, but this would be a mistake. Climacus respects Christianity because, *if true*, it is the most serious and important thing a person will face in existence, since Christianity claims that a person's relationship to it will determine his eternal destiny. He also respects Christianity because he can see that it is a strenuous way of life; existing as a Christian requires a rare courage and determination. But Climacus never says that Christianity is true, nor does he claim to know that it is. In fact, he argues that if one attempts to settle the question of Christianity's truth objectively, no result is possible.

3. *The* Fragments *as an Example of an "Experiment"*

The *Philosophical Fragments* is a good illustration of what Climacus means when he refers to himself as an experimenter. The *Fragments* is expressly called "not doctrinal but experimental" (VII, 312; p. 323). In the book Climacus attempts to clarify what is distinctive about Christianity by pretending to "invent" it. He assumes, first of all, that there was (and is) something distinctive about Christianity compared with philosophical and religious thought in paganism. The Christian faith cannot reasonably be regarded as a "Jewish" version of the speculative thought of Plato and Aristotle or even the practical moral reflection of Socrates. In attempting to isolate what is distinctive about Christianity, Climacus first characterizes pagan thought under the Platonic-Socratic principle of immanence: Essentially, the truth is *within* man already.

Socrates as a teacher honestly and consistently expressed this principle by his maieutic method: He helps others "give birth" by discovering the truth for themselves. In such a case Socrates' own significance as a teacher is vanishing, as is the significance of the "moment" the learner gains the truth. For the learner who really discovers the truth simultaneously discovers that the truth was already *his* possession (thus he essentially owes Socrates nothing) and that the truth is an eternal possession (hence the moment the discovery is made is of vanishing significance.)

In characterizing pagan thought in that manner, Climacus is referring to much more than the Platonic theory of recollection. In speaking about "the truth," he is referring to "ultimate or essential truth." The person who has the truth in this sense has fulfilled her destiny; she has become all that a human being can be. The principle of immanence thus designates any religious view which holds that the divine is already within the individual, who is essentially grounded in God, whether God be understood personally or impersonally. In Kierkegaard's day this sort of religious position was exemplified not only by Hegel but by thinkers like Schleiermacher. Many contemporary religious perspectives would fit as well. With a little imagination one can even extend Climacus' analyses to forms of religious humanism, which limit themselves to "this-worldly" hopes, or even to political ideologies such as Marxism. For these views would essentially agree with Socrates that the truth is "within" man in the sense that people can discover and achieve their destiny essentially by themselves and through their own efforts. (Of course Marxists would not say that the individual can do this, but they affirm that it is possible for mankind through historical action.)

In contradistinction to this principle of "immanence" Climacus explicates Christianity by a set of coherent concepts, which he pretends to be developing in the form of an "experiment" to see if there is really any alternative to immanence. The question he raises is simply this: Can we imagine a view that would be genuinely different from the Socratic? Such an alternative must emphasize the importance of "the moment." Rather than viewing the truth as the individual's eternal possession, the essential truth must be something one can acquire (or fail to acquire) in time. Since the truth must be acquired, it follows that the individual's condition is that of lacking the truth, of being essentially in error, a condition that Climacus decides to call "sin." In such a case the learner will need more than a maieutic teacher; he will need a teacher who can totally transform him by giving him the ability to understand the truth. Only the God himself could so re-create the person; hence, the teacher must be the God himself.

In developing these concepts Climacus suggests that the God's historical appearance would be essential if a total transformation of the person is to be effected. For only in this way would the individual get the God "outside him," so to speak. If God relates to an individual through the person's immanent moral and religious consciousness, then that moral and religious consciousness is not essentially in untruth. If the human condition *is* essentially that of untruth, then the need for a transcendent, authoritative revelation makes sense.

Thus the early Christians proclaimed Christianity as true by divine authority; they affirmed Jesus as *lord.* Climacus makes no attempt to argue that they were right in doing so or that Christianity is true.[12] He is simply attempting to make clear what Christianity is by exploring the meaning of a set of concepts which cohere and which clearly are different from pagan thought. These include such concepts as "the moment," sin, the incarnation, and authority.

The sting of this account is felt only when applied to the Hegelians who proclaimed that their speculative interpretation of Christianity was essentially Christian. For their interpretation of Christianity was essentially within the principle of immanence. On the Hegelian account Jesus could not be God in any unique sense and does not represent a transcendent revelation. Jesus may have been the first person to recognize man's essential oneness with God, but once this truth was recognized, it is essentially true of all human beings. Man's divinity is being concretely actualized through history. But this is an expression of the principle of immanence.

The Hegelian theologians claimed to be Christian, to have made an advance on pagan thought. Climacus' response is clear. "But to go further than Socrates, when one says essentially the same as he, only not nearly so well — that at least is not Socratic" (IV, 272; p. 139). The Hegelian view may well be true, or more true than Christianity, but Climacus says it is unjust to call it Christianity. Such an importation of immanence into Christianity does an injustice to both Christianity and paganism.

> That someone prefers paganism to Christianity is by no means confusing, but to discover paganism as the highest development within Christianity is an injustice both against Christianity, which becomes something other than what it is, and against paganism, which doesn't become anything at all, though it was really something (VII, 313; p. 323).

It is important to note that Climacus' attack, if justified, applies not only to Hegelianism, but to a tremendous amount of classical liberal theology and even to a great deal of theology today. For the Hegelians were certainly not the only ones to deny Jesus' divinity and to transform Christianity into either a speculative doctrine or moral teaching (or both) whose truth can be recognized through mankind's immanent moral and religious consciousness. Such a view, which obviates an authoritative revelation or transcendent acts by God in history, is widely prevalent even today. Though there are many different forms of moral teaching that are identified as Christianity, as widely different as Marxist revolution and individualist bourgeois conformism, the acceptance of the principle of immanence is common to all of them. Climacus' question to these "immanent" versions of Christianity is still pertinent: Why do you call your view Christianity?

This is one illustration of a point the careful reader will discover again and again in all of the Kierkegaardian literature. When the problems addressed there are untangled from their specific historical context, we discover that they are still relevant and pertinent, even if we do not agree with the views expressed. Kierkegaard's problems to a large extent are still our problems.

In the *Fragments* Climacus has attempted to clarify the essential difference between Christianity and all "immanent" ways of thinking. He does this, however, without so much as mentioning Christianity, except on the last page of the book. To understand the book, it is necessary to be able to do far more than recapitulate the conceptual contrasts drawn between Christianity and immanence, which Climacus calls the "dialectical movements" (although someone who can't do that has certainly not understood the book.) There is in a sense nothing very new or original in the content of the *Fragments*. Climacus himself says that

> It is well-known that Christianity is the only historical phenomenon which, in spite of the historical, nay, precisely by means of the historical, has intended itself to be for the single individual the point of departure for his eternal consciousness. . . . No philosophy (for it is only for thought), no mythology (for it is only for the imagination), no historical knowledge (which is for the memory) has ever had this idea. . . . it did not arise in any human heart[13] (IV, 271; pp. 137-138).

The originality of Climacus' account lies mainly in the form, which is, as we have said, the form of an experiment or hypothesis. Climacus pretends to "invent" Christianity, without calling it that, by imaginatively constructing a coherent alternative to Socratic immanence. The attempt is really impossible, since the very content of the hypothesis demands that the alternative to Socrates must be a revelation from God which no human being could invent. Readers who recognize this truth will in a sense understand the book as "recalled," in the sense of "revoked" or "called back." They will then see, not that Christianity is true, but that it is clearly different from immanent systems of thought. They will see this not because Climacus says it, but for themselves.

Climacus thinks that the problems of his contemporaries were not due to lack of knowledge, but lack of understanding. Any of the leading churchmen and theologians (or laymen for that matter) could have provided him with the information that Christianity was a religion based on an authoritative, historical revelation. The problem was that the contemporaries who *said* this did not seem to understand the implications of what they were saying. Climacus says that when a man has his mouth so full that he cannot take in food, one helps him by taking food out of his mouth. Similarly when people have knowledge but are not able to understand and perceive the significance of what they know, then they must have some knowledge taken away. The *Fragments* does this by presenting to the reader what he *knows* (by heart, objectively, by rote) in such a form that he will not recognize it until he has thought through the implications for himself (VII, 233-234n; p. 245-246n). This is accomplished through the presentation of Christianity in the form of an experiment.

4. The Postscript: *Combatting Intellectualism and "Christendom"*

At the end of the *Fragments*, Climacus makes a rather weak "promise" that in the sequel to the piece he has written, if he ever writes such a thing, he intends to "call the matter by its actual name, and to clothe the problem in its historical costume" (IV, 270; p. 137). The *Concluding Unscientific Postscript to the Philosophical Fragments* purports to be this promised "sequel," which gives the problem of the *Fragments* its historical costume by explicitly discussing Christianity. In reality, as Climacus himself admits, the *Postscript* is far more than this, and not mainly this at all. The discussion of the historical costume is limited to the relatively small sections of the book at the beginning and the end. The *Postscript* is really devoted to a different but closely related problem: "How does an individual become a Christian? What might bring a person to become a Christian?"

The *Fragments* had contrasted Christianity and immanence without pretending to decide which is true. The *Postscript* does not attempt to decide this objectively either, but it attempts to help the individual get clear as tö how she ought to approach the problem of Christianity subjectively. In the course of doing so a host of significant concepts with existential significance are considered: communication, truth, the ethical, reason, paradox, suffering, guilt. All of these are explored for the sake of clarifying something that is not really a concept at all in the ordinary sense — existence. To ensure that the discussion has this existential aim, Climacus focuses the key question of the book by zeroing in on his own existence.

Putting it as simply as possible (I shall use myself for the experiment): "I, Johannes Climacus, born in this city and now thirty years old, a common ordinary human being like most people, assume that there awaits me, just the same as a maid or a professor, a highest good, which is called an eternal happiness. I have heard that Christianity is the condition for someone's achieving this good, and I now ask how I can come into relation with this teaching" (VII, 7; p. 19).

Climacus asks about how he can relate himself to Christianity. But he actually writes a book that is for the most part not about Christianity directly, but about what it means to *exist*. His detective work in puzzling out the criminal wrong done to Christianity by Hegelianism has led him to the conclusion that the key error is failing to understand that Christianity is a communication with an essential relation to existence.

My principal thought was that in our age, due to the great amount of knowledge possessed, we had forgotten what it means to *exist* and the meaning of *inwardness*, and that the misunderstanding between speculation and Christianity could be explained on that basis (VII, 210; p. 223).

As Climacus saw it, not only the Hegelians, but even many orthodox defenders of Christianity, had transformed Christianity into an essentially learned and scholarly affair. Being a Christian had been confused with philosophical speculation over the meaning of dogma or historical investigation of ancient manuscripts and texts. If the precondition for becoming a Christian is the completion of this learned process, then Climacus recognizes that the individual is in trouble. For both philosophical speculation and historical inquiry are ongoing processes which in a sense never achieve final results so that further reflection and investigation become unnecessary. Yet Christianity is supposed to be the determinant of the individual's eternal destiny. And, of course, individuals do not live forever.

This intellectualist understanding of Christianity is helped by another misunderstanding, the misunderstanding of "Christendom." This is the assumption that becoming a Christian is something that happens automatically, by birth or baptism or just by residing in a "Christian" land. This error makes the intellectualist view much more acceptable. Since "we are all Christians," there is no need to worry about a person's existential relationship to Christianity. There is time and leisure for the

Christians to become superior Christians by gaining a deeper intellectual understanding of their faith. In this case the learned investigation becomes the content of the Christian's life (or at least of some Christians) rather than a precondition for becoming a Christian.

It is this connection between the two misunderstandings of Christianity, that of intellectualism and of Christendom, that explains some of the mixture of topics in the *Postscript,* which as a book continuously jumps from the consideration of philosophical questions to the consideration of distinctively theological and religious issues. In one section the nature of the self and its relation to truth are considered; this is soon followed by discussions of baptism, asceticism, etc. This can be explained thusly: The misunderstanding of baptism (the belief that being baptized as an infant makes one a Christian, regardless of the later orientation of one's life) is one of the factors that takes away the urgency from the consideration of Christianity, thus making possible its transformation into a learned affair instead of remaining an "existential communication."

This error of "Christendom" is also rooted in a failure to understand what it means to exist. The individual who accepts the root idea of "Christendom" is simply identifying what it means to exist as a human being with what it means to exist as a Christian. This Climacus sees as a radical error, which is perhaps only made possible by the fact that the individuals in Christendom have a very mediocre concept of what it means to exist as a human being. For an individual to decide whether or not he wished to exist as a Christian, he must be helped to understand Christianity as a way of existence. But Climacus sees that the Christian mode of existence presupposes a developed understanding of what it means to exist *religiously.* And existing religiously presupposes an understanding of what it means to exist as a human being at all. Hence, properly to help himself (and any others who might benefit) to determine his relation to Christianity, Climacus is forced to go "back" to a basic understanding of what human existence as such amounts to.

Fortunately, a good deal of this task was already done for him in Kierkegaard's previous pseudonymous works, where the various spheres of existence had been explored. This does not mean that these earlier works had dogmatically developed and straightforwardly presented the theory of the three stages or spheres of existence. They too are "indirect," an attempt to help the reader understand existence for himself. Climacus does not violate this indirectness. He does not claim to know for sure whether the pseudonymous authors of these books intended to present what he discovered there. But he does present one possible way of reading the works, a reading that sees a significant unity present in all of the works and that gives them a close connection to the *Postscript*.

In a sense the ideal introduction to the *Postscript* would be the whole of Kierkegaard's previous pseudonymous authorship. It is perhaps expecting a little too much to assume that the reader of the *Postscript* will have mastered *Either/Or, Fear and Trembling, Repetition, The Concept of Anxiety,* and *Stages on Life's Way,* not to mention the *Fragments* itself and a series of "edifying discourses" Kierkegaard wrote under his own name to "accompany" the pseudonymous works. Nevertheless, as Climacus employs one section of the *Postscript* to review these works, and as his own discussions frequently employ concepts that are developed in these other works, it is necessary to discuss the relationship of Climacus' work to these other works, however inadequate such a discussion will inevitably be.[14]

In beginning his investigation of the relation between Hegelianism and Christianity, Climacus proposes first to let "the existential relationship between the aesthetic and the ethical come into being within an existing individual" (VII, 211; p. 224). Much to his embarrassment, before he could even begin, *Either/Or* appeared. This provides the pattern for his "review" of the pseudonymous books. Just as he himself is about to undertake another step in his project, another pseudonymous book appears that accomplishes precisely what he had intended and even helps him become clearer about what he had intended (VII, 212; p. 225). We shall begin our examination of Climacus' writings then by taking a look at his view of the other pseudonymous writings of Kierkegaard. We shall focus particularly on the pseudonyms' exploration of existence, and the spheres of existence. Even more particularly, we shall give close attention to the aesthetic "sphere," since the concept of the "aesthetic" is one that Climacus employs frequently, but does not really analyze himself. Contrariwise, he has a great deal to say about the ethical and religious spheres.

---

[1] See, for example, the "Introduction" to *Lectures on the Philosophy of Religion,* where Hegel insists that "the re-establishment of the doctrines of the Church" is "truly the work of philosophy." *G.W.F. Hegel on Art, Religion, Philosophy,* ed. by J. Glenn Gray (New York: Harper and Row, 1970), p. 157. Also see p. 205, where Christianity is called "the perfected, absolute religion."

[2] Critics such as Hegel's own left-wing followers, David F. Strauss, and Ludwig Feuerbach, who expressed their attacks soon after Hegel's death in *The Life of Jesus* and *The Essence of Christianity* respectively. Though these critics wrote after Hegel this sort of criticism was already "in the air" in Hegel's time.

3   See Hegel, *Religionsphilosophie, Werke,* Vol XII, pp. 323 ff.

4   Hegel accepted the claim that Jesus is divine in some sense, or at least the significance of this *belief* for the church, but he does not understand this dogma as implying that Jesus as an individual person is uniquely divine. While it is essential for the divine to become concrete and therefore to incarnate itself, this incarnation is not a one-time historical event, but a picture of a universal truth. See Hegel's *Phenomenology of Spirit,* trans. by A.V. Miller (Oxford: Oxford University Press, 1977), pp. 461-463.

5   See the *Introduction to Hegel's Philosophy of Fine Art,* contained in *G.W.F. Hegel on Art, Religion, and Philosophy.* p. 106.

6   See the "Introduction" to *Hegel's Lectures on the History of Philosophy,* contained in *G.W.F. Hegel on Art, Religion, and Philosophy,* p. 280. Also see the *Phenomenology of Spirit,* p. 463.

7   "Latest of all philosophy permits full justice to be done to the content of religion through the speculative notion, which is through thought itself." *Ibid.,* p. 282.

8   Recall in the sense of "calling back," "revocation."

9   Josiah Thompson, *Kierkegaard,* p. 146.

10   VII, 152-157; pp. 163-167.

11   VII, 197-211; pp. 210-224.

12   One place where he seems to do this is IV, 191; p. 27, of the Swenson translation. "This strange fact deeply impresses me, and casts over me a spell; for it constitutes a test of the hypothesis and proves its truth." The word translated "truth" here is *"Rigtighed"* and is more properly rendered "correctness" or "soundness." Climacus means, I think, that his hypothesis has been proven to be correctly formed; i.e., it is a genuine alternative to Socrates. To the individual of faith who is open to transcendence, this suggests that the hypothesis is true in a deeper sense, but to the individual who lacks faith this will hardly be a proof that the content of the hypothesis is true, but rather a proof of its falsehood.

13   An allusion to I Corinthians 2:7-9, which is frequently referred to in Kierkegaard's works.

14   For better, more extended treatments I recommend Gregor Malantschuk, *Kierkegaard's Thought* and Louis Mackey, *Kierkegaard: A Kind of Poet.* These are very different, but, in my opinion, complementary works. Though I disagree with Mackey's overall thesis, his "readings" of individual works of Kierkegaard show a genuine sensitivity to their literary form. Malantschuk, as the title of his book would suggest, is a more reliable guide to Kierkegaard's thought.

Chapter III

EXISTENCE AND EXISTENCE – SPHERES:
CLIMACUS' READING OF KIERKEGAARD'S
PSEUDONYMOUS LITERATURE

1. *The Aesthetic Life*

Despite Climacus' claim that the other pseudonyms had already accomplished his task of presenting the existence-spheres, he himself gives an analysis of this concept which the other works lack. He characterizes these spheres in a number of different ways, employing different principles of classification. The spheres are classified, for example, with respect to their relationship to time, to the dialectical, and to the comic.[1] This is not an inconsistency; since the spheres represent entire modes of living, they are complex and can be viewed from more than one direction. One of the most helpful characterizations for attaining an initial understanding is the following:

> While aesthetic existence is essentially enjoyment, ethical existence essentially struggle and victory, religious existence is suffering, not as a temporary moment, but as continuously accompanying it (VII, 246; p. 256).

We shall take these three concepts of "enjoyment," "struggle," and "suffering" as the key to understanding the three spheres.

Before analyzing the aesthetic sphere, a comment on Kierkegaard's (and Climacus') use of the term "aesthetic" is perhaps in order. It is helpful initially to distinguish three different usages of this term in Kierkegaard's literature, although deeper study will show that there is a unitary meaning underlying all three usages. The term "aesthetic" is first used as we have used it above — to refer to a sphere or stage of existence. But the term is also used in the more standard sense of designating that which pertains to the arts or to the discipline that reflects on the arts. Finally, Kierkegaard uses the term to refer to a large section of his own authorship. Those works that attempt to communicate indirectly to the reader must have an "artistic" form; they imaginatively reproduce existential possibilities in an artistic medium. In all three usages "the aesthetic" emphasizes an imaginative play of possibilities.

The aesthetic as an existence-sphere or mode of living is in a sense where every person begins; it is the lifestyle of the person who wants to enjoy life. Its initial form consists in trying to satisfy or cultivate one's natural desires and impulses. The basic categories by which Climacus characterizes the aesthetic life are those of "happiness-unhappiness" (in the sense in which these depend upon fortune-misfortune)[2] and the category of "the moment" (used in a completely different sense than in the *Philosophical Fragments,* where it designates the period of time at which the disciple of the God receives the truth). The aesthete begins by embarking on the project of satisfying his natural wants; the very term "aesthetic" seems to be used here in its etymological sense — in Greek *aesthesia* designates "sensation." Since pleasure of this sort is necessarily spasmodic in character, the aesthete's life has a spasmodic character to it as well. It is essentially a search for satisfying "moments," which cannot by their very nature endure. Being singular and unique they resist "repetition" as well, a concept that has a profound meaning in Kierkegaard's writings.

The aesthete, is by no means simply a hedonist, however, in the sense of either Epicurus or English utilitarianism, though the hedonist certainly is a type of aesthete. The categories "pleasure" and "pain" are much too simple as well as ambiguous to describe the content of the aesthetic life. Kierkegaard's pseudonyms are well acquainted with the deviousness and complexity of the human psyche. The range of things that human beings can "enjoy" includes far more than pleasure, if that term is used to refer to any definite type of feeling or sensation, and is not simply used as a synonym for "whatever is desired." When it is used in this last sense, it can no longer be taken as a contrast term to pain, for there are many people who desire pain, as the psychologists tell us.

The aesthetic life can take many forms, ranging from crude sensuality to refined, cultured sensibility. The two ideal limits to this range would be pure sensuousness on the one hand and pure imaginative reflection on the other. The aesthete does not necessarily seek satisfaction only through fulfilling her physical drives such as sex, hunger, and so on. This type of aesthetic life is in fact unsatisfying and even impossible since it quickly becomes boring, and in any case a mature human being is scarcely ever impelled to act by "raw urge," unmixed with any reflection. The cultured aesthete does not merely seek food and drink; she wishes her food to be beautifully prepared and served; her wine to be exquisitely unique. The more developed her imagination, the more variety she can incorporate into her life. The really skilled aesthete learns to enjoy her own imaginative creations. The real world becomes a set of "occasions" for the exercise of her creative fancy. The end result is still the production of feelings and moods. These moods are certainly not limited to pleasure in any ordinary sense of that word. The aesthete learns, for example, that sorrow can be as aesthetically satisfying as joy; more so, perhaps, since it is a mood more easily sustained.

All of this is well illustrated for Climacus in *Either/Or.*In that work a range of possible aesthetic lifestyles is portrayed. Following the Diapsalmata, aphoristic lyrical expressions of moods, which constitute a type of "overture" to the book, there follows an essay on Mozart's *Don Giovanni.* Don Giovanni, or Don Juan, as most English readers know him, is the embodiment of raw sensuality, a type of "immediacy" that is not a real possibility but that forms one ideal limit to the aesthetic life. This sort of sensuous immediacy is completely spontaneous; it cannot be artfully achieved by reflection. There is a sense in which a person becomes conscious of it only when it is gone! The aesthete in *Either/Or* is far from being Don Juan, who is as remote from him as a lost paradise. The aesthete in *Either/Or,* whom we know as "A," nostalgically longs for some of the spontaneity of Don Juan, but he achieves this only vicariously through listening to Mozart's music.

The aesthetic life as it develops then inevitably relies heavily on the imagination. A life lived in imagination offers two definite advantages. First, by means of the imagination the aesthetic life takes on variety and attempts therefore to defeat the boredom which quickly drags down the "immediate" aesthete. Second, the imagination gives the aesthete a certain degree of independence from the real world, which of course she cannot ever completely control. Even if reality does not always offer the enjoyment she seeks, that enjoyment may be achievable through a poetic (imaginative) transformation of reality. Here we get a clue as to why the aesthete is represented as having a special interest in the arts, and why Climacus (and Kierkegaard) may have employed the term "aesthetic" in the way which they did. For the aesthete the arts may become a substitute for the real world.

The other ideal limit to the aesthetic life will then be a purely reflective life, a life lived in imagination. This type of aesthetic life is approached in the conclusion of volume I of *Either/Or*, in the infamous "Diary of a Seducer," which must be the least erotic such essay ever written. The seducer pictured here is almost purely intellectual; he achieves his satisfaction not really by deflowering virgins, but in the art by which he woos a girl. He is the completely reflective counterpart to Don Juan's immediacy. That a purely intellectual and imaginative life is also an impossibility for actual human beings is hinted at in the Diary itself, where the seducer finds himself tiring of his elaborate intellectual game and desperately seeks to recharge his desire by reading erotic books, observing women in semivoyeur fashion, and even making a false promise of marriage to a servant girl to get her in to bed with him.[3]

The aesthetic life of course does not usually take such exotic forms. Most people who live life at this level (and this probably includes most people) live a rather humdrum existence. However, Kierkegaard felt it was important to exhaust the possibilities of a mode of existence, and thus his authorship contains forms that are unusual but significant in pushing this life-form to its limit.

2. The Ethical Life: Existence and Passion

Whatever form the aesthetic life takes, it is judged by the ethical life (and Climacus concurs in this judgement) to be essentially in despair at bottom. Though in both *Either/Or* and the *Stages on Life's Way* there is no clear "result" in the sense that the ethical is acclaimed to be superior at the conclusion of the book, this by no means entails that these two views of life are portrayed as equally worthwhile. An objective result would be radically inconsistent with the principle of inwardness that underlies indirect communication.

A reader who needs the reassurance of a warning lecture to see that a standpoint is erroneous, or an unlucky outcome (such as madness, suicide, poverty, and so on), he really sees nothing; he merely imagines that he does (VII, 254; p. 263).

The aesthetic life is nonetheless judged by Climacus to be "perdition" even when "a milder light falls over it" (VII, 253; p. 263).

In both *Either/Or* and the *Stages on Life's Way* the ethical life is represented by Assessor William, a happily married judge. With respect to both *Either/Or* and the *Stages* Climacus says that the judge "easily wins" over the aesthete (VII, 252; p. 262) and even that all the mistakes of the aesthetes are answered and corrected in the ethical sections of the books (VII, 255; p. 264). This victory is not grounded in the judge's superior intellect (since he is actually inferior to the particular aesthetes considered) but in the inherent superiority of his "ethical passion and pathos" (VII, 252; p. 262).

What is the problem with the aesthetic life? The primary flaw is that the aesthete ultimately fails to *exist*. (We shall give this term a much fuller treatment later in several connections, but we can already see here the distinctive and significant way that "exist" is employed.) The English language regrettably does not have as many terms for "existence" as Danish (and some other languages). As is probably known by anyone who has studied Kierkegaard at all, he uses special terms for "existence" and "exist" (*eksistens* and *eksistere*)[4] which focus on the distinctiveness of human existence. Human beings do not merely exist in the sense of being actualized in space and time, as do rocks and plants, nor merely in the still broader sense of merely having some kind of "being." Human existence is a *becoming*; moreover, a special type of becoming. Though human beings by no means have the power to create themselves out of nothing — they begin with and always possess a given "nature" as humans as well as a quite definite and specific hereditary and environmental "deposit" — they nevertheless have the ability to shape their own development by exercising free choice. By becoming self-conscious and by imaginatively considering possibilities that are not actual, human life can achieve the dignity of a process that is to a certain degree, but only to a certain degree, self-conscious and self-directed. Existence is the process of becoming a subject, a process Climacus calls "becoming subjective."

Climacus thinks that in a sense all human beings "exist," but for many the term is deservedly put in quotation marks. Many people exist in the same sense that a drunken peasant who lies asleep in a wagon "drives" the wagon (VII, 267; p. 276). In fact, the horses run wherever they please. Similarly, many human lives are simply blown around and dissipated. The individuals are controlled by their environment or by their immediate impulses. Their "choices" are made for them. There is no unifying focus to their personalities, consequently no genuine growth or development. In the deepest sense this sort of person lacks a self and hence does not really exist—or does so only in a mediocre sense. The only solution to this problem is to recognize the significance of choice in life. One must seize the responsibility for one's own life by consciously recognizing who one is and choosing to become the person one should be. To take choice seriously is to recognize the significance of, and take responsibility for, the commitments one makes.

This is essentially the ethicist's message, and it contains his charge against the aesthete. In living life for the moment the aesthete's life becomes just that—a series of disconnected moments. A person of whom this is true really has no self, since for human beings a self is something that must be acquired. A self is not a gift of either heredity or environment; rather, as long as the person is *purely* a product of these factors, it is certain that this person lacks a self and only possesses the possibility of becoming one. It is because the aesthetic life lacks this process of development that it can be judged as a whole to be "immediate," even when it is most reflective. The aesthete simply "is what he is," while the ethical person "becomes what he becomes."[5]

The aesthete is in despair (VII, 214; p. 226), even if she is not fully conscious of it, because despair in the last analysis is the lack of a self, an emptiness or hollowness where there should be fullness. Most individuals think of despair as the outcome of an accidental occurrence. The girl lost her love, so she despairs; the man lost his fortune, so he despairs. However, if a person is brought to despair by accidental circumstances, does this not show that her life was essentially despair all along, since if she had not despaired it could truly be said to have been an accident? And yet the typical aesthete, whose life is based on those immediate goods whose distribution is subject to fortune, is in precisely the position of depending upon such accidents to achieve her goal of "enjoying life."[6]

It might appear that aesthetes are capable of a type of growth and development. For we have seen that the aesthetic life can shift from a more immediate and sensuous form in the direction of a more reflective and imaginative lifestyle. It is important to see what is wrong with this suggestion. It is certainly true that for Climacus the imagination is an essential component of existence, and even that the aesthete's imaginative development can be an existence-possibility that points toward existence so nearly that "one feels how every moment is wasted, in which a decision is not yet arrived at" (VII, 213; p. 226). Still, imagining something is clearly not the same as being or becoming that something. Otherwise the young girl who imagines she is an astronaut would be an astronaut; the distinction between play and reality, poetry and existence would disappear (IV, 186n; pp. 20-21n). Therefore the aesthete's imaginative development is not existential development.

Although both thought and imagination are essential elements of existence, neither is existence itself. It is possible to imaginatively conceive many possibilities and to have clearly thought through the meaning of these without having in the deepest sense existed. To exist means to choose; choice requires resolution; resolution requires what Climacus calls passion. "Passion," which is often used synonymously with "inwardness" and "subjectivity," is one of the most significant terms in Kierkegaard's authorship, but it is a term that is very apt to mislead the English reader.

The term "passion" is apt to suggest some sort of spontaneous and involuntary emotion that sweeps over a person in a flash, disappearing just as suddenly and involuntarily. "He murdered her in a fit of passion." This is very far from what Kierkegaard has in mind. Though there is certainly an element of passivity in passion, one of the chief characteristics of the highest forms of passion is that they endure. Kierkegaard's usage has a little in common with the old novelistic sense in which characters in a novel were understood by grasping their "ruling passion." Passions, as Kierkegaard understands them, can and must be developed and acquired, and the individual is responsible for them. To have a passion is to care deeply about something or someone. A passion is the wholehearted realization of what we sometimes call, rather colorlessly and palely, a value.

Patriotism might be seen as a type of passion, albeit a frequently degraded one. People who genuinely value their country care deeply about it. Their lives are oriented towards their country's preservation and betterment. The two passions Kierkegaard discusses most frequently are the passions of romantic love and of faith.

The passive element in passion consists in the fact that a human being can never simply will a passion into being. This is the mistake contained in that popular "existentialism" and humanism which assumes that the individual can decide for himself what he values. The individual does decide for himself, but he cannot value what he knows is valueless; there must be a basis or root for his caring concern. Passions must be "called forth." In a more immediate passion, such as erotic love, this is clear. This sort of love cannot simply be willed into being. True romantic love has an element of spontaneity in it; this was recognized by the Greeks, who ascribed love to the work of a god; even today a religious young man may regard his loved one as a gift from heaven.

True romantic passion is never purely immediate or purely passive, however. Although just about all human beings have erotic impulses and opportunities, not every human being becomes a great lover, worthy of being immortalized by a poet. What do most of us lack? What distinguishes the great lover from the mediocre one? It is precisely the quality of his passion. It is passion alone that deserves to be praised as love; raw physical desire is no special distinction, since it is something humans share with the animals. And passion in this sense is a quality that may be developed. It is not mere raw feeling but an enduring emotion which could almost be described in dispositional language as a capacity.

It is passion in this sense that makes existence in the strongest sense possible. Only through passion can a person begin to collect herself and give her life a unified direction so that she actually *becomes* something—and in so doing becomes a self. This process has something in common with what contemporary psychologists call, again rather colorlessly, personal integration. And it is this task the ethicist has embarked upon.

Why cannot the aesthete *choose* the aesthetic life? Why can't she develop her immediate and reflective enjoyments? In a sense, she can, as we shall see. But in a deeper sense the ethicist is correct in concluding that the aesthete lacks a self and fails to exist. The primary problem with the aesthetic life is its fragmented, spasmodic character. The aesthete can never truly collect herself into a unified personality, since by definition the content of her life is scattered into a series of moments. She can never will "one thing" since the objects of her desires are necessarily multiple and episodic.[7]

If the aesthete is unaware of the true character of what he seeks, then he cannot truly be said to will what he wills with passion, since this presupposes a conscious awareness of what one wills. If, on the contrary, a person is consciously aware of the fragmented character of what he wills, yet continues to will it, then he is no longer simply an aesthete. His life can now be described as *demonic*, since it is characteristic of the demonic to will the evil while knowing it to be the evil. As the judge says in the *Stages*, demoniacal resolution "is also ethical—that is, ethically bad" (VI, 142; p. 148).

The ethicist sees clearly that "the difficulty for the exister is to give his existence the continuity without which everything merely disappears." It is passion that gives the individual "that momentary continuity, which at the same time maintains and is the impulse for the movement." The distinctive passion that is characteristic of the ethical life is the passion for "the eternal" (VII, 268; p. 277). Climacus discusses at some length the nature of the eternal. We will give this concept a more thorough treatment in the next chapter, but at this point let us say that he is claiming that the values a truly integrated personality must embody cannot be regarded simply as particular, temporal goods a person happens to find attractive. That would be a return to the aesthetic life. The ethical life must consist in the attempt to realize those values that are universal and timeless, though of course those values must be actualized in particular and temporal modes.

The ethicist must begin by "choosing himself," the act by which he transforms the "given" self into a task. By doing so the ethicist reveals himself (the aesthetic life is a type of concealment). He takes time into account in a serious way by accepting responsibility for his commitments, thereby achieving the possibility of *"gaining a history,"* which is "continuity's ethical victory over hiddenness, melancholy, illusory passion, despair" (VII, 214; p. 227). This task of becoming a self constitutes the "struggle and victory of the ethical life." But the ethicist can only truly choose himself if he recognizes who he is—an individual with the capacity for realizing eternal values and who therefore himself possesses eternal significance.

The contrast of the aesthetic and ethical spheres is made clear in Kierkegaard's pseudonymous literature through concrete illustrations. The paradigm of the aesthetic life is the love affair; hence the first volume of *Either/Or* ends with the "Diary of a Seducer." The ethical life is symbolized in marriage, where love "acquires a history" and the ethical ideal of commitment can be progressively realized in the marriage relationship. It is significant that Judge Williams, who argues the ethicists' case, by no means regards the ethical life as excluding the enjoyment and immediacy of the aesthetic life. Rather, he argues that, when brought under the control of ethical resolution, the aesthetic ideal of love is secured against time and chance.

3. Religious Existence

As Climacus sees it, the existential conflict between the aesthetic and ethical spheres of existence, as illustrated in *Either/Or* and *Stages*, has a close relationship to his own task. This was, the reader will recall, the investigation of the crime done to Christianity by its transformation from an "existential-communication" to a speculative philosophical doctrine. The root cause of this is the failure to understand Christianity as a mode of existence, which in turn presupposes an understanding of existence itself. Hence it is essential for Climacus to focus his attention on "existence" itself and such closely related themes as passion and inwardness.

As Climacus sees it, however, an understanding of the Christian mode of existence presupposes an understanding, not merely of ordinary existence, but of a specific mode of existence, religious existence. To a large extent his own *Postscript* is devoted to the clarification of this mode of existence. This was, however, also a task the other pseudonymous writers had worked on, at least as Climacus views them, and it is proper for him to review their accomplishments.

The relationship between the ethical and religious stages is more difficult for the reader to understand than that between the aesthetic and the ethical. The difference is not merely that the religious exister believes in God and the ethicist does not. On the contrary, Kierkegaard represents his more developed ethicists as being religious believers in the ordinary sense of the word; Judge Williams, for example, is a churchgoer. And one can imagine genuinely religious existers whose conception of "the eternal" is not precisely in line with traditional theistic conceptions of God. The distinction between the ethical and the religious is made more difficult by the fact that Climacus distinguishes two kinds of religiousness. The first is that "immanent" religiousness he terms religiousness A; the other (termed religiousness B) is the distinctive kind of religiousness characteristic of Christianity. These two, however, are not always clearly separated in the other pseudonymous writings.

A still further complication is the fact that the ethical and religious stages are essentially related. In his Journal Kierkegaard says *"Three stages and still one either/or"* (*J. and P.* V, 5805). This is echoed by Climacus, in commenting on the *Stages*, which added a third "religious" section to the two possibilities presented in *Either/Or:* "Despite this triple division the book is nevertheless an either/or. The ethical and religious stages stand in an essential relationship to each other" (VII, 252; p. 261). This "essential relationship" is one we shall have to unpack.

The difference between the ethical and the religious life is grasped most clearly through two contrasts. First, the ethical life is described as a life of action and victory, while the religious life is one of suffering (VII, 252; p. 261). The ethical life, in its most developed and adequate form, is like the religious life in containing an "infinite interest." The ethicist is infinitely interested in *himself,* however; the religious individual's infinite interest is focused on "the actuality of another" (VII, 278-279; p. 288). These two contrasts are essentially the same. The heart of the ethical life is the ethicist's project of becoming a self through resolution. This presupposes a view of the self as active and as essentially self-sufficient. The ethicist may believe in and relate to God, but he does so essentially through his relation to himself.

A good example of this would be the purely ethical religiousness which Kant outlines in his *Religion Within the Limits of Reason Alone.* There the religious individual's knowledge of God is completely derivable from his understanding of the moral law. His relation to God is purely one of moral service. *"Whatever, over and above good life conduct, man fancies that he can do to become well-pleasing to God is mere religious illusion and pseudo-service of God."*[8]

The religious individual, on the other hand, sees himself as essentially separated from those moral possibilities he identifies with; he is alienated from himself and "unable to come back to himself by himself." Thus a God-relationship acquires a significance for him that it does not possess for the ethicist. The religious exister relates to himself through his God relationship instead of relating to God through his relation to himself.

Originally the ethical life is seen as the self's victory over despair: the victory of revelation and reality over aesthetic concealment. But what if the individual discovers he cannot conquer despair by willing it—that the decision to live the ethical life cannot be carried on in the individual's own strength? At this point the need for divine assistance becomes clear. The paradox of the ethical life is that the more intensely it is lived, the more likely this is to be the case. The most ethical person is not the person who passes over his failings by thoughtlessly assuring himself that he is no worse than "the others." He is precisely the person who is the sternest with himself; the most relentless in uncovering his ambiguous motives, who is not content with his ability to "fool the others" and hence may accuse himself when no one else does.

This paradox of the ethical life is expressed very well in *Fear and Trembling:* "An ethics which ignores sin is an absolutely useless science; but if it takes account of sin then it is *eo ipso* well beyond itself" (III, 146; p. 108). The reason for this is given in a footnote on the same page. "As soon as sin makes its appearance ethics perishes, precisely upon repentance; for repentance is the highest ethical expression, but precisely as such it is the deepest ethical self-contradiction" (III, 146n.; p. 108n.). The most ethical person can be precisely the person who feels most ethically inadequate. This is expressed by repentance, but repentance as an act transcends the positive, self-confident striving characteristic of the ethical life.

Fear and Trembling is the pseudonymous work that most clearly draws the distinction between the ethical life and the religious life. To make the distinction clearer, Abraham is pictured in *Fear and Trembling* as a man who has completely lived up to his ethical responsibilities; he has "fulfilled the universal." Abraham is a righteous man (III, 146; p. 108). It was not, however, through his ethical life that Abraham became the "knight of faith," a "guiding star which saves the anguished" (III, 73; p. 35).

Abraham's *faith,* his distinctively religious passion, shows itself rather through an act that, from a purely ethical standpoint, would have to be condemned—namely, his willingness to sacrifice his son because God asked him to do so.

Abraham here becomes the paradigm for those who must relate themselves to the "universal" (ethical duty) through the "absolute," (God) rather than relating themselves to the absolute through the universal (III, 119; p. 80). Abraham acts as "the individual." That is, Abraham's God-relationship was primary in his life. He did not merely perceive God through morality; he related to morality through God. Actually, as a man of faith Abraham does everything, including his ethical acts, because of his God-relationship. But the observer can only see the *difference* between Abraham and an ethicist in the situation where Abraham is "tested," a distinctively religious category. In the test or trial that Abraham experiences, his moral duty to his son was "teleologically suspended," that is, suspended for the sake of a higher goal. But the higher goal in question is not merely another ethical responsibility. Abraham does not sacrifice his son, as does the tragic hero, to save his country (III, 109; p. 69). He is willing to sacrifice Isaac for the sake of his own relationship to God. He acts because God commands him to act.

The real significance of *Fear and Trembling* is only hinted at in the book itself. There, as we have noted, Abraham is represented as a morally righteous man, and the "suspension of the ethical" appears as a temporary, exceptional moment in his life (VII, 226; p. 238). The possibility of a relationship to God that does not consist simply in a life of positive moral action is nonetheless delineated, since how long the suspension lasts is not so important as the fact that it is possible (VII, 226; pp. 238-239). Climacus sees that the *significance* of that possibility appears only when it is recognized that the ethical life cannot successfully be carried through by the self's own resolution. Then the individual truly finds himself "suspended" from the ethical:

> The suspension lies in the fact that the individual finds himself in just the opposite state of that which the ethical demands, so that, far from being able to begin, every moment he remains in this state he is more and more prevented from being able to begin. He relates himself [to the ethical demand] not as possibility to actuality, but as an impossibility. Thus the individual is suspended from the ethical in the most terrible way; he is in the suspension heterogenuous with the ethical which yet has an infinite claim on him. . . (VII, 226; p. 238).

It is the person who finds himself in this condition who truly discovers

Abraham as "the guiding star which saves the anguished." For the person in this guilty condition, which is illumined in *The Concept of Anxiety* by Vigilius Haufniensis, the religious life will not be a mere temporary moment; rather, the whole of existence becomes a trial. Each individual becomes "the exception."

Climacus describes the specific character of the religious life in detail as "suffering," a concept we will examine later at much greater length. The fact that suffering is regarded as the essence of the religious life makes intelligible the third section of *Stages on Life's Way*, which represents the anguish of an individual who falls in love, becomes engaged, but then feels compelled to break off the engagement. "Quidam's Diary" or "A Story of Suffering" is not obviously religious on its face; its religious significance lies in the fact that it points to "resignation," and "suffering," and "guilt," which are the distinctive elements of the religious life on Climacus' view.

More will be said about this later. Here we will merely note that the suffering of the religious life will clearly bear an essential relationship to guilt. The religious individual no longer sees himself as self-sufficient, hence no longer merely as *active*. He recognizes his lack of self-sufficiency and suffers. The remedy is a relationship to God through which the individual is refashioned, a relationship in which God is essentially active and the individual is active in learning the necessity for God's action rather than his own.

The religiousness sketched in the pseudonymous writings outside of the *Fragments* and the *Postscript* does not clearly distinguish between what Climacus calls religiousness A and the distinctive sort of religiousness characteristic of Christianity. The major difference between these two in the *Postscript* is that religiousness A is described as a religion of immanence, which does not rest on any special historical revelation of God. In comparison with the ethical life religiousness A seems to emphasize man's lack of self-sufficiency and need of God. But in religiousness A the exister at least views himself as able to recognize and realize his own guilt and need for God and through that recognition to allow his life to be transformed. Religiousness B, or the Christian type of religiousness, asserts that the individual cannot do even this; his "immanent" understanding of God is radically defective, and he is incapable of truly transforming his life through that understanding. Hence here there is need for God to reveal himself to the individual; to break into history himself. The individual's saving transformation is then dependent on a relation to the God in time; he can no longer rest content in his own moral-religious consciousness.

Obviously much more could be said about the stages and about

Kierkegaard's pseudonymous authorship, particularly books like *Repetition,* which we have ignored, and *The Concept of Anxiety,* touched on only in passing. More will be said in later chapters. But the preceding will perhaps serve as an introduction for the reader who lacks an acquaintance with these works and these concepts, yet wishes to read the *Fragments* and *Postscript.* It is particularly the latter work where these concepts are constantly in the background. In reviewing these works Johannes Climacus does not know for sure whether their pseudonymous authors' intentions corresponded to the meanings he found in the books, since they are all attempts at indirect communication (VII, 212; p. 225). It should be clear that in my discussion of these works I have attempted to view them as Climacus views them.

4. *The Nature of the Spheres of Existence*

A few questions remain about the general character of these spheres or stages. First, are they spheres or are they stages? That is, are they to be regarded as phases of the life cycle, or are they independent modes of existence from which the individual must choose? The answer is that they must really be seen in both ways. Climacus does see the stages as forming a "natural" progression. That is, it would be more or less normal for a person to begin life as a child in the aesthetic sphere, progress to ethical striving as a young person, and reach religious faith as a mature exister.

If the stages are understood only or even mainly in this way, however, they will be misunderstood. The reason for this is that Climacus does not see human development as a natural process in the sense in which a tree develops from an acorn. Human development is made actual through the free choice of the individual. Hence there is nothing automatic or necessary about it.

This is where the famous Kierkegaardian category of "the leap" emerges. In popular usage this concept is applied mainly to Kierkegaard's description of the transition to the Christian faith. The leap in Climacus' writings has a broader meaning, however. It is simply the category of decision, a concept that metaphorically emphasizes the decisiveness human existence demands. The transition from each sphere to the next demands a leap. One of Kierkegaard's earliest achievements as a thinker was the demarcation of what he calls "dialectical and pathos-filled transitions."[9] It is one thing in thinking through a series of positions to make a transition in *thought* (dialectics). It is quite another to make a transition in existence. The latter kind of transition is "pathos-filled"; that is, it is only achieved through the sort of passion we discussed earlier as the key element in the subjectivity or inwardness that an exister must develop.

It is for this reason that the stages must also be understood as spheres, existential possibilities a person can remain in for a lifetime. The transition from one sphere to another is only achieved via a passionate decision. Thus these transitions are by no means inevitable. Nor is it necessary for a person to go through the stages in a step-by-step progression. It is conceivable, for example, that an experienced aesthete might jump from the aesthetic life directly to a religious mode of existence.

A second general question about the spheres concerns the extent to which they are mutually exclusive. Can one person be aesthetic, and ethical, and religious? The answer is really yes and no, depending upon what is meant by the question. In existence, as the spheres are characterized in Kierkegaard's pseudonymous literaure, the spheres certainly oppose each other. The choice between the aesthetic and the ethical is an either/or, and the ethicist in the *Stages* is represented as defending himself against the religious life as well as the aesthetic (VII, 252; p. 262). Even a highly developed religious individual may be offended by the Christian kind of religiousness and choose to remain within the sphere of immanence. Climacus emphasizes, however, that it is only *in existence* that there is a decisive struggle between the standpoints. Abstractly seen, this is not so (VII, 253; p. 262).

What I think he means is this. There is no reason in principle why the contents of the aesthetic, ethical, and religious ways of existence cannot be achieved in one life. The difficulty lies in the way these elements are chosen, the *form* of these ways of life. To exist is by definition to be interested, to possess passion. And interests and passions are in the nature of the case imperialistic. This is particularly true of the supreme and ruling interests of a person's life. "No man can serve two masters." To be supremely committed to pleasure excludes a supreme commitment to moral duty, for example. But it is precisely this supreme type of commitment that is demanded by the moral life and the religious life. To be only partially willing to do what is morally right is precisely to be immoral. To regard God as one commitment among others is not to regard God as God. It is for this reason that the choice between existence spheres must always be a choice.

There is one sense, however, in which the commitments that are supreme in one sphere can be included in another sphere as relative. In fact, I believe this may be part of the justification for Johannes Climacus' "ranking" of the spheres. While the ethical life cannot be subordinated to the aesthetic life without becoming unethical, it is by no means certain that the converse relationship is the same. Judge William, Kierkegaard's leading ethicist, argues strenuously that there can be a "balance" between the aesthetic and the ethical in the composition of a personality.[10] The judge understands that this synthesis cannot be achieved through a compromise; it can only be gained on ethical terms. But when ethical resolution is allowed its supremacy, he argues that the relative aesthetic values remain and are even deepened. Thus he defends "the aesthetic validity of marriage." Of course one will not expect an existential aesthete to concede this claim, but that does not mean it is not true.

A similar relation is sketched in Climacus' writings between the ethical and religious spheres and, within the religious sphere between religious-ness A and B. Though the religious life is not reducible to the ethical life, it is normally reached through ethical striving (when that striving is recognized as unsuccessful), and it retains the ethical as an essential component (VII, 335-338; pp. 347-349). Again it is possible that an existential ethicist would deny this, under the grip of an imperialistic passion which by no means wishes to be displaced by something higher, even if preserved in another form. But that denial again does not entail that the religious claim is wrong.

With regard to religiousness A and B Climacus is quite clear. Although religiousness A can exist independently and exclusively (VII, 486; p. 495), it is also an essential component of the Christian kind of religiousness. "Religiousness A must first be present in the individual before there can be talk about becoming attentive to the dialectical in B" (VII, 486; pp. 494-495). "Every Christian has pathos as in religiousness A, and then this discriminating pathos [B]" (VII, 507; p. 516). Though again one would not expect an existential proponent of religiousness A to admit these claims, they are nonetheless made by the Christian. And similar claims cannot be made by religiousness A, which as a religion of immanence cannot accept the dethronement of immanence, which lies at the heart of B.

Climacus sees these relations as holding across more than one sphere. He explicitly claims, for example, that the aesthetic can appear as a relative aspect of the religious life. In commenting on Kierkegaard's *Edifying Discourses*, which are religious in character, Climacus says that some have objected to them because they were so poetic. Usually, he says, the religious address leaves out this poetic factor. But, Climacus says, this may leave the reader with the feeling that something is missing and make him seek it elsewhere. Why not include the poetic within the religious? The distinctiveness of the religious will remain in that the poetic has as its *telos* an aesthetic *telos*—beauty, along with psychical truth—while the religious address will utilize this aesthetic *telos* as a *means* toward its own *telos*—the upbuilding (VII, 217n; p. 230n). Here again we see that what is the highest *telos* within one sphere is capable of being incorporated in a relative way in another.

The answer then to the question as to whether the spheres are mutually exclusive is as follows: They are exclusive if the distinctive content of each sphere is absolutized. But if what is absolute is allowed to be absolute, the relative can be retained as relative. Actually, this relationship between the aesthetic and the religious which Climacus notices in the *Edifying Discourses* is characteristic of the whole of Kierkegaard's authorship, particularly the pseudonymous section, which Kierkegaard himself described as "aesthetic." This is so, at least, if the reader gives any credence to Kierkegaard's own statement that he was from the beginning a religious author. Such was his claim in *The Point of View For My Work as an Author*, where he affirms that "the whole of my work as an author is related to Christianity, to the problem of becoming a Christian, with a direct or indirect polemic against the enormous illusion: Christendom, or that in such a land as ours all are Christians of a sort" (XIII, 517-518; pp. 5-6).

5. *Climacus and Kierkegaard Again: Viewing the Pseudonyms*

This statement may rouse a question in the mind of a curious reader. What is the relationship between Johannes Climacus' view of Kierkegaard's pseudonymous authorship and Kierkegaard's own view of this authorship? And this in turn raises the general question of the relation of Climacus to Kierkegaard again. It should be remembered that this question is an historical one with no essential significance to the reader who aspires to be the "ideal reader" Climacus longingly imagines. Readers who have really been helped to see the truth for themselves by reading Climacus' works will not find it essentially important whether the opinions found there are Kierkegaard's or not. Nevertheless, it would be a rare individual who would not find his curiosity piqued by Kierkegaard's pseudonymous production.

The general relationship between Climacus and Kierkegaard seems to me to be as follows: The two are very similar but not identical. The close relation can be seen in many ways. For one thing the problem of the *Postscript*—how can an individual become a Christian—is affirmed by Kierkegaard to be the essential problem of the whole authorship.[11] The *Postscript* and the *Fragments* contain Kierkegaard's own name as editor on the title page, which he claims is an indication that these works, while not strictly religious, are not merely aesthetic in the sense that the other pseudonymous work is. This is said to be a "hint for him who is concerned about such things and has a sense for them."[12] One can in addition find a tremendous amount of the content of the *Postscript* in Kierkegaard's *Journals and Papers*, expressed initially as his own personal thoughts. In many cases these expressions are almost verbally identical. Another striking parallel is the extent to which the *Postscript* reflects, in the humoristic fashion to be expected of a Climacus, the content of Kierkegaard's *Edifying Discourses*,[13] of which S.K. expressly affirms that he is the author of "every word" (VII, 547; p. 552). It would not be extravagant to recommend the *Edifying Discourses* as perhaps the best guide or commentary to the *Postscript,* so striking are these parallels. There are also Kierkegaard's later statements about the *Postscript* in his *Journal,* where he sometimes straightforwardly refers to the book as his own.[14]

This general congruence of Climacus and Kierkegaard also holds with respect to the interpretation of the pseudonymous authorship. The reading of the pseudonymous works Climacus offers is that they have a unified purpose, which is the development of the inwardness or subjectivity that is demanded if Christianity is to be understood as an existence-communication. Though Climacus offers this view only as a third party, since he cannot be sure of the other pseudonymous authors' intentions, his perception of the works' significance is confirmed by Kierkegaard as substantially identical with his own intentions in producing them, at least as he sees them in retrospect.[15]

Kierkegaard describes his whole authorship as a twofold movement in one direction: "*from* 'the poet'—from the aesthetic, *from* 'the philosopher'—from the speculative *to* the indication of the most inward determination in Christianity."[16] This movement must necessarily be accomplished "indirectly," since the intended audience is in the grip of an illusion that must be dispelled before they can perceive the truth, and since in the deepest sense all one human being can do for another is to force the other to take notice.[17] The decision always lies with the other person.

We can see here the closest connection between Kierkegaard and Climacus, not only as to the content, but even as to the form of the pseudonymous works. The theory of indirect communication which Climacus develops at such length is specifically appealed to by Kierkegaard himself to explain and justify his use of the pseudonyms to point his readers in the direction of Christianity.

This of course is only Kierkegaard's testimony, which he himself would emphatically assert is valueless if the meaning he and Climacus see in the authorship (obviously, Climacus cannot comment on the later part of the authorship) cannot be seen by a third party.[18] The objection has often been raised that the view he presents of his authorship in *The Point of View* is hindsight, since it can be seen from his *Journals and Papers* that he by no means clearly understood the initial works in this way at the time he began to write them.[19] This objection is not really an objection, however, since it is clearly affirmed in *The Point of View* by Kierkegaard himself (XIII, 561-562; pp. 72-73). He admits that at the outset of his work he by no means understood his task clearly and precisely. Rather, the development of the authorship constituted his own education. In other words, the existential relationships that constitute the existence spheres were not necessarily clearly present at the beginning as a scheme around which the works were planned, though a good deal of the scheme clearly did exist. Kierkegaard learned as he wrote. That the whole thing acquired the unity and meaning it did Kierkegaard ascribed to "Governance" (XIII, 562, p. 73). This is of course an explanation that nonreligious readers will find implausible. However, it at least seems fairly noncontroversial to conclude that Kierkegaard's own understanding of the meaning of his works when completed is close to the meaning Climacus sees in them.

However close Climacus and Kierkegaard may be, they are not simply identical on this point or on others. Climacus sees the pseudonymous works in relation to *his* purposes, which are the elucidation of existence and clarification of the relationship between Christianity and speculation. Climacus is not a Christian, and he does not know and probably does not care whether his work will draw people toward Christianity or repel them. Kierkegaard, on the other hand, expressly affirms himself to be an author in the service of Christianity, one who recognized, however, that he was more in need of Christianity than Christianity of him.[20] Though Climacus is not a Christian and is not consciously attempting to serve the cause of Christianity, Kierkegaard sees his own creation of Climacus and Climacus' works as such an attempt, part of the attempt to "reintroduce Christianity into Christendom."

Climacus then is *not* Kierkegaard, and Kierkegaard expressly affirms this. "It [The *Postscript*] is by Johannes Climacus, and what stands at the back of the book is valid again here, that the pseudonym is not me; he permits himself a heedlessness which I neither can nor will."[21] Attributing the *Fragments* and *Postscript* to a pseudonym serves at least three important functions that are lost if the distinction between Kierkegaard and Climacus is not maintained. First, since Climacus is a non-Christian, he can function as a somewhat neutral arbiter in the dispute between Hegelianism and Christianity. One of his criticisms of the Hegelians is that in their relationship to Christianity they play the role of both opponent and arbiter. If Climacus spoke from the distinctively Christian viewpoint that is Kierkegaard's own, a similar criticism could be leveled against him.

Secondly, one of the errors, perhaps the central error, Kierkegaard is aiming at is the illusion of "Christendom." This illusion is grounded in the idea that being a Christian is something easy, something that everyone is as a matter of course. By personally claiming not to be a Christian, Climacus illustrates what he affirms about the difficulty of becoming a Christian. This is an essential aspect of Kierkegaard's "attack from behind."[22] In *The Point of View* he explains that an illusion such as Christendom can only be expelled in this manner. It is no good to thunder at people and affirm that they are not true Christians (thereby affirming that you are). Such a tactic only arms them by making them defensive. The correct tactic is to begin by accepting their illusion as "good money" and subjecting it to examination. One must take people's word if they say they are Christians, and then, by humbly confessing that you personally are not a Christian, since it is so difficult, lead them to the perception of the truth.[23] This is precisely the standpoint Johannes Climacus realizes.

Thirdly, the Climacus pseudonym is a realization of the ideal of indirect communication; it is the means whereby Kierkegaard personally withdraws from the reader so as to guarantee the reader's freedom, and make it possible to grasp the truth for himself.

Despite the close connection, then, between Climacus and Kierkegaard it is a mistake to conflate their personalities and attribute to Kierkegaard without question the content of the *Fragments* and *Postscript*. It is true that for the reader who is interested in such historical questions there are many points of agreement that can be demonstrated by comparison with Kierkegaard's *Journals* and his other writings. But historians would do well to limit their attributions to what can be certified in this manner. For there are also many things Climacus says in his character as a humorist, that would not be said by Kierkegaard personally. The "revocation" at the end of the *Postscript*, for example, is an act that is specifically characteristic of the humorist, and it must be understood in that light.[24]

Even when Climacus says something that Kierkegaard would personally agree with, there is still very often an important difference in *how* he says it. This is not so significant when Climacus is discussing the aesthetic and ethical spheres. It is very significant, however, where Climacus discusses Christianity. Climacus affirms quite clearly that it is possible to know what Christianity is without being a Christian. But he affirms just as clearly that there is a difference between knowing what Christianity is and knowing what it is to be a Christian (VII, 322; p. 332). It follows from this that it is a great mistake, though one frequently made, to look to Climacus as

Kierkegaard's definitive spokesman for Christianity. Climacus' viewpoint on Christianity is definitely an outsider's view; Kierkegaard's is an insider's view.

This outsider's point of view is signaled by Climacus for himself in the *Fragments,* where he uses the odd construction "the God" (*Guden*) to refer to the deity in describing God's entrance into history. The term "the God" is an abstract term with philosophical overtones of Plato and Socrates. Essentially, as we shall see, Climacus is a "humorist" who exists in the same region as philosophical speculation. Christianity is by no means his home turf.

This does not imply that what Climacus says about Christianity is *false,* since he does indeed understand what Christianity is. What it entails is that the innermost existential meaning of what he says may be totally opaque to him. He understands what faith is, but he does not understand what faith means to the believer. Therefore his descriptions of the Christian life are not distinctively Christian. The specific events of Christ's life do not have the meaning for him that they do for the believer. Hence it is a great mistake to look to Climacus for accounts of the Atonement, the work of the Holy Spirit, or other distinctively Christian concepts, which take on their full meaning only in the context of the Christian life.

We shall return now to Climacus' own exploration of existence, which he regards as the key to understanding Christianity and its proper relation to philosophical speculation. Indeed, readers may find Climacus' exploration valuable even if they are completely uninterested in Christianity, so long as they are interested in existing. And well they might, since Climacus himself affirms that there are a range of existence-possibilities outside of Christianity that are significant in their own right and therefore worthy of consideration.

---

[1] See VII, 256, 401-403, 434-436, 453-455, 498-499 (pp. 265, 413-415, 446-448, 463-465, 506-508), for some examples of these characterizations of the spheres or stages.

[2] The Danish terms are *lykke-ulykke. Til lykke* is the standard Danish expression for "best wishes," "congratulations," or even "happy birthday."

[3] *Either/Or,* vol. I (I, 381-382, pp. 409-410).

[4] This is modern Danish spelling.

[5] *Either/Or,* vol. II (II, 161; p. 182).

[6] This argument actually is employed most clearly by Anti-Climacus in *The Sickness unto Death* (XI, 136-141; pp. 155-161).

[7] See *Purity of Heart Is to Will One Thing*, which illustrates Climacus' views here very well.

[8] Translated by Theodore M. Greene and Hoyt H. Hudson (New York: Harper & Row, 1960), p. 158.

[9] Malantschuk, *Kierkegaard's Thought*, pp. 79-82.

[10] The second major section of *Either/Or*, vol. II, is entitled "Equilibrium Between the Aesthetical and the Ethical in the Composition of Personality."

[11] *The Point of View* (XIII, 517-518; pp. 5-6).

[12] Ibid. (XIII, 523; p. 13).

[13] A particularly striking example can be seen in "The Expectation of an Eternal Happiness," which sheds much light on Climacus' discussion of this concept. See IV, 139-156; pp. 75-100.

[14] See *J. and P.* I, 7, for example

[15] See *The Point of View*(XIII, 517-542; pp. 5-42).

[16] "My Activity as a Writer," *The Point of View* (XIII, 494; p. 142).

[17] *The Point of View*(XIII, 537-538; pp. 34-35).

[18] XIII, 524; p. 15.

[19] See, for example, Josiah Thompson, *Kierkegaard,* p. 121.

[20] *The Point of View* (XIII, 556-558, 561-564; pp. 64-47, 72-75).

[21] *J. and P.* V, 5884.

[22] Kierkegaard uses the imagery of approaching or attacking someone from behind frequently in this context—for example, in *The Point of View* (XIII, 535; p. 30) and in the title of the third section of his *Christian Discourses*—"Thoughts Which Wound from Behind—for Up-building."

[23] *The Point of View* (XIII, 531-533, 541-542; pp. 24-27, 40-41).

[24] See chapter 10, especially pp. 201-205.

Chapter IV

EXISTENCE AND PASSION:
"REDUPLICATING ETERNITY IN TIME"

1. *Existence as a Contrasting Synthesis*

Johannes Climacus sees the root problem of the speculative mis-understanding of Christianity to lie in a misunderstanding of existence. In his own work, therefore, he reviews the contributions of the other pseudonymous authors in their elucidation of the spheres of existence. This review corresponds closely with Kierkegaard's own assessment of his authorship as directing the individual in a two fold movement "away from the poet" and "away from speculation" (*The Point of View*, XIII, 563; p. 74). What the individual is being called away from appears to be different in the two cases. (But we shall see there is a close connection between the aesthetic and speculative views of existence). But what the individual is being called *to* is the same; it is existence, understood as ethical existence. When existence is used in its strong, pregnant sense by Climacus, it becomes practically a synonym for ethical striving. In this chapter we shall focus on the structural components of this activity, and in the next we shall examine the activity itself as a process.

One point that Kierkegaard and nearly all of his pseudonyms seem to agree on is that existence, understood in that special sense in which it refers to the type of existence human beings have, is a synthesis of contrasting factors. This is expressed most famously by the pseudonym Anti-Climacus in *The Sickness Unto Death.* "Man is a synthesis of infinitude and finitude, of the temporal and the eternal, of freedom and necessity" (XI, 127; p. 146). Anti-Climacus hastens to add that these are merely the elements of which man is composed; man's actual being as *spirit* consists not merely in the contrasting elements of which he is a synthesis, but in the fact that the synthesis is "a relation which relates itself to itself" (XI, 127; p. 146). This rather formidable language means that man is a self-conscious relationship. He not only is what he is—i.e., a relation or "bringing together" of contrasting elements—he is also his awareness of what he is. Man, as a self-conscious being, is capable of "relating himself to himself." In short, he is capable of self-conscious reflection which makes it possible for him to choose to be what he will be. *The Sickness Unto Death* provides the most complete and systematic analysis of these elements of existence in Kierkegaard's writings and sheds a great deal of light on the discussions of existence in the *Postscript.* This theme is also present in *The Concept of Anxiety* by Vigilius Haufniensis, who uses the terms "soul" and "body" as well as "temporal" and "eternal" to describe man (IV, 355; p. 76).

Johannes Climacus agrees with these other pseudonyms. He repeatedly speaks of the self as a synthesis of the temporal and the eternal. The theme is present already in *Johannes Climacus, or De Omnibus Dubitandum Est,* which is an early work of Kierkegaard's, unfinished and unpublished in his lifetime. The work is a kind of intellectual history of Johannes Climacus, and it really is a biography as well, since Climacus is represented as a person wholly devoted to reflection. Climacus here is represented as enunciating the characteristic Kierkegaardian view of man, though the terminology is different. Climacus talks about "consciousness" instead of existence, but it is clear that the concepts are the same. Consciousness is represented as a relation between two elements. This contrasting relation is described in two ways: between immediacy and language and between reality (*Realiteten*) and ideality.[1] Immediacy and reality here refer to the temporal and finite components in the human synthesis; language and ideality refer to the ideal, eternal element. That Climacus here is thinking of what he later terms existence is made clear when he asserts that the distinctive characteristic of consciousness, the one that distinguishes it from mere reflection, is that consciousness is interested.[2] This "interestedness" corresponds to what he later terms "passion."

This view is just as prominent in *The Concluding Unscientific Postscript*. "What is existence? It is that child, which is begotten of the infinite and the finite, the eternal and the temporal, and is, therefore, a continuous striving" (VII, 73; p. 85). Why does such a synthesis produce a continuous striving? As Climacus sees it, a striving requires both change and continuity (VII, 267-268; p. 277). A striving is by definition a process; human growth and development are characterized by successiveness and gradualness. Therefore some kind of continuity is necessary as well, since a being who changed *completely* every moment could hardly be described as developing. As Climacus sees it, the continuity is provided by the direction of growth, by the *ideals* the person seeks, while temporality denotes the incomplete, successive character of the achievement of the ideal. This temporal realization of the ideal is made possible by passion, which is equivalent to interestedness (VII, 164; p. 176).

To fully understand existence as a self-conscious, inner-directed synthesis one must understand the concept of "doubleness." The thesis that existence (and communication and thought about existence) contains a doubleness plays a major role in the whole of the Kierkegaardian authorship. We meet this doubleness already in the *Philosophical Fragments*, where Climacus explicates the concept of "coming into existence" (*blive til*). Everything that has spatio-temporal actuality has "come into existence" (IV, 238-239; pp. 92-93). According to Climacus this sort of change is never necessary; if it were necessary for a thing to be, it would always exist. What comes into existence, therefore, does so because of a cause; and the whole of nature possesses the characteristic of contingency. The ultimate cause of such an event must for Climacus be a "freely effecting cause" (IV, 239; p. 93).

Among the natural objects that have come into existence in this first sense there are some, human beings, whose lives contain the "possibility of a second coming into existence within the first coming into existence" (IV, 240; p. 94). Human existence is thus a "reduplication" or "doubling" (*Fordobling*). Human actions are doubly contingent. They are contingent not only because they are part of nature and hence point to an ultimate "freely effecting cause;" they are also themselves free acts.

How is it possible for an event to be a "coming into existence within a coming into existence?" Climacus says that "the coming into existence which here is held in common with the coming into existence of nature is a possibility" (IV, 240; p. 94). That is, human beings as part of nature (the first coming into existence) are endowed not only with actualities but possibilities. These possibilities are in a sense actual; they have "come into existence" in the sense that they are actually present in the individual. But it is up to the individual to actualize or fail to actualize these possibilities in the decisive sense. He thus acquires the capability of being a "relatively freely effecting cause." When he chooses to actualize a possibility, that actualization is a "reduplication" of what is already present—as a possibility.

What makes it possible for human beings to make choices this way is their self-conscious awareness of these possibilities. This awareness of the possible is the "eternal" element in man. It is possible for a human being to consciously reflect on the possibilities with which he is endowed. Man not only has possibilities (as do other animals); he *is* in part his awareness of these possibilities. Thought in the sense of conscious awareness is therefore an essential aspect of being human. It is the power of thought that introduces a duality into human existence, for the thought of a possibility is not identical with existing in the possibility. "So to think is one thing, and to exist in the thought is something else. Existing is in relation to thinking just as little something which follows of itself as it is something thoughtless" (VII, 215; p. 228). Thought is an essential component in existence, but it is not existence. Existence, as a successive, temporal striving, involves the separation of thought and being. For God, on the other hand, no such separation exists; God is the one whose being coincides perfectly with his thought (VII, 287; p. 296). Human existence contains "the idea"; this makes it possible to strive toward ideals. But since these are ideals, the exister's being never perfectly coincides with them.

We shall now attempt to look at the structural components of this process of reduplication: eternity, the ideal component; temporality, the limiting component; and passion, which provides both the "glue" and the motive power to existence. Climacus' discussion of these three concepts is strongly shaped, as is all of Kierkegaard's authorship, by Greek thought, particularly that of Socrates, Plato, and Aristotle in this case. Existence is explicitly described by Climacus as identical with the Platonic conception of eros, as developed in the *Symposium* (VII, 73; p. 85). Here love is described as the child of "poverty and wealth," whose essence "partakes of both." Love here, says Climacus, evidently signifies "existence, or that whereby life is in its wholeness, that life which is a synthesis of the infinite and the finite" (VII, 73; p. 85). In another discussion that clearly points toward a familiar Platonic metaphor, Climacus describes existence as a wagon with two horses attached, one a Pegasus and the other a worn-out hack. "Eternity is like that winged horse infinitely quick; temporality is the worn-out hack; and the exister is the driver" (VII, 267; p. 276). As we discuss Climacus' usage of these terms, we shall cast sidelong glances at the significance they had in Plato's writings.

2. The Eternal

The significance of the eternal element in the human synthesis is lyrically expressed by another of Kierkegaard's pseudonyms, Johannes de Silentio, in *Fear and Trembling*:

> If there were no eternal consciousness in a man, if at the base of everything there only lay a wildly seething power, which writhing in obscure passions brought forth everything that was great and everything that was insignificant, if a boundless emptiness, never satisfied, hid itself in everything, what then would life be but despair? (III, 68; p. 30).

Johannes Climacus is no less convinced of the significance of "the eternal" in human life. It is not, however, an easy matter to determine just what he means by the term. But it is beyond doubt that he perceives the exister as an "eternal spirit" (VII, 189n)[3] whose intended destiny is an "eternal happiness."

A careful study of Climacus' usage leads to the conclusion that he uses the term "eternity" in several distinct ways, but that there is also an underlying unity of meaning. In each of the uses Climacus gives to "eternity" the word denotes what is unchangeable, perfect, and complete as opposed to what is changing, imperfect, and in process. The eternal is what is self-identical; it is that which perfectly is what it is. It therefore suffers no essential change. The term "eternal" is then primarily a qualitative adjective. In the course of his writings Climacus refers to several types of things that possess this qualitative completeness. I believe there are four significant uses, that "the eternal" refers to (1) abstract logical possibilities, (2) moral obligations, (3) God, and (4) man's future life.

The first usage has to do with eternity as applying to logical entities. This is the kind of "eternity" that is the medium of abstract thought, which focuses not on actuality, but on possibility. Like any good Platonist Climacus (and Kierkegaard on this point) assumes that when one reflects on an entity with regard to the kind of thing it is (and how else can one reflect on it?) one focuses on its universal character. These universal characteristics, as distinguished from the particulars that realize them, are in themselves timelessly eternal. This sense of "timelessness" is a familiar one to modern logicians, who deal with such abstract entities as "propositions," which can be distinguished from the sentences that express them.

Climacus discusses this sort of eternity in the course of his attack on the Hegelian treatment of immortality. In the Hegelian view the Absolute Spirit that manifests itself in history is immortal. The individual, insofar as through intellectual thought he himself becomes spirit, participates in this immortality. The basic problem Climacus saw in this is the relation between the existing individual and the Absolute, when the Absolute is understood as "pure thought." There is no problem in accepting the thesis that "pure thought" is immortal, since eternity is essentially the medium of thought (VII, 258; pp. 267-268). The difficulty lies in the supposition that an existing individual could be or become "pure thought." To put it another way, it is clear that for Climacus such intellectual entities as ideas and propositions are eternal, but it is just as clear that human beings are not entities of this type.

A thought reality is a possibility (VII, 276; p. 285). As such the eternal becomes a constituent of human life through reflection and imagination, whose medium is the medium of the possible. It is important to understand the relationship between thought and existence for Climacus. This relationship is an essential one, since thought is an essential element in human life. But the relation is never one of identity, since the thinker's thought does not necessarily coincide with his *being* and does not in any case do so merely by virtue of his thought. This is well expressed by Climacus, again in Platonic language, when discussing "what it is to exist as an individual person."

> It [individual existence] is not to be in the same sense as a potato is, but neither in the same sense as the Idea is. The human existence has Idea in itself, but is yet not Idea-existence. Plato places the Ideas on the second rank as middle-links between God and matter, and as existing the person must participate in the Idea, but is not himself Idea (VII, 285; p. 295).

From this it can be inferred that Climacus places the person as a "middle" between the ideas and the material, in much the same way as Plato himself. The person possesses some of the characteristics of the eternal Forms, which the person can participate in, make a part of his life in thought, and even realize in action, though the person never becomes pure Form. It is the human ability to conceive universal qualities and structure life around conceived universal qualities that raises human existence above the level of the animals, which simply act on impulse.

These universal qualities are logical possibilities. In the process of knowing, a person transforms actualities into possibilities by attempting to abstract from the particular and understand physical objects in their essential character (VII, 275-276; pp. 284-285). When a person acts, the process moves in the other direction; through passion, conceived possibilities are transformed into actualities (VII, 293; p. 302).

It is when action is introduced that the second usage of "eternity" comes into play—this is "the eternal" understood as the eternal moral obligations which impinge on human existence. Climacus frequently uses the phrases "the eternal" and "the ethical" synonymously. The relation between these usages is as follows. From a purely intellectual perspective eternity appears to man simply in the guise of universal possibilities. However, man is not merely an intellectual creature but a being who acts. As an agent man reflects on possibilities, not as merely intellectual concepts but as possibilities for action. These possibilities for action cannot merely be contemplated in a detached fashion; they must be reflected on as worthy or unworthy of fulfillment. In the course of man's practical life some of these possibilities can be grasped as universal and timeless, according to Climacus. These moral possibilities, which transcend personal whims and cultural fashions, are those possibilities the exister encounters as eternally binding. Therefore, for an exister eternity does not consist merely of ideas, but of ideals, norms, or goals which he must strive to realize. "The ethical is the very breath of the eternal" (VII, 125; p. 136).

The fundamentally moral character of eternity here also comes loaded with Platonic overtones. The Platonic concept of the "Forms" seems to function in both of Climacus' two usages of "eternity." The Forms are both ideas and ideals. Plato seems at times to regard them as simply logical possibilities, speaking of the Forms of horseness, dogness, tallness, and so on. But the Forms also seem to function as ideals or norms, the standards that particular things more or less successfully imitate. It is noteworthy that in this respect Plato seems to be much more successful when dealing with moral concepts such as "justice." Of course the Forms are in some sense all value-impregnated; in *The Republic* their source is said to be the "Form of the Good." It is therefore not surprising that it is the universal moral qualities that are most plausibly viewed as eternal Forms. Plato even seems at times to doubt himself whether it makes sense to regard anything other than moral qualities as Forms.[4]

Climacus' first two usages of "eternity" can be understood as an attempt to separate and at the same time show the relation between idea and ideal, between mere logical possibles and standards of value. Both ideas and obligations are eternal in nature, since they both possess the qualities of the self-identical. They are timelessly complete and therefore perfect. When man thinks from a detached intellectual standpoint, he apprehends the eternal in the form of the Idea, the logical possibility. This, however, is merely what Climacus calls the "eternity of abstraction." When an individual acts, he encounters the eternal in the form of moral ideals. These are eternal possibilities that have concrete relevance for the ethical exister. Thus in a concrete human life "the eternal" is synonymous with "the ethical."

The third usage of "eternal" in Climacus' writings is in connection with God. God is said to be eternal, and at times he is even said to be "the eternal." The reason for this is that for Climacus God is primarily, at least within the compass of the sphere of "immanence," that reality which the individual discovers in discovering moral duty. God is essentially a moral being, and he is known as the source and guarantee of moral obligation. This is of course very controversial with respect to both morality and God. In our analysis of the ethical and religious life we shall give an account of Climacus' reason for thinking of God and morality as connected in this way. At this point we simply want to say enough to make sense of Climacus' terminology. God as moral reality possesses the self-identical, complete character of the eternal.

God is for Climacus a reality, even though he does say that "God does not *exist*." We must recognize that Danish has more than one word that must be translated by "exist" in English. The term here (*existere*) is used by Climacus almost always to designate the special type of existence that humans possess. This type of existence is expressly used to designate the necessity for incompleteness and perpetual striving. Thus in denying that God *exists* (in one English sense) Climacus by no means denies that God is a real being. Taking the quote as a whole, the point is how much more perfect God's being is than man's:

> God does not think, he creates; God does not exist, he is eternal. Man thinks and exists, and existence separates thought and being, holds them apart from each other in succession (VII, 287; p. 296).

Climacus is not saying that God has no independent being but that God's being is superior to man. God's actions completely coincide with his being; there is no distinction between what he thinks, what he wills, and what he does. It is precisely this which constitutes God's perfection and completeness, hence his eternality.

Climacus' conception of God seems at times to be purely Platonic or

Aristotelian, since he emphasizes God's eternality and makes such a sharp distinction between time and eternity. "The eternal" is discovered by the individual who makes "the absolute venture" of willing moral duty absolutely. At this ethical level it probably does not matter much whether the individual conceives of God as a personal being or merely in terms of abstract moral qualities, since God as "the eternal" is known only through those moral qualities. However God is conceived, he is nonetheless conceived as a reality. A close look reveals that God is seen as a distinct being who has a relation to the space-time world. God is said to be "he, who himself is outside existence (*Tilværelse*), who in his eternity is eternally complete and yet encloses existence in himself" (VII, 97; p. 108). Climacus does not regard God's eternality as precluding any change. He says that the true religious conception of God, as distinguished from paganism, is that the religious person views God as himself moved or changed inwardly, while the pagan said that God, unmoved, moved everything else (VII, 375n; p. 387n).

The fourth usage of "eternity" concerns man. What role does eternity play in human existence? Eternity figures in human existence as both a *constituent* and *goal*. These are not unrelated since man's goals as a reflective being permeate his present actions. Climacus sees man as a being whose intended destiny is eternal life. Man's highest *telos* is the possession of an eternal happiness, which is a state that Climacus defines without attempting to describe. He does, however, tell us his reasons for not describing it (VII, 339-341; pp. 350-352). *Descriptions* of an eternal happiness that would be intelligible to human beings in general would inevitably take on an aesthetic color. This would make it impossible to strive for an eternal happiness, which must be attained precisely through the renunciation of the relative aesthetic values in favor of doing one's duty whatever the cost. An *eternal* happiness is only a meaningful concept to the person who is *committed* to the realization of "the eternal." The eternal in this sense is simply the ethical, when the ethical is understood not in terms of prudential action but in the sense of the absolutely binding duties man discovers. Eternal life is therefore conceived as the perfect, endless realization of the eternal moral qualities man discovers as exister and conceives as realized in God. An existing individual can only relate himself to the eternal as something future (VII, 368; p. 380), and thus Christianity properly proclaims eternity as a future life (VII, 263; pp. 272-273). Yet this future life involves a qualitative change in the mode of the individual's existence, and it should not be conceived simply as an infinite extension of time, with its constant incompleteness.

Let us try to summarize. The concept of eternity is used by Climacus to refer to four different sorts of things: (1) abstract logical possibilities, (2) moral duties, (3) God, and (4) man's intended future state. The common meaning in these different references would seem to be that each of the four entities described possesses a kind of being, that, contrasted with other things, can be described as perfect and complete. These entities are essentially unchanging, though Climacus does not think of God and human beings as possessing the kind of static unchangeability possessed by a logical concept.

3. *Is Climacus a Metaphysician?*

Many readers may find it surprising to find Climacus, the great "existential thinker" and vehement opponent of "speculative philosophy," employing concepts that seem so obviously drawn from the great speculative philosophies of Greece. A careful reading of Climacus shows that this surprise is unwarranted, however. He consistently refers to himself as a humorist, making it clear that a humorist is essentially a *thinker* who hails from the same general region as Hegel and other speculative thinkers. In Climacus' attacks on the Hegelians he never challenges the validity or value of abstract thought. What he attacks is the fantastic notion that an exister can become a purely abstract thinker. He does not deny that abstract thought plays a significant role in the life of an exister. On the contrary, he is himself a special type of thinker who acknowledges the value of speculative thought.

> Honor to speculation; praise to everyone who in truth occupies himself with it. To deny the worth of speculation (though one might wish that the money-changers in the courtyard, etc. be banished as profane) would in my eyes be to prostitute oneself; and it would be especially miserable of one, most of whose life is in proportion to its poor opportunities devoted to its service, especially miserable of one who admires the Greeks (VII, 42; p. 54).

Some may object that Climacus is thereby engaging in "metaphysics" or "ontology." I believe that this is correct in a sense but that it is hardly an objection or difficulty. Climacus is trying to clarify the fundamental concepts that he feels are needed to describe the nature of existence. It may well be that in looking at these conceptual tools Climacus gives us at least the outlines of a "metaphysic" or "ontology." However, it is hard to see how one can avoid an ontology in this sense. Certainly Climacus is not engaging in some sort of illegitimate pseudoscientific enterprise, of the sort metaphysicians are sometimes accused of attempting. His "metaphysic" is a descriptive one that in no way involves any confusion with the scientific enterprise. It is possible to challenge the value or worth of his particular description, but it is difficult to see how one could avoid doing the kind of thing Climacus is doing.

Nor are these reflections of Climacus a desertion of his primary goal. He is not a speculative philosopher but an existing humorist. Hence he pursues these abstractions, not for the satisfaction to be gained from speculative thought itself, but to illuminate existence. It would be possible, I think, to take Climacus' conceptual structure and develop a full-blown philosophical system from it. Climacus' discussion of God and "the possible" raise many questions that he does not himself answer, since he is not interested in pushing the ideas any further than is necessary for his existential purposes. Nevertheless, I believe that the following outline of how the four kinds of things said to be eternal (logical possibles, moral ideals, God, and man in his intended future state) are related is at least consistent with Climacus' fragmentary comments.

What I shall do here by way of summary is to attempt to fill in some of the gaps for those who would like a more unified and systematic understanding of Climacus' conceptual universe.

In its widest sense "the eternal" simply refers to all the logical possibilities there are, all actual or potential objects of reflection. Climacus, along with a great many other classical philosophers, accepts the notion that the possible has a kind of reality. Universals exist, not as space-time objects, but as possibilities. The possible has a kind of being also. How do these possibilities relate to God? God, as the being "for whom all things are possible," must be seen as the ground of all possibility. God is supremely real in the sense that every possibility depends on him for its realization. As supremely *perfect* he actually embodies or realizes in his own character all the *highest* possibilities. These possibilities are moral; hence "the ethical is the breath of the eternal." That is, God as the eternal realization of these highest or supreme possibilities is identical with those universal characteristics that are truly the "core" of the eternal. *Man's* intended destiny is an embodiment or "reduplication"of these eternal possibilities which make up the very being of God.

This reconstruction of Climacus' views makes good sense of his usage. Both logical possibilities and God are thus eternal without God being reduced to logical possibility in general. The close connection between God as the eternal and the ethical as the eternal is explained, and the role each plays in human existence is clarified. Man, in encountering the ethical, encounters God, since God is the supreme realization of the ethical. Man, in seeking an eternal happiness, is seeking a relation to God.

Some may object that such knowledge of God is just what Climacus denies is possible for human beings. In the *Philosophical Fragments* Climacus argues that God can be known to human understanding only as the "unknown" and that the attempt to know God inevitably leads to idolatry (IV, 212-213; pp. 55-56). However, it must also be noted that Climacus describes in great detail a type of immanent religion, which he says was possible in paganism, in which the individual life is transformed through a God-relationship. Is this not a contradiction? Chapter 8 includes a full account of Climacus' view of God and how he is known. I will here anticipate by giving the conclusion of that account. Climacus certainly does deny that God can be "known" immanently. But he means by "know" something rather specific; what is known is known through detached, objective thought. God cannot be known in this sense. But God can be discovered in *action* and committed striving. Climacus does not choose to call this "knowledge." But it is certainly a true awareness of God's character and reality. From the Christian perspective even this "existential" awareness is radically defective. Such immanent knowledge of God is insufficient to truly transform a person's life, and thus is not from a Christian perspective a true awareness of God. A true awareness of God comes only through God's historical self-disclosure. Nevertheless, even the Christian must admit that a type of God-consciousness is a possibility for existing human beings.

Thus, the eternal is the element in human life that distinguishes man from the brute. Man's life partakes of the eternal in that he lives in light of his consciousness of universal possibilities. Among the possibilities or Ideas he encounters are those supremely moral possibilities that God himself perfectly embodies and that God commands human beings to realize. It is supremely in the ethical life, therefore, that man takes the eternal into his life in its most significant sense. It is here he discovers God, and it is here he discovers those possibilities that constitute his own true self and provide the ideal he is trying to realize in his existence.

4. *Temporality*

Of the three terms employed by Climacus to characterize existence— "eternity," "temporality," and "passion"—it is "temporality" that presents the fewest problems. It is not that temporality itself is easy to analyze, as Augustine always stands ready to remind us. But the temporal character of human existence is so strongly felt that most people have little trouble in understanding what Climacus is getting at. That human existence is temporal shows itself in the character of a human being's successive struggles to accomplish something. One must do one thing at a time, first things first, the simple before the complicated. The baby must crawl before learning to walk; the child must know the alphabet before learning to read. It is not successiveness *per se* that is in focus here — that is, I do not think that Climacus commits himself to the thesis that a being who is fully eternal, whether God or man in his future state, would have no successive consciousness (through certain passages suggest this). What is significant about temporal existence is the incomplete character of its achievements. Human actions must be successive because of the imperfect character of those actions. Because man always fails to realize his ideals fully and perfectly, he can only conceive of their realization in a continued striving. The incomplete, successive character of human existence is crucial in distinguishing existence from imagination and thought. In one's imagination one can become a doctor (or anything else) in a flash; actually to become a doctor takes time and work, even if one has the talent and the opportunity.

The incomplete, successive character of existence implies many things. For example, as Plato said, not only is the person who lacks something he needs in want, but also someone who possesses something he needs — since he "wants" to continue possessing it. In the realm of cultural accomplishments maintaining an achievement may be as difficult as the achievement itself; the person who learns a foreign language, such as Danish, discovers that it requires work to maintain one's facility just as it did to learn the language originally. Ethical and religious qualities must be constantly renewed in order to be preserved. Thus it is one thing to say at one time, "One ought always to be thankful to God," quite another thing always to be thankful to God (VII, 147-149; pp. 158-160).

Temporality is also connected by Climacus with limitation and finitude. Here it becomes clear that not only temporality but spatiality is being referred to, or rather that spatio-temporality, thought of as a unity, is the referent. Not only are man's achievements successive and gradual; they are everywhere bounded by the limitations imposed by being finite. Temporality is bound up with "necessity." The limitations include not only the general one imposed by physicality, but all the special limitations imposed by the particular environmental and hereditary factors that shape individuals and continue to limit their potentialities.

The temporal in this sense is linked by Climacus with what is seen as accidental and inessential to the person. Temporality itself is an essential component of selfhood. It is essential for a person to be a definite, concrete subject with a set of definite accidental characteristics. But the fact that a person has blue eyes or brown, is tall or short, or is born rich is itself accidental. This does not mean that these factors become insignificant to the individual, since we shall see that one aspect of the universal ethical task is precisely the person's acceptance of herself with all of her accidental traits. Her task is to express what is universal through and in the particular and the concrete.

Since human beings are self-conscious, with a consciousness of eternal possibilities, it is logical that man's temporality is of a different quality from the time-consciousness of creatures which lack this "eternality." Some of the other Kierkegaardian pseudonyms take this into account by making a distinction between time and temporality, using the latter as a distinctive term to refer to human existence. Man's self-consciousness, with its participation in the eternal, adds a new quality to time. Human existence is not only successive (time), but *tensed* (temporality). Man is capable of consciously reflecting on what he has become. In his self-consciousness, however, man becomes aware not merely of actualities but of possibilities. The self-consciousness of man as he is engaged in choosing provides a fulcrum point that transforms time from a mere infinite succession of moments into qualitatively different phases. In his present self-consciousness man separates time into past and future. The present is the moment when in reflecting on himself as he has become (the past), man chooses what he will be (the future).[5] Climacus does not explicitly expound this time-temporality distinction, but it is at least consistent with his reflections on human existence and, in my opinion, underlies his reflection at certain points.

All of the aspects of temporality for Climacus come powerfully to consciousness in the individual who becomes aware of the fact that she must die. This is not a reference to the individual who is merely aware in a general way "that everyone must die," but the person who actually attempts to think through and understand the implications of her very personal death for her life (VII, 137-147; pp. 147-159). The awareness of death is an awareness of the uncertainty that attaches itself to all human existence in virtue of its temporal character. In becoming aware of death as a boundary to my time I become all the more aware of the fragmented, incomplete, and episodic character of my achievements. I become aware of the *time it takes* to exist and am forced to reflect on the value of my past actions and the potentialities that still exist for me in the future.

5. Passion

Man's life in general is a synthesis of the temporal and the eternal. Being temporal, man's life is a *successive* process in which he attempts to realize ideals. Being eternal, it is a process in which *ideals* are realized. But one must remember that man is not merely a passive synthesis but an active synthesizer. He himself shapes the direction he travels. The process of "reduplicating" the ideals is a self-conscious one.

How does this active shaping take place? How does the individual synthesize the eternal and the temporal by reduplicating timeless ideals in time? The answer revolves around the concept of passion: "Only momentarily can the single individual exister be a *unity* of the infinitude and finitude which transcends existence. This moment is the instant of passion. In passion the existing subject is made infinite in the eternity of imagination and yet is also most definitely himself" (VII, 164; p.176).

To be a *unity* of finitude and infinitude, temporality and eternity, lies beyond mere existence, which is a *synthesis* of these elements. As a synthesis in time it must be a *successive* achievement, which must be renewed and repeated. Existence thus contains momentary unities of the temporal and the eternal. It is in these moments that the eternal can truly be said to be duplicated in existence. The momentary union of the temporal self with the eternal is made possible by passion. It is important to recall here our earlier discussion of passion. A passion is an emotion but not just any emotion. A passion is an enduring emotion that is capable of giving shape and direction to human life. Though passions must be called forth (they cannot be created *ex nihilo*), they can be cultivated or suppressed. A passion is not necessarily an irrational force that simply sweeps over a person and directs his life "from without." True passions are inward possessions.

Climacus is striking a fine balance in his account. The issue really concerns what role values, "Ideas," and ideals play in human life. Are values (ideals) objective objects to be cognized (Ideas), or are they simply expressions of human emotions and feelings? Climacus says that they are neither. On the one hand he recognizes the intimate connection between values and emotions. "Value" is a verb; the person who does not *value* something has no values. Values and ideals are not simply objects to be known, since they enter human life through the emotions. The person who has not acquired the capacity for caring deeply and feeling authentically can never recognize the eternal.[6] Hence the hope for a "scientific ethics" is a vain one. Values can only be recognized and actualized in subjectivity.

However, this by no means entails that values are themselves *subjective*. Many readers of Kierkegaard go wrong at this point. What can only be recognized through subjectivity is not necessarily only subjective in itself.

The fact that values are only realized in and through passion does not entail that values are reducible to human passions. Many thinkers conclude from the fact that values cannot be justified by an appeal to "objectively" observed evidence that they must be merely subjective preferences. They ignore the possibility that values in themselves eternally valid might make contact with human life through the emotions. They ignore the possibility that human emotions and attitudes, as C. S. Lewis says, in themselves could be warranted or unwarranted, profound or trivial, in tune with the nature of reality or out of tune, "true" or "false."[7] This is precisely what Climacus affirms. It is true that values are a reality only to the "interested" person, but it by no means follows that her values are reducible to her interests.

The subjectivist view ignores what the phenomenologist would call the intentionality of passion. The person who truly values something values *something*. The object she values is by no means reducible to the act of valuing itself. Nor can the valuer believe that the value of the object is bestowed upon it by the act of valuing. If I care deeply about something, I do not regard that something as in itself valueless, but only acquiring value because I care about it. If I admire an action and regard it as worthy of emulation, I cannot believe that it is my admiration that makes the act admirable. The object of passion is always viewed by passion as *worthy* of its passion. The passion is called forth by its object, though not in a mechanical way, of course. Climacus himself comments on this by noticing the etymological connection between passion and passivity. In Danish the term passion (*lidenskab*) contains as its root the verb *lide*, which means, among other things, "to suffer" (in the sense of "to permit"), "to be receptive."

Through imagination the person conceives for himself the eternal. In passion he binds himself to these imagined possibilities and thus "infinitizes" himself. It is through this process that a person begins to "collect himself," to become a unified person, to exist in the pregnant sense. The intimate relation between existence and thought or existence and imagination shows up here again. Imagination is for Climacus "the faculty of all faculties." The imagination is simply man's ability to present to himself the nonactual, the possible. Without such an ability man could not truly think or reflect. Imagination and reflection are thus essential characteristics of existence. But they are never identical with existence. The exister does not merely imagine and reflect; he acts. To act he must bring to a close the process of conceptualizing possibilities and reflecting on them. This closure occurs not through thought itself but through interestedness. The person passionately links himself with an imagined possibility and makes it his own. Existence is certainly not devoid of thought (VII, 101; p. 112), but existence without passion is a contradiction in terms (VII, 267; p. 276). The true reduplication of eternity is not thought but true action. This notion we will encounter again in the discussion of truth and subjectivity.

In uniting the temporal with the eternal, passion gives to the exister both of the characteristics existence must have, movement and continuity. The following rather lengthy quote nicely summarizes much of what we have said so far.

> Insofar as existence is movement it holds that there still is a continuity which underlies the movement, otherwise there is no movement. Just as the assertion that everything is true means that nothing is true, thus the fact that everything is in motion means that there is no motion. The unmoveable belongs to the movement as the movement's goal, both in the sense of *telos* and *metros* [end and measure] . . . The difficulty for the exister is to give his existence that continuity without which everything merely disappears . . . passion is the momentary continuity, which at one time holds fast and is the impulse of the movement (VII, 267-268; p. 277).

In the passionate attachment to the object of passion, the individual acquires a goal and a direction that gives continuity, while at the same time it provides the impulse for action by closing out the possibility for further reflection and uniting the individual to the object of passion. One can see from this why passion is itself action, since such a passionate linking must continually be renewed by a temporal being.

There are, however, passions and passions. Climacus by no means regards it as a matter of indifference what sort of passion one has and what its object is. These two, the character and object of the passion, are closely linked, since there are certain objects that can only call forth passions of a certain type, and reciprocally there are certain kinds of passion that demand a certain type of object. It is here that the connection between existence and the ethical comes into view and the essential connection between the ethical and eternal values appears. Passion directed to what is momentary and temporal necessarily takes on a momentary and temporal character itself. It thus fails to provide the continuity and wholeness the exister seeks. This is well illustrated in some of Kierkegaard's discourses, particularly *Purity of Heart*, where it is argued at length that the person who would will one thing can only will "the good," which is eternal. Thus the "integrated" personality that is the goal of existence requires a passionate attachment to eternal values. This is generally more assumed than argued for by Climacus, but he clearly accepts the thesis that existence in the true sense can only be constructed around eternal values, and is therefore ethical existence. "All idealizing passion is an anticipation of the eternal in existence for an exister in order to exist; (VII, 268; p. 277). In a footnote to this sentence he explains that only this "idealizing" passion has this power to make existence possible: "The earthly passion prevents existing by changing existence to the momentary." Thus in the strict sense existence and ethical existence are synonymous. The passion that can truly form a human life can only be the passion for ethical ideals—i.e., ideals that are recognized as more than ephemeral or transitory.

Human existence is thus a synthesis of the temporal and the eternal, finite and infinite. It is a successive process in which the individual can recognize and attempt to actualize "the eternal" (ethical values). The recognition and realization is made possible in and through the passion the individual develops in the course of living. This passion then makes up the inwardness or subjectivity that is the actual content of a person's existence. In the next chapter we shall give a fuller account of the ethical striving that constitutes existence.

---

[1] *Johannes Climacus eller De Omnibus Dubitandum Est* (Copenhagen: Gyldendals, 1967), pp. 78-79; English translation by T.H. Croxall (Stanford, Calif., Stanford University Press, 1958), pp. 148-149.

[2] *Ibid.*, p. 81; English translation, pp. 151-152.

[3] The Danish sentence referred to here is omitted from the English translation on p. 202n.

[4] See the *Parmenides*, 130 b-e, where Socrates is confident that there are forms of value qualities and logical ideals, unsure about significant particulars like human beings, and fairly sure there are no forms for insignificant or valueless particulars.

[5] See for example *The Concept of Anxiety* (Dread) (IV, 355-360; pp. 77-81). This distinction between time and temporality is clearly discussed in Mark Taylor, *Kierkegaard's Pseudonymous Authorship. A Study of Time and the Self* (Princeton: Princeton University Press, 1975), pp. 123-125, and by Johannes Sløk, *Kierkegaard—Humanismens Tænker*, (Copenhagen: Hans Reitzel, 1978), pp. 187-193.

[6] This connection between values and emotion is especially well treated by C. S. Lewis in "Men Without Chests" in *The Abolition of Man* (New York: Macmillan, 1947; paperback ed., 1965), pp. 33-35.

[7] See *The Abolition of Man*, pp. 25-32. It is the fact that human subjectivity can be "true" in this sense that underlies Climacus' discussion of truth and subjectivity. See Chapter 7.

Chapter V

EXISTENCE AND THE ETHICAL:
BECOMING A SELF

1. *The Ethical as the Sphere of Responsible Choice*

Before looking at the task of existence, understood concretely as the ethical life, let us first attempt a rather formal description of the ethical life. Actually, Climacus says more about the form of the ethical life than about its content. There is really nothing in his writings that corresponds with what contemporary writers would call normative ethical theory, though as we shall see, there is some content to his concept of the ethical life. His major thrust is to remind his readers about the nature of the ethical as a pattern of life.

The ethical conceived as the task of existence must be conceived as a universal task. This is one of the criteria that distinguishes the ethical from the aesthetic. Aesthetic life-views are recognizable in that they make the meaning of life depend in the final analysis on fortune or fate. The aesthete, whether he cultivates money, sensuality, fame, artistic imagination, or even scientific knowledge, always determines the significance of his life in relation to the "differences" between individuals. Some individuals are born with beauty, others without. Some are born with brains, others are not. Some are placed in advantageous circumstances for succeeding in their projects, others are not. This is the dialectic of fortune/misfortune (*lykke/ulykke*), which attaches itself to any person who evaluates the significance of his life in terms of what he possesses or achieves that other people do not possess or achieve.

The ethicist, in contrast, repudiates the significance of these accidental distinctions.

> Every person must essentially be assumed to be in possession of what essentially belongs to being human. The subjective thinker's task is to transform himself into an instrument which clearly and definitely expresses the human in existence. To comfort oneself with respect to differences is a misunderstanding, for the business of having a little better mind and other such things is purely insignificant (VII, 309; p. 318).

Since we are discussing the essential task of existence, it would be a contradiction to assume that the capacity for the task is an accidental possession, which some existers have and some do not. The task is essentially to become a person; every person must be assumed to be capable of such a personal existence. There are of course special cases, such as infants, who are not yet existing in the strongest sense but merely possess a potentiality to exist. But I believe that Climacus would hold that even those individuals society designates "mentally retarded," if they are capable of conscious choice at all, can fulfill the "universal human," and may even do so to a far greater extent than people with rich intellectual and aesthetic gifts. Though there are no doubt boundary cases (severe brain injuries, for example) where it is impossible for an observer to decide whether a person exists in the pregnant sense or not, this does not mean that there is no qualitative difference between human existence and existence that lacks this quality.[1] Within this qualitative sphere quantitative differences are seen as insignificant.

The universal task of "becoming what you are," to use Nietzsche's phrase, is distinctively ethical in character. It is the task of becoming "the individual":

> To want to be an individual human being (which is what one undeniably is) by help of and in power of one's differential distinctions is cowardice; but to want to be an individual human being (which is what one undeniably is) in the same sense that every other person can is the ethical victory over life and over all illusions (VII, 309; p. 319).

Climacus' concept of "the individual" is therefore not a glorification of personal idiosyncrasies. It highlights what is universal in human existence: the power of the individual to shape her life through choice. The significance of life is determined by the choices the individual makes for herself. But responsible choice is precisely the realm of the ethical. Ultimately what counts is not what one is *given*, but what one does with what one is given.

This "what one does" must be more closely defined as well. For Climacus by no means wishes to equate the ethical with what he terms the outward result. There is one sense in which "what one does" is largely dependent on "what one is given" through heredity, upbringing, and circumstances. The result in this sense is not within the individual's power, and thus has no essential relevance to the ethical life. Climacus goes so far as to say that a truly ethical person, while striving to develop his powers to the utmost, might perhaps thereby achieve remarkable results in the world, but he would *choose*, if that were possible, to remain ignorant of the results (VII, 110; p. 121). The case is probably purely hypothetical, since it is hard to envision how someone could truly strive and act without any knowledge of the consequences of his actions. But the point is that whether those results are great is not directly determined by the quality of the individual's striving, but by a host of other factors; ultimately the result is in the hands of providence (VII, 110; p. 121). Thus an individual who by the help of fortunate circumstances produced a wonderful outcome might easily be tempted to evaluate himself more highly than he should.

2. "Soul-Making" vs. "Society-Transforming" Ethics

It is by now quite clear that the description of the ethical life Climacus is offering is neither new nor uncontroversial. Climacus' view is decidedly in the line of those ethicists who have taught that life's task is "soul-making." In the final analysis the highest value in life is the cultivation of character —specifically, moral character. The existence of truly humane individuals is good in and for itself. This is the type of ethic that is associated with the great world religions, and it is the type of ethic found in Greek philosophy, particularly the thought of Plato and Socrates. It would seem today to belong to the family of deontological ethics as opposed to consequential or utilitarian ethics.

Despite this pedigree much ethical thinking in Western, technological, progress-oriented society is very much against this "soul-making" view, both in capitalist and socialist societies. The soul-making view is charged with being subjectivistic, individualistic, even selfish. Is it not immoral for a person to be so concerned over his own petty self? The challenge is plainly laid down by a social-minded thinker such as John Dewey:

> This constant throwing of emphasis back upon a change made in ourselves instead of one made in the world in which we live seems to me the essence of what is objectionable in "subjectivism". . . . All the theories which put conversion "of the eye of the soul" in the place of a conversion of natural and social objects that modifies goods actually experienced, is a retreat and escape from existence. . . The typical example is perhaps the other-worldliness found in religions whose chief concern is with the salvation of the personal soul.[2]

Though Dewey is a secular writer, similar views may even be found among some theologians today, particularly those who repudiate pietistic concern for the individual soul by identifying true religion with the quest for social and political progress. And the sort of view Dewey represents is common, but not universal, among Marxists, who are often charged, sometimes justly, with subordinating the good of the individual to society, or worse, future society.

This soul-building ethic of Climacus is criticized sometimes as part of a psychologistic attack on Kierkegaard's writings and Kierkegaard himself. More than one critic has charged Kierkegaard with inserting an essential selfishness into the heart of ethics and religion. The following statement from H. J. Paton is all too typical: "If ever a person was self-centered it was Kierkegaard: he hardly ever thinks of anyone but himself. Selfcenteredness is the very antithesis of religion."[3] It would be pointless to argue over whether or not Kierkegaard was personally selfish, whether he had poor motives in breaking his engagement, attacking the church, etc. The question at issue is the viability of a soul-building ethic. Is such an ethic essentially subjectivistic, even selfish, as the advocates of what we might call a "society-molding" ethic charge?

In arbitrating such a dispute it is important not to caricature either position. A disinterested observer will immediately notice that the two sorts of ethics are not completely exclusive. For example, a society-molding ethic does not have to deny the significance of individual transformation. Dewey, for example, clearly affirms the importance of transforming individuals; he objects only to regarding these transformations as an end in itself.[4]

Nor is it completely fair to analyze this dispute as one between an ethic that cares about individuals and one that cares only about the abstraction called "society." For Dewey could quite justly point out that the ultimate purpose of the social changes he is seeking is to benefit individuals. Dewey's view culminates in the affirmation of aesthetic individual enjoyments, though not just any old enjoyments, but those approved by critical reflection.[5]

Still, even after these qualifications are added, there is a marked difference between Dewey's type of view and that of Climacus. The difference concerns what is valued absolutely and what is valued relatively. What is man's highest good? For Climacus this highest good is moral transformation. He by no means denies that aesthetic goods are goods — all other things being equal, it is reasonable to prefer health to sickness, wealth to poverty, enjoyment to pain. But these aesthetic goods are only relatively good, and all other things are not always equal. It is quite possible that there are circumstances where poverty and suffering are more conducive to the development of moral character than wealth and pleasure. In such a case it is better for a person to experience poverty and suffering. Though these are no doubt things that no one wishes for "immediately," Climacus thinks it is possible for a person who achieves true moral character to realize on reflection that these "unwished" elements have benefited him.

It is important not to caricature Climacus' view at this point. His position here is strikingly similar to Kant's, and Kant has often been subjected to similar criticisms. Kant also holds that the chief aim of a moral agent is the perfection of his own moral character. Is such moral self-concern selfishness? Does this mean that the moral agent is indifferent to others and the world around him?

These conclusions do not necessarily follow. What one must do is to examine the nature of this self-concern. Suppose I believe that it is my moral duty to act unselfishly toward my neighbors. Suppose that fulfilling my moral duty was my highest value, more important to me than anything else. In such a case I would have an intense concern over my self, but surely it would be wrong to call this concern selfish. For the content of my concern would be precisely over whether I was living unselfishly. It is hard to imagine any great moral personality who would not manifest this sort of self-concern. A healthy suspicion of oneself is necessary if traps like laziness and pride are to be avoided (even pride over how suspicious of oneself one is.)

If one's moral duties are duties toward one's fellow human beings, then it cannot be maintained consistently that a person who cares absolutely about whether she fulfills her moral duty does not care about her fellow human beings. If she does not care about her fellow human beings, she has not fulfilled her moral duty. Though her concern over her own moral character is absolute, that concern is a concern over how she relates to others.

The claim that moral character is valued as the highest intrinsic good does not mean that the moral individual regards other individuals as merely occasions for his own self-improvement. There is an analogy to the famous hedonic paradox here. The person who aims for pleasure does not get so much as the person who simply aims at other things and gets pleasure as an accompaniment. Similarly, the moral individual who is obsessed with improving his own character does not improve it so much as the person who simply learns to care about others and is improved in the process. Virtue must be understood, not as the immediate end of every moral action, but the long-range, higher-order end a reflective moral person sets himself, reminds himself of from time to time, and which he can in retrospect see realized in the pattern of his moral choices.

3. Are Ethical "Results" Important?

A critic might admit that this sort of reply is valid for Kant, who says explicitly that a moral act of willing is "not a mere wish, but the straining of every means within our control."[6] However, is this line of thought consistent with Climacus, who says explicitly that the moral individual does not care at all about "results" — that is, results in the outward sphere of society (VII, 110; p. 121)? If we look carefully at what Climacus says about the result, we will see that his view is fully consistent with the line of thought advanced here.

Why are "results" disparaged by Climacus? There seem to be two reasons. First, there is the problem that results are not completely within the control of the agent. Whether moral action succeeds in an external sense depends upon hosts of factors beyond the control of the individual. Since the result in this sense is not completely in the individual's control, it follows that the individual is not morally responsible for it, and should not employ it to judge the morality of his action. The most praiseworthy moral act can lead to nothing; morally dubious actions, on the other hand, can through fortuitous circumstances lead to wonderful results.

Of course, from the fact that the individual is not responsible for what he cannot control, it does not follow that he is not responsible for doing what he can. It is thus completely consistent with Climacus' disparagement of the moral significance of results to claim that the individual should strive for results with all his power, paradoxical as it may sound. The truth is that in the final analysis very little in the way of results, if anything, is *completely* within the individual's power. For no individual can by willing guarantee that he will not be struck down by disease or accident that will take away all his powers at the very moment he begins to act. It is for this reason that Climacus would hold that the person totally paralyzed in a wheel chair may accomplish more morally than a politician who transforms half the world. For in the final analysis all the paralyzed person or the politician can do is to will the good; the result is not in their hands. But this does not mean that the individual who truly *wills* the good and does not merely wish does not strive with all his might to realize it.

It seems to me that this implies that there is a sense in which the moral individual does care about "results." To the moral individual the important thing is not what he manages to accomplish but what he earnestly attempts to accomplish. Hence Climacus depreciates resuslts. However, if the individual is truly earnestly attempting to accomplish something, he is attempting to achieve results of some type. I believe this sort of concern with results is consistent with Climacus' main point, which is that the individual should not evaluate his own moral purity with reference to the success of his projects, which depends upon a multitude of factors beyond his control. That is surely compatible with asserting that the individual is responsible for doing what is within his power, and even with claiming that the moral individual earnestly yearns for the success of his projects, and in that sense "cares about the result." (No one who earnestly attempts to achieve something is indifferent to whether that achievement is realized.) However, Climacus does not really take the trouble to show in what ways a truly moral individual might care about the result. Had he done so, it certainly would have strengthened his description of the ethical life and prevented many caricatures of his ethic as selfish, subjectivist, or whatever.

A second reason Climacus disparages "results" is that he employs a different standard in evaluating the result than does the advocate of the society-molding ethic. Since the highest value is the realization of moral character, it follows that the highest thing one person can do for another is help him become more moral. Of course this does not entail that one does *not* have moral duties to help those in physical need, to prevent suffering, and even to increase others' pleasure as far as possible. And these sorts of duties, though they may be valid in their own right, are not unrelated to helping others to be moral, since it is by showing compassion that one may help another to be compassionate, and a person who does not have enough food to eat may be incapable of reflecting on moral duties. Thus, saying that the highest thing one person can do for another is to help the other become moral does not entail that this exhausts one's moral duties. It is, however, in Climacus' view the highest moral duty.

Helping another person to become more ethical is a difficult thing to do, however, since one of the characteristics of a truly moral person is that the person himself freely chooses the good. The person who is compelled or bribed to act morally does not act morally, at least in the highest sense.[7] From this Climacus concludes that however much one strives to help another person become moral, one can never be sure of the outcome. The other person's freedom must be taken into account. If the other person's freedom is not considered, then he may be hurt rather than helped. It is for this reason that the moral teacher must employ the maieutic method that Socrates practiced. He must view himself as a midwife who is merely an instrument to help the other realize himself. He cannot guarantee his results without ceasing to act morally. Therefore moral action and results do not necessarily correspond with one another.

Furthermore, since the ultimate aim of the maieuticist is the other's inward transformation, the results can never be *known* with certainty anyway. Even the noblest acts can be done for base motives; it is possible to find oneself in a situation where one must bring pain to another as well as to oneself if one's love for the other person is truly unselfish. Thus, no human being can be absolutely sure about another person's moral character. Indeed, it is only with the greatest amount of effort that a person can become clear about himself, and even that may not be totally realizable.

We can thus see that there are genuine differences between Climacus' type of ethical view and utilitarian moralities and other moralities that emphasize social results or changes as the primary end of moral action. Both sorts of views sometimes make unjust charges at the other. It ought to be realized that the society-molding view can recognize the importance of changing individuals and that the soul-making view can affirm that the moral individual cares in one sense about the results of her actions. The difference lies in what is considered relatively important and what is considered absolutely important. The soul-making view considers the cultivation of moral character to be the highest intrinsic good — which contrasts sharply with views that only value moral character as instrumentally good — or as one relative good among other.

Incidentally, if Climacus is taken as a type of deontological thinker, perhaps his insights provide us with a way of restating and clarifying the quarrel between the deontologist and the utilitarian. Frequently the distinction is drawn in the following way: The utilitarian claims that the rightness of an act is determined solely by the results or consequences; the deontologist denies this. When characterized in this way, the deontological position seems implausible to me. Perhaps the issue can be better described in this way: Both the utilitarian and deontologist view the morality of an action as linked to the consequences of an action, but they measure those consequences by different standards. For the deontologist the highest good is the achievement of moral character — on the part of the agent and others. Hence the *moral* outcome of an action is absolutely important in determining the morality of the action; the achievement of aesthetic goods, while important, can be only relatively important. For the utilitarian just the reverse is true. In evaluating the morality of an action, the amount of nonmoral goodness produced is ultimately decisive. The production of moral character may be valued as well, though it is not valued absolutely, but relatively; i. e., it is valued as a means to nonmoral goodness and perhaps for itself when its production does not require any net sacrifice of nonmoral goodness. Both types of moralities may recommend similar actions for many circumstances. The significance of the dispute only becomes clear where there is a conflict between moral and nonmoral goodness — where the achievement of moral character requires a sacrifice of pleasure, beauty, knowledge, or other aesthetic goods.

   4. *The Content of the Ethical Task: Supplying Matter for the Ethical Form*

   As mentioned earlier, Climacus actually does not say very much about the content of the ethical task, and one looks in vain in his writings for something resembling contemporary normative ethical theory. The reason for this is that he is primarily interested in helping people to realize the nature and significance of the ethical life. The content of the ethical life was not something he had to invent, since on his view he could presume that every one of his readers would already have knowledge about it. The ethical is an essential component in all human existence and is present to everyone. The ethical is easy to understand, so that everyone can understand it, and in order that "no time may be wasted but a beginning made at once" (VII, 339; p. 350).
   Climacus makes a sharp distinction between what one might call "civic morality" and the ethical in the true sense.[8] It is quite possible for a person to grow up in a culture, learn the prevailing social rules and taboos, and live by them, thus acquiring a reputation as a fine, upstanding citizen, without ever discovering the ethical in the deepest sense (VII, 205; p. 218). The problem with such a person is not necessarily so much what she does, but why she does it. If she follows the principles she does only because "everybody else does," then she fails to discover the ethical in its "infinity." Even if the cultural principles she follows are ethical, the individual is not

truly ethical if she does not follow them *because* they are ethical.

There is certainly a Kantian strain here in Climacus' thought, which other commentators have noticed. The truly ethical person not only does his duty, he does it because it is his duty. And just as was the case with Kant, the absolute duty cannot be identified with any particular set of moral rules; the absolute duty is to duty itself. And, somewhat like Kant, Climacus thinks that this formal principle itself gives the key to the content of the ethical life. But he recognizes more fully than Kant that it is not up to reason to invent the moral life, and hence that concrete moral duties cannot simply be deduced from a formal principle. His perspective is that the ethical life has the passions for its matter, reason for its form. In his discussion of the ethical life the existence of passion is presupposed. The task of reflection is to penetrate this passion with the formal demands of duty and thus to arrive at actual duties.

It might be thought that Climacus has two different ethical views which are not completely congruent. On the one hand he talks about self-actualization; the ethical task is the task of existing, of becoming oneself. On the other hand he talks of the absolute character of duty in a way reminiscent of Kant. The key to understanding his view is to recognize that he is saying both of these things: Actualize yourself and do your duty for the sake of duty. They are unified in this way: The essential self that you are to become is your ethical self; the person only realizes himself through ethical commitment. Ethical commitment is the decisive criterion of "selfhood."

To understand the relationship between self-actualization and duty we must look at the content or matter of the ethical life as well as the form. If the ethical form is to become existentially concrete, it demands material content. This content is in one sense highly individualized, since in order to describe an individual's duties concretely one must understand the particular situation the individual finds himself in. The content in a sense is "given" to the individual.

The way the content of the ethical life acquires form is well illustrated by the relationship between the aesthetic and the ethical. This is treated much more fully by Judge William in *Either-Or* than by Climacus, so we will take a brief look there, for the sake of illuminating what Climacus does say. Judge William says that the aesthetic life is a life in which a person is what he is, while the ethical is that whereby a person becomes what he becomes (II, 161; p. 182). But what does a person become? The answer is "himself." But what is this self? It is the self as conscious of its eternal significance, which is realized through the choice of one's duty. But what do these duties consist of in the concrete? Where do they come from, so to speak? From the judge's point of view, this content is discovered within the self by the self. It is present at least in the form of potentiality within the "immediate" self.

The relationship of marriage illustrates this nicely. Since marriage is for the judge the paradigm of the ethical life, it could scarcely be said to be an untypical example. The "form" of marriage is ethical duty; like all truly ethical duties the individuals who get married by a responsible choice impose upon themselves a commitment that is absolute in character. The content of marriage, on the other hand, is romantic love. Where does this love come from? Romantic love as immediate is not invented by the ethical; it is discovered. But romantic love alone is not marriage. Marriage is made possible only when the individual discovers the eternal element in love, only when the individual makes a commitment of himself. Thus, love, whose content is immediate and already present, becomes a duty by receiving the ethical *form*. The form does not invent the content; it rather takes it as the material content of life and seeks to penetrate it. Immediacy that cannot be transformed in this way is unethical; it lacks the eternal. What is true here is true of *every* aspect of the ethical life. If a person has talent, for example, the aesthete takes this as given and remains within it. An ethical person, however, takes his talents, which are immediate, as *tasks*, insofar as they permit of this. By the help of his talent he is to express what is universal and eternally valid. There is still a large degree of individuality present here; Climacus assumes that every individual has an awareness of "the eternal" and must himself use that understanding to clarify his own immediacy and discover the "task for him".

This view of the relation between ethical matter and form is again a little reminiscent of Kant, though it certainly has strongly Hegelian overtones as well. Kant's categorical imperative is a purely formal principle. It cannot generate material ethical maxims; one cannot logically deduce a set of concrete duties from it. Kant seems to view the categorical imperative more as a "test" to which material maxims must be subjected. From the variety of proposed rules for action that are presented to the person, some are selected as being those principles *through which* the individual can express his commitment to universal duty.[9] Those maxims have a matter; they direct the individual to concrete ends, and in willing to follow those maxims, the individual wills those ends. But his decision is not determined by these ends, as things he finds pleasing or desirable, but by the fact that in willing these ends he acts in conformity with his duty. He acts out of reverence for the moral law, even though the moral law alone could not determine a specific action. In much the same way Climacus assumes that the aesthetic, immediate elements in life provide a multiplicity of content;

it is up to the individual to discover and select that content given to him *through which* he can express his commitment to the eternal. In so doing he ceases to live merely aesthetically; he no longer has his life in the immediate categories of the desirable/undesirable, but chooses what he chooses because of its relation to the eternal. He has developed not merely aesthetic passion, but ethical passion — passion for the eternal. Marriage, for example, is the concrete form in which love can *endure*, which is the form in which the eternal is realized in time.

I believe these reflections illuminate the self-actualization ethic that Climacus presents.

> Ethics concentrates upon the individual, and ethically understood it is every individual's task to become a whole person; just as it is the presupposition of ethics that every person is born in such a condition that he can become one (VII, 300; p. 309).

Obviously it is only if "being a whole person" is defined in terms of ethical character that this can be so. Any concrete elements one might list, such as the potentiality for artistic appreciation or brilliant thought, might well be lacking for many individuals, either because of their genetic endowment or because of life's circumstances. Hence one cannot identify becoming a whole person with any specific content, but only with the formal characteristic itself. Nevertheless, for every specific individual there will be such specific content.

This content can even be described in a general way. That is, it is possible to pick out those potentialities that seem genuinely and universally human in the sense that they would be present in an ideal human life. Climacus himself mentions thought, imagination, and feeling as universal dimensions of the human personality (VII, 300; p. 310). The whole person is thoughtful; she has an appreciation for knowledge and is capable of reflection on her own life. She is imaginative, she appreciates poetry and the arts, and she is capable of imaginatively putting herself in different situations and presenting alternative choices to herself. Lastly she is capable of deep and genuine emotion; she has within herself pathos. She cares about the good and feels sympathy for those in pain. This last element would seem to be more than just an element, since Climacus holds that passion is not merely a part of existence, but the decisive part that makes existence possible. If, however, we distinguish between pathos in general and the absolute ethical pathos that has the ethical itself for its object, we can make sense of passion as "part" of the concrete content of the ethical life and yet also as the form of the whole. It must not be forgotten that it is the absolute ethical passion, the passion for the eternal, which provides both the cohesive and motivating power in the ethical task of self-realization. But there must be concrete ethical passions as well, feelings of sympathy and benevolence, which the individual will discover as concrete forms that can express the eternal and that will motivate specific actions.

Climacus says that the task of existence is the unification of these human potentialities. In a mediocre existence the person will be imaginative as a child, reflective as an adult, perhaps feel pathos when elderly. The truly ethical person, however, sets himself the task of achieving an "ennobling of the successive in contemporaneity. To have been young, and then to have become older, and then finally to die, is a mediocre existence; for the animal has this merit also" (VII, 302; p. 311). The person who loses his imagination is as bad as the person who loses his reason.

Where does Climacus get these elements? They are not invented by him, but discovered. They are the general characteristics "immediately" present in human beings, which the ethical then takes as a task. But being general they of course do not eliminate the necessity for the individual to concretely understand those potentialities that are uniquely his, and which he can take upon himself as duty. Climacus is aware that none of us are ideal human beings. "That every person is somewhat one-sided I know well, and I do not regard it as a fault; it is a however a fault when a fashion wants to make a one-sidedness into the total norm" (VII, 302; p. 312). No individual or even a nation should take their own peculiar gifts as the norm for all mankind. Every distinguished individual has something one-sided about him; though this one-sidedness is not his greatness, it may be an indirect indication of his real greatness (VII, 302-303; p. 312). If the individual is morally great, that greatness consists in what is universal: the ethical responsibility with which the individual discovered the possibilities for the eternal that lay within him and chose to become himself, by taking his potentialities as duties.

If we focus on the matter of the ethical life, Climacus' ethics seem like an ethic of self-realization, perhaps reminiscent of Aristotle. If we focus on the form, Climacus' ethic seems more like a Kantian ethic of duty for duty's sake. Actually, in synthesizing these elements it is like neither. It differs from Aristotle in seeing moral character as *the* decisive end of existence and in understanding that moral character is a devotion to duty as eternal and absolute. But it differs from a Kantian ethic in seeing the need for duty to express itself and individualize itself in the individual's concrete immediacy; the self has content as well as form. This content cannot simply be objectively codified. Climacus does not thereby seem to give much significance to concrete ethical principles such as might be found in the ten commandments or other moral codes. It seems to me that this lack is significant and points to a difficulty in Climacus' view. It is hard to see just how one goes about deriving specific ethical duties from the concrete immediate possibilities, which are ultimately transformed into ethical tasks by imposing the ethical "form". (There is an analogous problem with Kant, of course.) Climacus himself seems to see this process as artistic in character. Ethical existence is an art form (VII, 304; p. 314), which is not to say that it is aesthetic. The existential artist is the one who, with an eye on the eternal present within himself, takes on and shapes his aesthetic immediacy in such a way that the eternal *exists*. In that sense ethical existence, the synthesis of the temporal and the eternal, is itself a paradox.

5. *Soul-Making Ethics: A Humanistic Ethic for Today?*

It would be a mistake to think that Climacus is trying to demonstrate the truth of a soul-making ethic. Such an attempt would violate his thesis about how moral truth is acquired. Understanding moral truth is not like grasping a "fact" that can be directly passed on. To recognize the value of something means to value it yourself. It is an affair of passion, not just thought. The process of coming to understand the absolute significance of the achievement of ethical character is not separable from the process of acquiring the character. Moral understanding and moral growth go hand in hand. This is the theme we encountered in discussing Kierkegaard's theory of existence-spheres and his use of indirect communication. These ideas are clearly part of Climacus' thought, too, and are closely tied to the necessity for maieutic action on the part of the moral enthusiast. So it would be foolish to think that Climacus would contradict himself by presuming to offer an objective proof of his view.

However, this by no means entails that thought has no role to play in coming to see the truth. One can and ought to think through a view — to penetrate its assumptions and follow its implications out with logical consistency to the very end. To a large extent this is what Climacus the dialectician is trying to do. It is by helping the individual become completely clear about his own view that Climacus attempts to help him. This action is nonetheless maieutic, since Climacus does not know what the person may do with his increased self-understanding. If a person's life-commitments are demonic, as the person gets clearer about himself, his response may be an intensification of his demonic passion rather than a conversion to the good.

When thought through in this manner there are certain features of Climacus' view that stamp it as at least a deeply humanistic ethic, in the sense that it maintains the dignity and meaning of all human life. There is first and foremost the characteristic with which we began our exposition: universality. It seems to me reasonable to hold that the ethical, as the essential task of existence, must be relevant to everyone. Climacus says that every person must be assumed to be in possession of what essentially belongs to being human (VII, 309; p. 318). On the soul-making view, what essentially belongs to being human is the ethical task, and this does indeed belong to every human being. There is a deep human equality here that makes it possible for the ethical to be "in the midst of solitude the reconciling fellowship with every man" (VII, 125; p. 136). The fact that there are countless human beings who live out their lives in obscurity, without experiencing great happiness or accomplishing notable results, is no cause for despair if the essential human task is that of becoming a self. "There is no wastefulness [of human lives], for even if individuals were as numberless as the sand of the sea, the task of becoming subjective is given to each" (VII, 131; p. 142). On this view it is possible that the simple and obscure accomplish far more in life than the wealthy and famous:

> In relation to the cleverest, most daring plan to transform the whole world, the principle is valid that it becomes great by virtue of the result; in relation to the simple and loyal resolution of an obscure human being the principle holds that this plan is higher than any result, that its greatness is not dependent upon the result (VII, 345; pp. 356-357).

The "principle of equality" that underlies Climacus' ethical view here is a very significant aspect of his thought, and indeed of Kierkegaard's whole authorship. (It also plays a key role in Kierkegaard's discussions of religiousness and Christianity.)

Not only is the ethical universal in the sense of being relevant to, and offering significance for, every human life; the ethical is also universal in the sense of being relevant to all of life's experiences. The society-molding ethic, even when it concentrates on the value of the individual, in the final analysis judges the value of the individual life according to aesthetic criteria (in Climacus' sense). If the individual is fortunate enough to have happy experiences, a secure environment, a long life, her life will be judged worthwhile. But it is in the final analysis accidental whether a person is born in comfort or poverty, in a secure, prosperous country or in an area ravaged by war and heartbreak. No one can be sure that disease will not strike in the prime of life. Climacus dismisses any life-view that could be destroyed by such circumstances as cowardly; the person who only sees her life as worthwhile if such and such does not happen lacks the courage and sympathy to identify with her fellow human being who is the victim of such and such. In effect Climacus is saying that no view of life that does not find room for the tragic elements in human life can stand. A contemporary psychologist such as Viktor Frankl would agree: "If there is a meaning in life at all, then there must be a meaning in suffering. Suffering is an ineradicable part of life, even as fate and death."[10]

On the soul-making view every element in life, including tragic suffering and death, is potentially meaningful. For who can deny that such suffering has given rise to the most ennobling virtues in those who face them? It is no doubt for this reason that Climacus, who writes for sophisticated people about the great difficulties of the ethical, does not think even the sophisticate who becomes an ethical enthusiast ever achieves more than "the simple" people who "bear feelingly the burdens of life in another way" (VII, 141n; p. 152n). Climacus and Kierkegaard show a deep respect for those oppressed by poverty and misfortune; the difference between the wise man and the simple man is expressed in an oft-repeated formula: *"The simple man knows the essential,* the wise man little by little comes to *know* that he knows it or comes to *know* that he does not know it, but what they know is the same" (VII, 132; p. 143).

If the ethical task is soul-building, then every person has plenty to do. There is no danger that anyone will finish the task and move on to more significant matters, since "where the time itself is the task, it certainly is a mistake to be finished before the time" (VII, 136; p. 147). The time is life, and the task is life. Thus, "to become finished with life, before life is finished with you, is precisely not finishing the task" (VII, 136; p. 147).

The danger that critics will see in such a view is that it may justify complacency with regard to human suffering. Since the truly ethical person does not care about the result, and since suffering may be meaningful and ennobling, is there any reason for human beings to try to change their world so as to prevent what suffering they can? That this may be a temptation to the truly ethical person cannot be denied. But it seems to me that it is only a temptation, not a necessary consequence of such a view. It is one thing to say that human suffering is not meaningless, quite another to be indifferent to human suffering. This is best illustrated by a love relationship in which one partner dies. It is quite possible for the physically healthy lover to appreciate and even marvel over the courage and beauty of soul the dying person may acquire and manifest. The lover would regard it as a crime against the beloved if anyone were to say that these sufferings were meaningless. But it would be an utter falsehood to say that the lover in this case would be indifferent to the beloved's sufferings, would not personally move heaven and earth if it were possible to alleviate those sufferings.

The lover in this case seems to me to be a model of the ethicist who sees the possibility of meaning in human suffering. Such a person may care more deeply than anyone. One must remember that it is only in one sense that the ethicist depreciates "the result"; the true ethicist strives as deeply as anyone, and genuine striving is the opposite of complacency. The deep humanism in the soul-building ethic is incompatible with such complacency. If I truly view every human life as significant and meaningful, I cannot be ethically indifferent to any human life. And though my highest hope for every human being is that he or she may "become a self" and achieve "purity of heart," this by no means entails an indifference with respect to human trials and struggles. Insofar as I recognize human beings as unified persons, true sympathy will be a sympathy for the person in every dimension.

When all is said and done, however, it cannot be denied that Climacus is not a social activist. Though I have argued that social concern is not logically precluded by his view and is even implicitly contained in it, the thrust of his view is towards turning the individual away from "world-historical concerns" and toward a concern for selfhood. This may be grounded in the thesis that the ethical task is something that can be carried on under any political or economic conditions. Climacus consistently maintains a sharp separation of "the inner and the outward," with a tendency to depreciate the significance of the latter. Sharp questions can and should be raised about this bifurcation, since it is dubious as to whether the inward life of a person can be understood in total isolation from outward actions, which in turn make it necessary to reflect on the social environment. It may be that it is this bifurcation that leads Climacus to minimize or even ignore the ways in which the ethicist is concerned about "results." Though I have argued that a concern with physical human needs and suffering, for example, is consistent with Climacus' view of the ethical life, it seems to me that a truly adequate version of a soul-making ethic will make an even stronger claim. Such outward activities are not merely consistent with soul-making; they are demanded by it, since they are the concrete activities through which the soul is formed. Otherwise the soul that is formed threatens to become a contentless abstraction, the individual an artificial monad. For the concrete individual is involved in a myriad of relations and acts in a host of contexts. He becomes himself in and through those activities, and insofar as he truly becomes a self, those activities and relations must be affected. None of this is to deny the significance of the inward struggle, nor does it reduce the individual to a set of social roles. It merely recognizes that as a concrete individual he necessarily fulfills a set of social roles.

This one-sidedness of Climacus' view becomes much more understandable if we examine the views he was reacting to, views that certainly have their twentieth-century counterparts. In part those views were those represented by the practical "men of common sense," who urged people to fill up their lives with the "pressing issues of the day"; one must get involved, see that the new sewer line is run, reform the insurance industry, lengthen the session of the legislature, concern oneself with changes in customs. There is of course nothing wrong with such concerns, and the person who lacks them totally may be condemned as a bad citizen. But one must remember that Socrates was also condemned as a bad citizen. Climacus views all such practical political and economic problems as of relative significance. He does not thereby imply they have no importance. I would argue in fact that what is absolutely significant must have an effect on such relative tasks. But it is possible for an individual simply to lose himself in relativities and thereby fail to gain an understanding of what is truly significant in human life. Such an individual becomes very busy with "important" matters and yet may fail to exist in the most significant sense, since he has no understanding of the goal existence sets for every person — and therefore for him as well.

An even stronger reaction on Climacus' part was called forth by the Hegelians, who seemed to him to ground the ethical (insofar as it is present at all) in world-historical development. Instead of the individual's quest to actualize his own *telos* there is the quest of the race to actualize its *telos*. Presumably the individual's task is to discover this goal of mankind and find meaning for his life in his relation to it, however insignificant that relation may be. The highest form of such a relation is regarded as intellectual understanding by Hegel himself. Climacus finds several things about this disturbing.

First, there is the fact that this world-historical process only seems understandable in retrospect. Because of the uncertainty that surrounds all human action, no one can tell for sure what the outcome of a revolution, for example, will be, or what significance it will have for human history as a whole. For Climacus this means that world history gives no ethical guidance, since the ethical asks about what I *should* do. This is so unless the ethical task is simply contemplative understanding of history, which, if taken seriously, would entail that history would end, since people would cease to act. Such a contemplative ethic is sometimes held; it seems to be the sort of view William James describes as the "subjectivist" option in "The Dilemma of Determinism." But I suspect it will not be attractive to many for the kinds of reasons given by James and Climacus.

The second element Climacus finds disturbing about dealings with the world-historical is that it inevitably compromises the purity of the ethical resolve. The person who desires to realize some significant historical accomplishment no longer wills *only* to become morally good. He wishes to become morally good *and* by his goodness to accomplish something outwardly great. The crunch comes when this cannot be done, when historical results can only be achieved through compromising one's moral intention. Becoming a self is ethically the absolute; it cannot be just "one more" good among others without ceasing to be what it is. To avoid this Climacus suggests that the true ethical individual wills the good and leaves the world-historical to God. The reality and significance of mankind's history is not denied, but this significance is only properly perceived by God (VII, 131; p. 142). The individual makes history through his ethical striving, but the *telos* of his ethical striving is not derived from history.

Of course the contemporary view that this discussion brings to mind is Marxism, one of Hegel's living descendants. The Marxist, like Hegel, claims to be able to discern a *telos* in human history and to discover the individual's task therein, thereby giving meaning to human existence. The Marxist at least has the advantage over Hegel that this *telos* is seen as a future achievement, and thus can be worked for.

When Marxism is viewed in this light, not merely as an economic and political program but as an attempt to give meaning to human existence, then it runs squarely against the soul-making view. The difficulties this raises have been glimpsed, both by Marxists themselves and people like Sartre who would like to be Marxists but do not find the Marxist treatment of the individual completely satisfying. In an early essay, for example, Sartre points out the uncertainty that attaches to all historical undertakings and questions whether the Marxist view that the individual can find meaning by relating himself to the future triumph of the proletariat is secure:

> Given that men are free and that tomorrow they will freely decide what man will be, I can not be sure that, after my death, fellow-fighters will carry on my work to bring it to its maximum perfection. Tomorrow, after my death, some men may decide to set up Fascism, and the others may be cowardly and muddled enough to let them do it. Fascism will then be the human reality, so much the worse for us.[11]

Adam Schaff, a contemporary Marxist philosopher, sees the difficulty in Marxist theory here and tries to import a kind of ethical humanism as the ground of Marxism.[12] One must at least pose a question, however, as to whether the Marxist can consistently import such ideas, and if not, whether Marxism can truly meet Climacus' challenge to produce a humanistic view of life, one that gives meaning to every human life and sees the possibility of meaning for any individual, even in suffering and death.

One reason this may be difficult for Marxism is the close affinity a soul-making ethic seems to have with religious perspectives on the person. The similarity between a soul-making ethic and a religious quest for salvation are apparent, and they are more than accidental. For both perspectives see the individual ultimately as an end-in-itself, to use Kant's phrase. This sort of conception of human life has always been closely associated with an understanding of human persons as more than biological or social products, but as responsible beings, made in God's image.

Climacus certainly sees his soul-making ethic as religious in character. It is his conviction that the task of actualizing the self is at the same time the acquisition of a God-relationship. In attempting to realize oneself as a being with eternal significance, the individual is attempting to fulfill the destiny of the creator. The "universal" possibilities an individual can realize are not her own invention. She discovers them as present beforehand. These moral demands thus disclose the innermost essence of reality, though the individual may not realize this; it is thus possible to live an ethical life without being conscious of the fact that one is thereby relating to God. In discovering "the eternal" the individual does discover God, however, and to truly understand oneself is to gain a consciousness of God. This does not imply that the self and God are identical; the individual is still conscious of a gulf between the self and the eternal which is the *telos* of the self.

In this way we can see how the religious life grows out of the ethical from Climacus' perspective. To attempt to prove God's existence or to quell doubts about God via speculative arguments is for Climacus totally wrongheaded. "God" is that "eternal," "infinite," and "absolute" reality that is disclosed to man in the course of ethical existence. God is discovered not through argument but through moral passion. To see God truly is to see him as Lord, but he is seen as Lord only when he is understood as moral ruler and judge. The role of thought is only to help the individual understand more clearly and more fully the nature of this moral reality, not to prove its existence. Climacus' view of God, how God is known, and the relation between God and morality will be given a more complete treatment in chapters 8 and 9.

[1] Even among those who lack this quality one might distinguish those who possess it potentially or did possess it in some sense (infants, severe retardation, brain damage) from animals that lack it completely.

[2] John Dewey, *The Quest for Certainty,* (New York: G.P. Putnam's Sons, 1929), p. 275.

[3] H. J. Paton, *The Modern Predicament* (London: Allen and Unwin Ltd.; New York: MacMillan 1955), p. 120.

[4] *The Quest for Certainty,* p. 275.

[5] See *The Quest for Certainty,* pp. 260-265.

[6] *Groundwork of the Metaphysic of Morals,* trans. by H. J. Paton, (New York: Harper & Row, 1964,) p. 62.

[7] Climacus does not in my opinion adequately consider the ways in which such rewards might be temporarily useful in preliminary ethical training, developing habits of moral character.

[8] In Kierkegaard's writings there is still another ethical level, the Christian "indicative ethic" in *Works of Love.*

[9] See the *Groundwork of the Metaphysic of Morals,* p. 88. The interpretation of Kant given here is similar to that Paton gives in the summation of the "Argument" in this edition of the *Groundwork.*

[10] *Man's Search for Meaning* (New York: Washington Square Press, 1963), p. 106.

[11] "Existentialism" in *Existentialism and Human Emotions* (New York: Philosophical Library, 1957), p. 31.

[12] See his *Marxism and the Human Individual,* (New York: McGraw-Hill, 1970), especially pp. 167-182, 240-256.

Chapter VI

SUBJECTIVITY AND COMMUNICATION

1. Communication and Existence

One of the most interesting features of Climacus' writing (and Kierkegaard's authorship as a whole) is his attempt to employ what he termed "indirect communication." Climacus tells us that certain kinds of objective truths can be communicated directly as a "result." These are contrasted with subjective truth, which must be communicated indirectly as a "way." The difference is that understanding the second kind of truth requires a type of personal appropriation or "subjective understanding" the individual must achieve by himself, which is not necessary in the case of direct communication of objective information. Climacus thought that Socrates' maieutic method, which involved a withdrawal from any would-be disciples to foster independence, was the classical example of indirect communication. In the *Philosophical Fragments* and *Concluding Unscientific Postscript* Climacus both discusses the concept of indirect communication and attempts to engage in it. And of course the mere fact that Climacus is the author of the books can be seen as Kierkegaard's attempt to communicate indirectly, withdrawing from the reader following the pattern of Socrates.

In what follows I shall attempt to give an analysis of Climacus' concept of indirect communication. The peculiar problems that arise in understanding communication reflect the peculiar nature of existence and the relation between existence and thought. As will be recalled from chapter 4, in Climacus' view existence involves a "doubleness" or "reduplication." Human existence is a "coming into existence within its own coming into existence" (IV, 240; p. 94). Man exists not only as a part of nature but as a free historical being. As a natural creature he has "come into existence" in the same sense as other natural creatures. But human existence, as part of its natural existence, contains not merely actualities but possibilities that enter human life through conscious reflection. Man not only *has* possibilities (as do other creatures); he *is* in part his awareness of these possibilities, which he may choose to actualize or fail to actualize. Existence, which is this process of actualizing what is already present or given (in the form of reflected possibility), is therefore a process of "reduplication."

The reflective consciousness that makes this process of reduplication possible also ensures that a duality remains in human existence. The thought of a possibility is not identical with its actualization. "It is one thing to think and another to exist in the thought. Existing is in relation to thinking just as little something which follows of itself as it is something thoughtless" (VII, 215; p. 228). It is essential to think to exist, but thinking is not existing. Existing, as a successive, temporal striving to reduplicate the possibilities reflected on (which have an ideal character on Climacus' view), involves the separation of thought and being (VII, 287; p. 296). Human existence contains the "idea" or "the eternal"; this makes it possible for an exister to strive. But since the eternal is for an exister an *ideal*, it is never perfectly realized. It is realized incompletely in a progressive temporal process — in moments of "reduplication."

2. Objective and Subjective Communication

With this understanding of existence as a backdrop, let us look at what Climacus says about objective and subjective communication and the understanding that the communication seeks to achieve. Climacus claims that subjective understanding which focuses on existence requires a "double reflection" which is rooted in the character of existence (VII, 56; p. 68). Direct communication, which aims at objective understanding, does not require this doubleness. What is communicated directly is essentially intellectual content, and when the recipient of the communication understands the ideas (possibilities), the communication is successful. The recipient only has to grasp the possibilities intellectually (first reflection); no double reflection is necessary. When the subject of communication is subjectivity itself, however, the matter is different. Here the aim of the communication is self-understanding. The individual in this case must not only understand the intellectual content (first reflection), but also relate that content to her own existence (second reflection). Since the self is existing, is in process, the communication cannot simply be in the form of "results," but must itself reflect the "process," "the way," which is the self. The recipient of the communication understands it only when she appropriates it by applying it to herself. The double reflection here mirrors the doubleness of existence, where the exister not only is aware of certain possibilities (ideas), but in her existence actualizes those ideas (reduplicates them).

Climacus frequently caricatures objective communication by describing it as "patter" and "rote-understanding." The idea here is that most people accept verbal agreement as the criterion of understanding. Verbal agreement can hide a tremendous misunderstanding, however, since the communicator and the recipient may not understand the words in the same way. Climacus felt that a great deal of what passed for higher education in his day (and no doubt in ours as well) was simply verbal; the learner gains the ability to parrot what the communicator says but has no genuine understanding of the content. However, though Climacus sometimes talks as if all objective communication were of this sort, it is clear that this is not the case. There is a tremendous difference between someone who has simply memorized the "results" of a geometrical system and someone who really understands the logical connections between the theorems, just as there is a tremendous difference between someone who can recite Einstein's relativity theory and someone who understands it. This shows that even objective understanding requires a type of personal appropriation on the part of the recipient.

I think that the distinction Climacus wishes to draw between subjective and objective communication can still be made, however, though I am not sure that it can be drawn so clearly and absolutely as he suggests. For the personal appropriation necessary to understand objective communication is an intellectual appropriation. Even though it is relevant to the thinker's existence, it is primarily relevant to his existence as a thinker. Suppose, however, that the subject of communication were itself existence, how to exist. Here again one could distinguish between someone who merely repeated the communication by rote and someone who had a more adequate understanding. In this case, however, if the understanding is only intellectual it will inevitably take on a rote character, to a greater or lesser degree. For the subject matter one must be familiar with in order to personally appropriate the content of the communication is existence itself. The person who does not employ his life to understand the communication and apply the communication to his life is to a certain extent "pattering," since he has not really appropriated the meaning of what he says. This application of the thought to existence constitutes the "second reflection." The distinction between subjective and objective communication is therefore the difference between what has an essential relationship to existence and what does not. This is for Climacus simply the difference between ethical and religious concerns and all others, since for him it is precisely the ethical and the religious which have an essential relation to existence (VII, 165; p. 177).

3. *Is Subjective Reflection Thought or Action?*

There is still a problem in understanding what is meant by the "second reflection," which Climacus describes as an "appropriation" of the thought (VII, 60; p. 73). Is this reflection a *reflection* on existence or is it equivalent to existence itself? Is it necessary for the individual to realize the subjective content in *action* to understand it subjectively? Or is the existential understanding still a form of understanding with which one's existence may not be fully in accord? How close is the link between understanding the truth and doing the truth? Climacus talks a great deal about subjective thought and the subjective thinker. Is this thought essentially thought, or is it equivalent to action?

If the "second reflection" is identified with action, it would seem to make it impossible for the individual to reflect subjectively on his actions prior to his actions, which would make his action blind and arbitrary. On the other hand, if the second reflection is essentially reflection, it would seem that the close connection between existence and the subjective reflection is severed. In this case it would seem possible for a person to understand intellectually what he should do apart from any existential *doing* on his part. But how would such an intellectual understanding differ from *objective* understanding (requiring only the first reflection), especially when it is recognized that genuine objective understanding also requires a type of personal appropriation (of an intellectual sort) on the part of the understander?

With a little work it is possible to construct an answer to this dilemma which is both plausible and consistent with Climacus' text. Climacus wishes to draw a distinction between thought and action and another distinction between thought that is essentially concerned with action and thought that is not. These two distinctions are not the same. Thought and action are both linked and separated by existence. Thought, no matter how closely concerned with action, is never equivalent to action. As we have seen, however, action is by no means devoid of thought; action is "an inwardness in which the individual revokes the possibility and identifies himself with the thought in order to exist in it" (VII, 293; p. 302). Thought and action are separate because action is never equivalent to merely having thought something; they are linked because genuine action is the realization of what has been thought. This separation and linkage makes it possible for the individual to reflect on what he should do and thereby understand his action prior to acting. One illustration of this is Climacus' discussion of what it is to understand Christianity; here he argues that it must be possible to understand what Christianity is without being a Christian (VII, 322; p. 332). This is so even though Christianity is primarily a way of existing.

Within the sphere of thought, however, a distinction can be drawn between thought that is "abstract," essentially disinterested and removed from existence, and thought that is *concrete*. "What is concrete thinking? It is thought where there is a thinker, and a definite, particular something which is thought, where existence gives to the existing thinker the thought, time, and place" (VII, 287; p. 296).

Though concrete or subjective thought is not action, it has an essential relation to action and thus differs from purely objective or abstract thought. This "situated" thinking is thinking about existential problems, and it is permeated and linked to the action by passion, which is what makes action possible. "To think about existential problems in such a way as to leave out the passion is not to think about them at all; it is to forget the point, which is that the thinker is himself an existing individual" (VII, 304; p. 313). This close connection between subjective thought and action which is due to the connecting passion even makes it legitimate to speak of a "boundary zone" of thought; a thought that is almost an action.

> If there is in general any difference between thought and action, it can only be held fast by relegating to thought the possible, the disinterested, the objective — to action the subjective. But now a boundary zone begins to appear. Thus when I think that I will do this or that, this thought is still not an action, and is for all eternity qualitatively different from an action; nevertheless, it is a possibility in which the interest of actuality and the action already reflects itself. Therefore the disinterestedness, the objectivity, are in the process of being disturbed, because actuality and responsibility want to take

hold of them. (There is therefore a sin in thought.) (VII, 293; p 302).

Subjective thought when viewed analytically is by no means equivalent to action. It is important to distinguish them, since action by no means inevitably accompanies thought. However, when viewed in the process of living, the sharp distinction does not appear. To the person who has acted, her thought appears to her as the first phase of her action; her action is the realization of this thought. (Of course, if she had failed to act, the thought would have remained a mere possiblity.) In existence subjective thought and action are thus linked, and to the exister the question as to what constitutes the "second reflection" (is it reflection or the act itself?) is artificial, since she sees her reflection and her action as the beginning and fulfillment of a single process. Hence it is understandable that Climacus, who is discussing existence, at times makes it seem as if the second reflection he is talking about is the actual "reduplication" involved in existing itself. It seems more plausible to conclude, however, that the second reflection is not the reduplication of existence itself, but the "existential thinking" that precedes the action. Subjective communication must be intellectually understood (first reflection), but its concrete relevance to the individual's life must also be thought through (subjective thinking — second reflection). This latter process is permeated with passion, has an essential relationship to action, and may indeed be the first aspect of an act, but it alone is not action.

4. A Type of Subjective Understanding That IS Equivalent to Action: Existential Understanding

This problem is further complicated by the fact that Climacus also holds that there is a type of understanding that is identical with action. For example, though he says one can understand what Christianity is without being a Christian, he claims one cannot understand what it is to be a Christian without being one (VII, 322; p. 332). I think that what he means by this is something like the following. Thought, no matter how concrete, always remains abstract to a certain degree. That is, the existential possibility that is thought always remains a possibility, no matter how closely related to existence. Thus, there is a sense in which *existence cannot be thought* (VII, 264, 283; pp. 274, 292). For when it is thought, it is thought as a possibility, not an actuality. This is true for all cases except the individual's own existence (VII, 272-273; p. 281).

Climacus has often been misunderstood here. The limitation he places on thought is not an attack on thought. The translation from actuality to possibility does not alter the content, and Climacus says that between thought and existence there may be no difference of content at all (VII, 295; p. 304). When he says that existential reality is incommunicable, he is not saying what thinkers such as Bergson have said, which is that abstract thought can never capture reality because thought falsifies reality. This is the sort of criticism that claims that abstract thought fails to capture the concrete particularity of the "real world." ("How can thought capture the taste of a potato chip?") To this sort of criticism the thinker could rightly respond with Hegel that unless these concrete characteristics *can* be thought, they become contentless, even meaningless, since nothing can be said about them. From Climacus' view the distinction between actuality and thought is one of mode, not content. The concrete particularity that Bergson and others try to discern in actuality is not a *characteristic* of actual things, but their mode of being itself, which Climacus calls their form (VII, 295; p. 304). This mode of being, since it is not a characteristic of things, cannot itself be captured by a concept. *It is not merely a concept, but the difference between the conceptual and the actual.* This is what I think is meant when Climacus affirms that one cannot by reason demonstrate the existence of something, since we "reason from existence, not toward existence" (IV, 207; p. 50). One can attempt to demonstrate that a certain object is a certain kind of object, but existence itself must be something that is *given* (in immediate sensation) or believed, which Climacus sees as a decisive action grounded in personal passion.

Can existence be thought? Is it knowable? Climacus' answer is yes —but not as existence, as possibility. The content of existence can be thought, but its specific character as existing cannot be (VII, 276; p. 285). This is what Climacus means when he urges that "the only thing-in-itself which cannot be thought is existence, which is something thought has no dealings with" (VII, 283; p. 292). What we think is a possibility, not an actuality.

There is, however, one actuality that is not transformed into a possibility by thinking it; that is the individual's own existential actuality. A possibility that I myself by my action identify with is not merely a possibility; it is actuality. This ethical actuality of the individual is "the only actuality which is not transformed into a possibility by being known and which is not known only by being thought, since it is his own actuality" (VII, 275; p. 284).[1] This is the reason why Climacus says that a person's own existential reality is incommunicable (VII, 61, 310; pp. 74, 320), an "essential secret." It therefore follows from this that a person who has actualized a possibility by his action understands and knows that possibility in a way that no one does who has not actualized it; for he does not merely know it as a possibility but as an actuality. There is therefore a type of subjective understanding that is acquired in and through action. There is a qualitative difference between understanding a lifestyle as merely a possibility and understanding a lifestyle as an actuality. I think this is what underlies the distinction Climacus draws between someone who knows what Christianity is and someone who knows what it is to be a Christian. Both know the same thing; it would be a great mistake to think that one can know what Christianity is without knowing it as an existential possibility. The person who only knows Christianity objectively — as a set of doctrines, for example, or as historical facts — does not even know what it is, since Christianity is essentially subjectivity, existential communication that is accepted by acting on it. But even the person who understands Christianity subjectively, which involves the "second reflection" or reflection about how Christianity applies to one's existence, may fail to be a Christian. This in fact is precisely the position of Johannes Climacus himself. Yet he sees that there is a type of understanding that is essentially a product of action, and thus the true Christian understands Christianity in a deeper way than even the subjective thinker who is not a Christian, since to the Christian, Christianity is not merely understood as a possibility but is known as an actuality. This deep understanding involves a doubleness as well, but not merely a double reflection; it requires the doubleness of existence itself.

It would seem advisable to distinguish these two types of subjective understanding, the one essentially understanding, the other an understanding that is realized in action, even though (for reasons we will examine later) Climacus often seems to conflate them. I shall term the first *subjective understanding;* the latter, *existential understanding.* Subjective understanding is reflective understanding that has been concretized by thinking it through in relation to existence. Existential understanding is subjective understanding that has been realized in action.

5. *Communicating Subjectivity: The Concept of the Maieutic*

What, then, is the task of the person who wishes to communicate subjectivity? The answer in general is that such communication must be artful or "indirect," since the communication to be understood must eventuate in a double reflection on the part of the recipient. The receiver must personally appropriate the content, and he is free to do this or to refrain. Hence the success of the communication cannot be guaranteed. The true subjective communicator practices the maieutic art, as did

Socrates. The maieuticist is a midwife; he does not give birth himself but helps others to give birth to their own "thought-children." The communicator cannot force or even seduce the recipient to perform the second reflection, since it is a characteristic of subjective appropriation that it must be truly one's own. The person who does not freely appropriate does not subjectively appropriate. Hence the true communicator recognizes the necessity to distance himself from the receiver, to help the receiver to grasp the truth on his own. The paradox of the maieutic life is that "the recipient by the help of another comes to stand by himself."[2] But if this is to be possible the communicator must find a way to reduce his own significance to the recipient to a vanishing nothingness. Socrates realized this through his ignorance, his irony, and above all by use of his method of questioning. In this way he discouraged would-be "disciples"; the person who had best understood Socrates was the person who realized that he owed Socrates nothing.

The other hero of indirect communication who captures Climacus' attention is Lessing, the famous eighteenth century German dramatist, critic, and man of letters. Climacus wryly acknowledges that he cannot be sure about Lessing, since if he could be sure, then Lessing would have communicated something directly and thus failed to realize the ideal of indirect communication. Lessing, in making his life and beliefs an enigma, perhaps expresses the essential truth that subjectivity must always be a personal acquisition, and therefore remains in a sense a "secret" to everyone who has not acquired the secret for himself.

To describe this maieutic form of communication in closer detail one must specify what sort of subjective understanding one is seeking to impart: the subjective understanding that is still a form of thought, or the existential understanding that comes about only through action. Both types will require maieutic communication, since both require a free appropriation on the part of the recipient if understanding is to be achieved.

There are two elements required to communicate subjective understanding. First, the communicator must be dialectically clear; that is, he must clearly understand the content of what he is to communicate by clearly understanding the subjective possibility itself. This means he must have an understanding of the key structural concepts that define the possibilities he is discussing in their interrelationships and in their application to existence. The second element is the "artful" element; the form of his communication must correspond to its content. Since the conceptual content of subjective communication is about existence, the communicator must, to prevent misunderstanding, avoid giving the impression that the content can be understood impersonally and abstractly. He must design his communication in such a way that the recipient is encouraged to apply the content to his own life and situation. If this is successful, the recipient will not simply appropriate the communication as a result, but will acquire the understanding for himself as a "way." But this second reflection cannot be guaranteed by the communicator; all he can do is communicate the existential possibility as a possibility. It is up to the recipient to think through the possibility with respect to his own life. The communicator really only provides an "occasion" for the recipient to gain self-understanding.

This inability to guarantee results is not a defect but an advantage. Not only must the individual apply the understanding to his life; he is himself Socratically responsible for making such an application. Whether or not he grasps the truth is essentially up to him.

The communicator can of course try to prevent misunderstandings that arise when he contradicts himself by failing to make the form of his communication correspond to the content. For example, it would be a contradiction for a teacher who wished to communicate that a man should have no disciples to seek disciples for his teaching (VII, 70; p. 57). It would similarly be a contradiction for a teacher of subjectivity to give the impression that his teaching could be directly and simply handed to his learners. This is where the artfulness comes into play. The artist seeks to make the form appropriate to the content. The artful communicator of subjectivity seeks to distance himself from the recipient and to prevent the misunderstanding that arises when the form contradicts the content.

What about existential understanding, the understanding that comes from appropriating an existential possibility in *action*? How can this be communicated? In a sense it cannot be, since it depends on the individual's free action. But this is true in a weaker sense of subjective understanding, too. The communicator can be the occasion for someone else achieving existential understanding, just as he can be the occasion for someone achieving subjective understanding.

How can a person help another to achieve existential understanding? If I thought, for example, that a certain ethical life form were true, how could I help another to realize this possibility in her own life? Obviously it cannot be done directly at all, but it would seem that it could be done indirectly by helping the individual achieve subjective understanding. I cannot guarantee that another person will choose the good or even that she will choose to understand the good, but if I can help her to gain a clearer understanding — in existence — of the alternatives that face her, I will have done something. But we have seen that even this cannot be done directly but only maieutically. All that can be done directly is to compel the other person to "take notice" by arousing her attention. Hence the person who wishes to help another existentially is twice removed; he can become the occasion for another's existential development by being the occasion for another's increased subjective understanding.

It follows from this that the person who does wish to help another existentially is indistinguishable from the person who wishes to help another achieve subjective understanding. It is no doubt because of this fact that Climacus often seems to unite these two kinds of understanding we have distinguished. From the existential communicator's point of view these are not two tasks, only one. (Though of course someone *might* seek to help a person acquire subjective understanding without caring about the existential understanding.)

The existential communicator must see his task as both positive and negative. He reflects not merely on what he must communicate but to whom he is communicating. If the recipient is in the grip of various illusions, this obviously makes his task much more difficult. Existential illusions cannot be directly dispelled any more than the truth can be directly communicated, since a person may will, consciously or unconsciously, to remain in the illusion. But the communicator can be the occasion for the removal of an illusion. His primary tools for doing so are humor and irony. Socrates ironically undermined the illusions of his contemporaries by accepting at face value their claims to have wisdom and then requiring them to think through their wisdom and see what it amounted to. This provided the occasion for the wise man to notice the contradiction between his profession and his reality. In an analogous way Climacus accepts at face value the claims of his contemporaries to be Christians and even to have "gone further" than Christianity. As a humorist, however, he cannot help noticing that those who claimed to be Christians contradicted their own assertions by the way in which the assertions were made and by their lives. In pointing up these humoristic contradictions Climacus again provides the occasion for the dispelling of the illusion for anyone who is willing to have the illusion dispelled.

6. Methods for Communicating Indirectly

How can such artful communication be accomplished? The most obvious example is Kierkegaard's pseudonymous authorship itself, which he explains in *The Point of View* as an attempt in indirect communication (XII, 540-541; pp. 39-40). Here we have the significant elements clearly displayed: The communication is a work of art in which the various pseudonyms do not simply talk about but exhibit the existential possibilities that make up their content. The literary form reflects the content. By the pseudonym Kierkegaard distances himself from the reader so as to allow for the reader's subjective appropriation of the content and to force the reader to assume responsibility for the manner in which he does this.

Many in fact have almost equated the concept of indirect communication with Kierkegaard's use of the pseudonyms. This is a mistake, however. The concept of indirect communication as the maieutic art is far broader than the use of pseudonyms, which should be understood as only one device or strategy for carrying out indirect communication. This is important, for it means that a reader who regards the pseudonymous literature as too "mystifying" does not have to reject the concept of indirect communication. It is even possible to imagine a person criticizing the pseudonymous books on the basis of their failure to successfully communicate indirectly. That is, it might be argued that the whole intricate literary form, with its puzzlelike structure, becomes too aesthetically enchanting. Rather than successfully distancing himself from the reader, Kierkegaard may have seduced some readers into endless fascination with himself and the aesthetic characteristics of his authorship.

In any case Johannes Climacus discusses indirect communication a great deal and pseudonymity hardly at all. The lack of any such discussion is only proper since he is himself one of the pseudonyms and could hardly be expected to understand or explain his own creator's ultimate purposes. Climacus himself discusses other devices for communicating indirectly. The primary such device is what he calls the experimental form, which we have already discussed to some extent. To write in an experimental form is to write "hypothetically." The experimentalist offers no results and thus forces the readers to come to their own conclusions, as, for example, Lessing perhaps does on Climacus' reading. Instead of direct, dogmatic assertions, the experimentalist employs freely acknowledged assumptions. He provides only "hypotheses," possibilities; he suggests that something *might* be the case. This tentativeness creates the necessary distance between reader and author so that the reader grasps the truth for himself, if he grasps it at all.

In the realm of psychology the experiment is exhibited by the delineation of a life-possibility about which the reader must form his own opinions, since no finite result is offered. (This is well illustrated by *Repetition* and especially "A Story of Suffering" in *Stages on Life's Way*.) Climacus himself employs the experimental form in the *Philosophical Fragments,* where the dialectical content of Christianity is presented in the guise of a thought-experiment. In the *Postscript* the hypothetical form is secured by the "revocation" in the Appendix, where Johannes Climacus "recalls" the book by asserting that "everything is to be understood in such a way that it is revoked" (VII, 539; p. 547).

Throughout his writings Climacus maintains the same hypothetical stance through the use of irony and humor. Humor is in fact defined by Climacus as always involving a "revocation." The communication that is a "unity of jest and seriousness" becomes a riddle to the recipient, which the recipient must solve for himself (VII, 68-69; p. 81). The ironical and humorous form once more is a way of securing the author's distance from the reader and thereby the reader's independence and responsibility. More will be said about irony, humor and "revocation" in chapter 10.

7. Types of Maieutic Communicators

It makes a great difference who is doing the communicating and which existential possibility is being communicated. Climacus discusses three different practitioners of the maieutic: the Socratic-type practitioner, the Christian, and God himself. The last is perhaps the most surprising and also the most significant. If God limits himself to "indirect" communication, this constitutes a strong limit to human presumptuousness. Who would dare to try to become something for another person that not even God permits himself to be?

How can God practice indirect communication? In one sense, of course, God is not a maieutic practitioner, since as Creator he is everything to the creature, and the creature therefore can never be totally independent. But, as Climacus sees it, man does have a certain relative independence of God; it is not an absolute independence since the independence itself is granted by God. But this independence is nonetheless real.[3] God, like any indirect communicator, distances himself from the recipient. His communication in creation is a "resigned" communication.

> To communicate in that way is the most beautiful triumph of resigned inwardness. Therefore there is no one so resigned as God, for he communicates through his creating in such a way that he, by creating, gives independence over against himself (VII, 220; p. 232).

It is this created independence that governs human communication as well.

The greatest degree of resignation a person can achieve is to recognize the given independence in every person, and according to his ability do everything in truth to help someone preserve it (VII, 220; pp. 232-233).

God is even compared by Climacus with a pseudonymous author.

For no anonymous author can more cunningly hide himself, and no practitioner of the maieutic can more carefully withdraw himself from the direct relationship than God. He is in the creation, everywhere in the creation, but directly he is not there, and only when the individual turns himself inwardly into himself (therefore only in the inwardness of self-activity), does he become attentive and able to see God (VII, 204-205; p. 218).

Just as God, though everything to the creature, is nonetheless only maieutically active in creation, so he is also only maieutic in re-creating the individual. At least this is how Climacus spins out the imaginative experiment in the *Fragments* which he later identifies with Christianity. The God here is represented as re-creating the learner who has forfeited the truth, in that the God grants to the learner the condition for grasping the truth. Here in an even more decisive way the person owes everything to the God and is really nothing apart from God. As Climacus imaginatively thinks it through, however, a God moved by love for the learner would not wish the learner to become nothing, but to become something. Such a God would not crush the learner by forcing him to receive the condition or deceive him by luring him into receiving it. Such a God would offer the condition by resigning himself — by lowering himself to the position of the learner. God in the form of a man — that is true resignation. By coming to man in the form of a lowly servant, God makes it *possible* for man to respond to God; but also possible for man to refuse to respond. Climacus says that the God-man would necessarily communicate indirectly. Even if he directly affirms, "I am God," there is the "counterargument" of his ordinary human form (IV, 255-256; p. 116).[4] Thus the reality of the God in time cannot be grasped immediately but only in faith. Again we have the paradox that man owes everything to God, yet man's freedom and selfhood are safeguarded by God himself.

Of the human practitioners of the maieutic, logically there are two possibilities with respect to man's relation to the essential truth — the truth about existing. The first is that man essentially possesses the truth; this is the view that underlies "immanence" and is philosophically expressed most forcefully in Idealism, and also in many religious perspectives. At heart man himself possesses the capacity to know God, or the Absolute, or the Supreme Moral Ideal, and relate himself to it. For Climacus this was understood most deeply and expressed most consistently by Socrates as described in the Platonic dialogues. Socrates' ignorance and irony, his repelling of all would-be disciples, his ironic puncturing of illusions, and his energetic attempt to assist others to "beget" by themselves, represents the highest and noblest manner of communication within the sphere of immanence. Socrates as teacher is only the "occasion" for the learner's own self-conscious realization.

The other possible assumption with regard to the essential truth is that man lacks this truth and needs to be given the condition for grasping it by God. It might seem that there are still other alternatives. Might it not be, for example, that man lacks the essential truth and is not able to regain it in any way? Abstractly considered, this is possible, but it is not a possibility that must be considered by the communicator, since on this view no understanding of the truth, and hence no communication, would be possible. The subjective, existential communicator believes there is a truth to be communicated and that it is possible for that truth to be understood.

The second alternative is that man must receive the truth directly from God. We have already seen how the God could be seen as communicating "indirectly" on such a view. Would there be any role for human communicators on this alternative? Or, to put it in explicitly Christian terminology, what is the role of the Christian communicator? Since on this view each person must receive the truth from the God directly, it is clear that the Christian will respect the maieutic ideal, since every human being who has received the condition from God is essentially equal. Each believer owes the other nothing, but everything to the God. The task of the believer in this case will be to *bear witness*. He will proclaim, "I believe that the God has appeared..." By proclaiming the news of the God's appearance he may become the occasion for another person to encounter the God for himself. This witness, however, provides only the occasion; if the recipient of the communication does not receive the condition, which is faith, from the God himself, he does not and cannot believe.

Actually, Kierkegaard himself sees a much greater role than this for the Christian maieuticist. Johannes Climacus is not a Christian, however, and can hardly be expected to understand the Christian life in all its compass. A much more elaborate discussion of the Christian maieuticist is found in Kierkegaard's *Works of Love*, where both similarities and differences between the Socratic and Christian maieutic are discussed in more detail.[5]

The maieutic as discussed here is not limited to subjective communication but centers around existential communication, since the primary aim of the Christian is to help others change not merely the way they think, even about subjective matters, but the way they live. The maieuticist is the one who "upbuilds" *(opbygger)*, but again who does so in such a way as to ensure the independence of the one helped. The art of the maieutic here consists in getting the other "to stand alone — with God's help."

The major difference between the Socratic and Christian maieutic in *Works of Love* revolves around the concept of "neighbor love," the distinctively Christian kind of love. When Socrates has helped the other, he can take a certain ironic satisfaction in observing the other stand alone — with his help. This satisfaction is bound up with Socrates' own independence. The Christian maieuticist, on the other hand, is bound to the one helped in a way that Socrates was not. For the Christian both the one who is helped as well as he himself stand alone — with *God's* help. The helper and the one helped are independent of each other but totally dependent on God. In thus sharing a total dependence on God's love they are bound together in a way. This binding does not compromise their independence of each other. The divine love they share is infinite and eternal; it does not make distinctions or draw boundaries around its love. It is this love that the Christian grasps as the truth, and it is this the Christian wants to communicate to others.

This is not explicit in Johannes Climacus' account of the Christian maieuticist, but much of it is implied. As Climacus sees it, in the Christian alternative to Socrates the disciple owes the God everything, and the condition he receives becomes a trust, since the learner owes his life to the God (IV, 186; p. 22). The content of that new life will not be hard to discern, since even Climacus sees that this view implies that the God is essentially love — a love that reaches to all human beings (IV, 193-194, 199; pp. 30-31, 39).

We conclude that the concepts of the maieutic art and indirect communication play a central role in Climacus' thought. They are intimately linked with his understanding of existence itself as a doubling and with the acquisition in existence of these existential capacities that constitute subjectivity. Climacus highlights both the value and limits of clear thought and understanding. On the one hand, subjective understanding is an essential condition for existential achievement and is indeed the first step toward such an achievement. But this subjective understanding can remain merely understanding, and as such is not itself the achievement. But as essentially related to existential understanding, subjective understanding shares the characteristic of being a personal appropriation. It reflects the passion that is the decisive element in genuine action. The communicator must recognize the personal existential character of subjective and existential understanding by communicating in an artful way: distancing himself from the recipient and ensuring that the form of his communication reflects the fact that what he is communicating is a way and not a result.

8. A Critical Note: Communication as a Relational Concept

A final note seems necessary in connection with the concept of indirect communication. This concept has inspired a great deal of confusion on the part of Kierkegaard commentators. Some have concluded that the artful character of Climacus' writings (and the Kierkegaardian pseudonymous literature in general) precludes any straightforward, meaningful discussion of that literature. This seems to me to be a blunder. It is not, for example, contradictory to reflect *objectively* on the nature of indirect communication and Climacus' *theories* about such communication. Of course reflection about subjectivity is not subjectivity, but the fact that such reflection is about subjectivity does not eliminate its reflective character.

Climacus' central worry seems to be that the communication of subjectivity is a type of communication that easily misfires. The communication may fail because either the communicator or the one who receives the communication has not concretized what is communicated by applying it to existence. In that case the communication becomes merely verbal, "patter."

Climacus thinks that there is a constant tendency for subjective communication to degenerate in this way. I am sure he is right. It is easy for the ethical or religious individual to become aesthetically interested in the abstractions of ethical theory or in the subtleties of systematic theology without asking what these intellectual conceptions mean for her own existence. Climacus thinks that this tendency is encouraged when ethical and religious truths are communicated in a direct, straightforward way. The individual who is handed a set of propositions is easily seduced into thinking that the ethical and religious life can be had as a "result," instead of beginning the arduous process of thinking through the truths she has received in relation to her own life, as a "way." Climacus therefore recommends that subjective communication be done "artfully," in such a way that the content is reflected in the literary form.

However, one must ask whether Climacus does not here translate a possibility or tendency into an inevitability. *Must* the individual who has just heard the ten commandments or a religious creed communicated "directly" fail to apply what she has heard to her own life? Surely it is also possible for the individual to subjectively appropriate what she has heard. It is true that there is a risk that she will not do so, but that risk is rooted in a possibility, not a necessity.

What must be kept clearly in mind is that communication involves a relation between two or more people. Whether someone successfully communicates subjectivity depends not merely on what the communicator attempts to communicate and how she attempts to do it, but also on how the communication is received. It is true that communicating moral and religious truth directly often results in a perverse missing of their point. But it is possible for the individual who receives such "direct" communication to receive it subjectively. *And* it is also possible that an "artful" communicator will meet the same fate as the unsuccessful "direct" communicator. It is even possible that the artfulness of the communication will itself be the source of the temptation to miss the point; the recipient of the communication may be aesthetically enchanted with the artistic skill and techniques and so fail to make the existential application. In fact, I think this has often been the case with Kierkegaard's own authorship.

There is a tendency in Climacus to dichotomize the objective and the subjective; to assume, for example, that if Christianity requires belief in doctrines, then it is *not* something to be lived. The underlying assumption is that objectively formulating moral and religious truth perverts it. Surely, however, such an objective formulation merely lends itself to such perversion, which therefore creates a problem moral and religious communities must be constantly on guard against. Moral and religious teachers and hearers must constantly remind themselves of the point that the teachings must be *appropriated*.

I am myself inclined to view Climacus' view on indirect communication and his use of it as just such a reminder. The primary value of the concept of "indirect communication" is not as a theory about how to communicate, though it can be helpful and suggestive here. It is even more helpful as a constantly needed reminder of how one should hear and respond to communication. The point is surely that the individual is responsible for seeing and accepting the truth herself. The ideal is not to be one who is the right type of communicator but to be one who is the right type of listener and responder.

---

[1] The Lowrie-Swenson translation here is incorrect and misleading.

[2] See *Works of Love* (IX, 261-266; pp. 256-260) for a penetrating discussion of this paradox, including the contrasting forms it assumes in the ethical life and the Christian life.

[3] See *Journals and Papers II*, 1251. Here Kierkegaard argues that it is a characteristic of being *almighty* to be able to "draw back." Only God can practice the maieutic art to perfection.

[4] This is later developed at greater length by Anti-Climacus. See many sections of *Practice in Christianity (Training in Christianity)* especially XII, 125-127; pp. 134-136.

[5] For what follows see particularly IX, 261-266; pp. 256-260.

Chapter VII

TRUTH AND SUBJECTIVITY

1. Truth and Salvation

Scarcely any aspect of Kierkegaard's writings has stirred more controversy than Climacus' assertion that "the truth is subjectivity." A "subjective" definition of truth is offered by Climacus in a famous passage: *"the objective uncertainty, held fast in the most passionate appropriation of inwardness, is the truth,* the highest truth there is for an *exister"* (VII, 170; p. 182). This assertion has commonly and unfortunately been understood as implying that truth is subjective, and it has been used to hang the stigma of a crude epistemological relativism around Kierkegaard. A leading textbook is all too typical here. W. T. Jones says that for Kierkegaard "the belief of a Hindu that Vishnu is God, the belief of a Mohammedan that Allah is God, the belief of a Nuer that *kwoth* is God—even the belief of an atheist that there is no God—are all true; providing only that in each of these beliefs an objective uncertainty is embraced with passionate intensity."[1]

Even a leading Kierkegaard scholar in a highly praised book despairs of taking seriously the thesis that "the truth is subjectivity." Louis Mackey tells us that the definition of truth offered by Climacus is actually to be taken as a satire, the point of which bears a distressing resemblance to the relativism usually ascribed to Climacus.

> When Climacus "defines" truth as "subjectivity, the objective uncertainty held fast in the most passionate appropriation of inwardness," he is writing a satire on definition to recall his reader from the illusory certainties of knowledge to the awareness that every belief and every truth claim has no surer warrant than the freedom and the fervor of him who asserts it.[2]

A careful examination of Climacus' text shows that these interpretations (which have engendered enthusiastic support for Kierkegaard as well as repugnance) are completely unwarranted. This is an area where it is crucial to pay attention to what Climacus actually says and not to assume that one already knows what he is saying. Here, as in many other places, Climacus shapes language to his own ends, and it is not wise to assume that one knows those ends in advance.

Most of the confusion in this area arises from the fact that Climacus is mixing two areas that are not usually mixed: the philosophy of truth and the theology of salvation. He is simultaneously discussing issues in logical theory and epistemology on the one hand and issues in soteriology on the other. He is not himself confused here; he is pointing to analogies between these two fields that most thinkers today do not see. But his discussion can be confusing to the reader who does not see the distinctions and the connections made and who misses the crucial transitions in the exposition.

To put the point clearly, Climacus begins by discussing the philosophical issue about the nature of truth in general and the various philosophical theories that answer this question. He ends by discussing the question as to how an individual can be "*in* the truth"; that is, how an individual can live in such a way as to have fully fulfilled his destiny as an existing person. This is the concept I described as the equivalent of the religious concept of salvation. It is Climacus' genius to see that these two apparently diverse areas are connected and that the term "truth" is not merely being used equivocally when used in the two contexts.

2. Classical Theories of Truth and Their Limitations

Climacus begins the chapter on "the truth is subjectivity" with a discussion of two classical philosophical treatments of the concept of truth. These two theories are called the empirical theory, which defines truth as "the conformity of thought with being," and the idealistic theory, which defines truth as "the conformity of being with thought" (VII, 157; p. 169). He seems to have in mind here views that are similar to the classical correspondence and coherence theories, respectively.

The classical correspondence theory, which is historically associated with empiricism, takes reality or being as a given and regards human thought as true when it "agrees with," or corresponds to, the real. It is noteworthy here that classical thinkers such as Locke tended to talk of truth in a psychological mode; hence the question of truth was the question of how thoughts, or beliefs, or ideas, understood as psychological events or acts, could be true. Contemporary philosophers prefer to think of truth as a "logical" relation; thus they usually talk of a correspondence between propositions (understood as logical entities) and reality. This shift in terminology tends to obscure the problem that Climacus wishes to address, so we will begin by using the classical type of terminology he himself employed. However, it will become apparent that Climacus is quite aware of some of the reasons for this shift in terminology, and would probably have approved of it.

The other theory that Climacus mentions, referred to as the idealistic theory, is at least a cousin of the coherence theory associated with classical idealism. The idealist, with his conviction that the ultimate essence of being is thought and, thus, that thought and being are one, understands the true as the fully rational. Being or reality must be what conforms to thought itself; hence the test of truth is the test of reason. For Hegel this meant that the truth emerges through his dialectical logic; for rationalist thinkers wedded to a more Aristotelian logic, this means that rational coherence becomes the essence of truth.

In both of these views the concept of truth seems to involve a "doubling" or "reduplication." What Climacus finds in common in the two definitions is the notion of an *agreement* or *correspondence* between two elements— thought and being. The difference in the two theories lies merely in the "direction" of this agreement. In either case Climacus feels that the crucial question to ask concerns what is meant by "being" *(Væren)* (VII, 157; p. 169).

Climacus consistently makes a distinction between being in the ideal sense and being as concrete, empirical actuality. What is distinctive about concrete, empirical actuality is that it is a process, a constant becoming. It follows from this that if by "being" we mean concrete, empirical actuality, then the truth, at least for man, becomes an approximation.

If being in the two given definitions is understood as that empirical being, then the truth is changed into something to be achieved, and everything put into process, because the empirical object is not finished, and the existing knowing spirit is himself in process, and thus the truth is an approximation (VII, 157; p. 169).

Climacus here cites two reasons for his claim. First, the object of true knowledge is constantly changing. Secondly, the knower himself is in process of changing. Since the object is unfinished, no human idea can claim to be the final truth about it; all human cognition of concrete being is "subject to correction and improvement." But a truth subject to correction and improvement is not the final truth but an approximation to the final truth. Since the cognitive subject is himself in process, he can attempt to correct and improve his thought, but this merely reemphasizes the incomplete character of his thought.

The only exception Climacus makes, and it is a significant one, concerns God. For God, presumably because he is eternal and sees from the eternal point of view, truth about empirical actuality may be perfect and not merely approximative (VII, 158; p. 170). This corresponds to Climacus' assertion that for God existential reality forms a system (VII, 97; p. 107). For human beings logical systems are possible, but never existential systems. Man is capable of constructing formal, logical structures that are complete and final, but when these logical structures are taken as models of reality, they become "hypotheses" or "approximations" to the truth (VII, 161; p. 173). Climacus does not denigrate the significance to humans of this approximative truth; he is merely reminding us of the nature of empirical knowledge.

It follows from this that if one is talking about truth for man in the ideal sense, one is not talking about actual, empirical truth but about the ideal which that truth attempts to approximate. That ideal is only realized for human beings when they are dealing with conceptual truth, or the truth that contemporary philosophers would call analytic. This is the sort of truth that depends merely on the ideal relations between concepts. In this case the conformity of thought with being or being with thought must be understood as an ideal relationship, and being must be understood as "ideal being." This ideal being is the object of thought which emerges when thought abstracts from the concrete particularity of the empirical world. Climacus mentions mathematics as an example of such an abstraction (VII, 161; p. 173). In mathematics the thinker does not consider three pears and three apples but merely the abstract number three. The mathematician's object of thought is a conceptual ideal which is therefore finished and complete in a way that no empirical object is. Climacus does not deny the possibility or value of such abstract thought; however, he claims that such abstractions are not empirical reality itself, but must be regarded as "an abstract repetition or an abstract model of what being *in concreto* is as empirical being" (VII, 158; p. 170). When being is understood in this ideal way, "there is nothing to prevent the determination of the truth abstractly as finished; for the agreement between thought and being is abstractly seen always finished, since the beginning of becoming lies precisely in the concreteness from which abstraction abstractly looks away" (VII, 158; p. 170).

Climacus admits that this sort of abstract truth does fit the classical definitions of truth. Abstract thought can correspond with abstract being. However, in this case he claims that there is no genuine "doubling" or reduplication. The definition of truth given is really a tautology, since thought and being here refer to the same thing. The "being" that is referred to is being as thought abstractly, but this being is identical with abstract thought itself. All that is really said by the classical definitions of truth is that truth *is;* the doubleness in the definitions merely illustrates the logical form of truth. It *shows* that truth involves a reduplication (VII, 158; p. 170). There is nothing wrong with this formula as an abstract formula, but it does not touch the question of the truth about actual entities.

3. *Truth and Existence*

The question Climacus is really interested in now can be asked: What is the relationship between the individual exister and truth? This is a question to which contemporary philosophy has not paid sufficient attention. Contemporary philosophy correctly sees that there is a problem in talking about truth psychologically. How is it that a belief, understood as a psychological event, can be true? It would seem that a belief, understood as a psychological event, is merely one more concrete empirical actuality, and it is mysterious how the relation of "agreement" is established between one such actuality and another. The solution to this problem usually takes the form of noting the ambiguity that attaches to the term "belief." "Belief" can refer to a psychological event or act, but it also can refer to a content, what is believed. This content can be expressed in a proposition, and thus the problem of beliefs being true or false is converted to the problem of propositions being true or false.

A proposition is, however, an abstract, logical entity. Propositions as such do not exist in Climacus' sense of the word, though they may well be regarded as real in some sense. What is the relation between a proposition and an existing human being? How is it that an existing human being can believe something; that is, how is it that a timeless, logical entity (like a concept or a proposition) can become an element in a person's psychological history? For Climacus this is what happens when a human being thinks abstractly.

Climacus by no means denies that human beings possess this power and that it is significant. He himself emphasizes that human existence contains "the idea." He claims that the capacity for considering abstract ideals is an essential aspect of existence, which is itself the process of reduplicating these eternal ideals or possibilities in actuality. But he emphasizes just as strongly that thought in this sense is only an aspect of existence, that existence is not reducible to thought. Why does he insist on this so strongly? It is because he thinks that there is a strong tendency to forget that the thinker is first and foremost an exister, and consequently to fail to consider the relationship between abstract thought and existence.

It must be recognized that for Climacus these issues are not merely interesting problems in logical theory. The issue of man's relationship to abstract ideas possesses existential, even religious significance. This is best seen if we examine the thinkers he is most interested in, Socrates/Plato and Hegel. In the Platonic dialogues Socrates' intellectual quest for conceptual understanding clearly possesses religious significance. In discovering the Forms Plato thinks man discovers eternity and at the same time realizes his own true character. The divine lies within him and can be reached in thought. In a similar way Hegel had claimed that abstract thought, Reason, is the most adequate means of grasping the Absolute, which Hegel identified with the object of traditional religious worship. The individual who embarks upon the reflective process therefore takes the path that leads to his own personal fulfillment. Abstract thought is really the pathway to salvation.

These views may seem foreign to contemporary logical theory and epistemology, which appear on the surface to be far removed from such religious concerns. However, a closer look reveals that there are still some who give "religious" significance to objective, abstract thought. Anyone who, whether consciously or unconsciously, regards the search for objective, intellectual truth as man's highest end is close to Plato and Hegel. For this view implies that it is through intellectual achievement that man most adequately fulfills himself and become truly human.

Bertrand Russell will serve as a good illustration of a thinker who ascribes religious significance to objective truth:

> The free intellect will see as God might see, without a *here* and *now*, without hopes and fears, without the trammels of customary beliefs and prejudices, calmly, dispassionately, in the sole and exclusive desire of knowledge—knowledge as impersonal, as purely contemplative, as it is possible for man to attain.[3]

Russell goes on to affirm that such intellectual contemplation ennobles the contemplator as well:

> Thus contemplation enlarges not only the objects of our thoughts but also the objects of our actions and our affections—it makes us citizens of the universe. . .

> Through the greatness of the universe which philosophy contemplates, the mind is rendered great, and becomes capable of that union with the universe which constitutes its highest good.[4]

Thus, Russell sees the highest human end to be the achievement of objective truth, and he stresses that such truth has an impersonal character which in turn demands a purely detached objective attitude on the part of the knower.

Russell's view may be thought extreme, but it is not that unusual. Anyone who speaks of a "duty to truth" and sees that duty as man's highest obligation is implicitly agreeing with Russell.

Without questioning the value of truth and the fact that there is such a thing as a duty to truth, one may question whether this duty is man's highest duty. What would that mean? Is man's *telos* qua man the acquisition of intellectual understanding? Does that mean a person who fails to know something she could know is less human than she could be? This seems implausible. There are surely millions of facts that no sane person would worry about knowing, unless she simply enjoyed knowing about trivia. Even in the case of ignorance of significant scientific theories, it would seem dubious to claim that the ignorant have necessarily failed to live the fullest kind of human life.

Climacus' response to someone who regards man's highest duty as the acquisition of objective truth seems to be something like this: "What kind of truth are you seeking? If it is empirical truth, then you must recognize that you can never find genuine truth in this region, but only approximation and probability. (Climacus also thinks that even this approximative truth cannot be gained through disinterested speculation, but requires personal commitment.) If, on the other hand, you are seeking abstract, formal truth, you must recognize that this truth is not about concrete actuality but about ideal being."

With regard to this formal, abstract truth Climacus agrees that it is to be found by means of abstract, disinterested thought. Some idealists had insisted that an "exhaustive reflection" or universal doubt was a possibility for man. Through this process the thinker could reach the realm of "pure" abstraction, the "pure I." It is this thesis that Climacus opposes, for he sees that though it is easy to *talk* of a universal doubt that leads to pure abstraction, it is impossible for a thinker to achieve this in actuality. Man as an exister is not and cannot be pure thought. He is capable of abstract thought, but that abstract thought is momentary in character and never completely "pure."

Climacus himself is struck by how mysterious man's ability to think abstractly is, but he fully acknowledges that it is nonetheless a reality. However mysterious and difficult to explain, it is possible for abstract logical entities, such as universal concepts and propositions, to become a part of an individual's temporal history. This is why human existence itself is described as a paradox. It is a synthesis of the eternal and the temporal. Existence is the double movement in which the individual conceives of ideas and then reduplicates those ideas in reality. But it is also possible for human beings to engage in intellectual reflection for its own sake. In so doing the individual abstracts from existence and "loses himself in the Idea." It is through this process that the individual exister realizes abstract, formal truth. But this realization of abstract truth is always momentary; even in the moment the individual has this truth, he does not have it *qua* exister but only insofar as he *abstracts* from existence, "looks away from" or brackets the fact that he is an exister. Thus it is a contradiction to urge that abstract truth is man's highest end *as exister,* since man only realizes this truth insofar as he momentarily "eternalizes" himself and ceases to exist. "If the existing individual could be outside himself, then the truth would be something completed for him, but where is this point? The "I-I" is a mathematical point, which does not exist at all. . ." (VII, 164; p. 176).

Climacus drives home his point about the relation between the exister and objective truth with some interesting reflections about insanity. Subjectivity is usually feared as the home of arbitrary passion; an insane person is thought to lack the capacity for objective reflection. Climacus points out, however, that objectivity alone is no guarantee of sanity, since an escapee from a mental institution would hardly prove his sanity by going around and constantly reciting such an objective truth as "The world is round" (VII, 162; p. 174). In fact, pure objectivity, if it could be realized, would be a type of insanity, for such an individual would be totally lacking in any human interest and emotion. Even if such an individual by some freak of nature uttered a steady stream of objective truth, he would still fail to be a human being. He would not be able to act and could not see the use or value of his knowledge. Climacus thinks some philosophers approximate this sort of insanity:

> When the insanity is the aberration of inwardness, the tragic and the comic lies in the fact that what infinitely concerns the unhappy person is a fixed idea which is of no concern to anyone. When the insanity however is the kind in which inwardness is excluded, it is comical that what the happy individual knows is the truth, the truth which concerns all mankind, but does not at all concern the much honored prattler (VII, 163; p. 175).

4. Moral and Religious Truth as "Essential Truth": Can a Life Be True?

What kind of relationship *is* possible between an exister and truth? How can the truth itself be realized in existence? In his answer to this question Climacus restricts himself to considering what he terms "essential truth." This is the truth that it is essential for an exister to have, the truth that itself has an essential relationship to existence (VII, 165; pp. 176-177). This is simply the truth about how to *live,* and Climacus says that the quest for this truth is identical with the quest for ethical and ethical-religious knowledge. It is crucial to recognize that Climacus' definition of truth as subjectivity is intended to apply only to this essential truth, as he makes it clear in a footnote to the crucial passage.

> The reader will observe that the discussion here is about the essential truth, or about the truth which essentially relates itself to existence, and that it is precisely to make it [this truth] clear as inwardness or subjectivity, that the contrast [with objective truth] is drawn (VII, 166n; p. 178n).

In other words the definition of truth as subjectivity is not intended to apply at all to logic, history, and other areas where the truth concerned does not essentially bear on existence. These areas Climacus terms accidental knowledge, since one cannot say that a person who lacks such knowledge, however valuable, has failed to exist in the highest sense. Presumably in these other areas if man as exister relates to the truth, it will be through the approximative inquiry and momentary abstraction from existence discussed earlier. (And these activities in their proper place are not to be denigrated.) These "objective" areas of knowledge are considered by Climacus only insofar as they become elevated to the level of moral and religious truth; only insofar as it is claimed that man's highest duty is to achieve such truth and that man fulfills his destiny as *exister* through such knowledge. It is these claims that Climacus has tried to deflate through his careful analysis of objective truth and its relationship to existence. To summarize and repeat his conclusion: Insofar as objective truth concerns existence, only approximations can be realized, not the truth itself. Insofar as final truth is achievable, it is achieved by abstracting from existence. In neither case does the truth *exist*, in Climacus' special sense, though truth may be nonetheless eternally real and, for God, actual.

To see the relationship between an exister and truth we must once again be reminded of the nature of existence as a synthesis of the temporal and the eternal. Human existence contains a double movement. This is first the movement from actuality to possibility, in which the individual becomes conscious of himself and comes to understand his actual self as containing possibilities. The second movement is the movement of choice in which the individual selects from among these possibilities some to be actualized and does so by passionately identifying himself with these possibilities in commitment. Action (the second movement) has just as much intellectual content as reflection (the first movement). The difference between action and reflection is the direction of movement; both are concerned with conceptual possibilities. In reflection the individual moves from actuality to possibility; in action he moves from possibility to actuality. The content of action and reflection can therefore be identical. Climacus insists that *existence contains content:* He says, for example, that when a religious believer exists in his faith, "his existence acquires tremendous content, but not in the sense of paragraph-material" (VII, 330; p.340).

Many contemporary philosophers claim that only propositions can be true or false in the proper sense. They often think of propositions as capable of being true or false because they possess intellectual content and are thus capable of being a "model" that agrees with, or corresponds to, reality. Climacus sees that human existence itself possesses content and therefore is capable of "modeling" reality; in fact, it is much more capable of modeling existential reality, which is a process, than is a proposition, which is an ideal logical entity. When the subject under discussion is moral and religious truth, the truth that essentially concerns existence—how to live—Climacus claims that existence itself provides the *only* adequate form for the realization of the truth. Since existence is a process or "a way," the only perfectly adequate form for the realization of the truth about existence is the process of existing itself. If the truth is to be more than an *ideal,* if it is to become actualized in time, it must be *lived.* When the truth is existentially realized in this way, the exister is *in* the truth, and his existence itself may be described as true.

The question then becomes, How can the truth be realized in existence? How can the individual come to exist true-ly, to be in the truth? Here Climacus poses two possible answers. One is that the individual is in the truth, has fulfilled the moral and religious ideal, if he knows objectively true things. The other possibility is that the individual is understood to be in the truth if he relates himself rightly to what he understands as true by actualizing that truth in his actions.

> *When the truth is asked about objectively, the truth is reflected on objectively as an object, to which the knower relates himself. The reflection is not upon the relation, but upon the fact that it is the truth, the true he relates himself to. If only this he relates himself to is the truth, the true, then the subject is in the truth. When the truth is asked about subjectively, the individual's relation to the truth is reflected upon; if only this relation's "how" is in the truth, then the individual is in the truth, even if he thereby relates himself to untruth* (VII, 166; p.178).

As we might guess, for Climacus the answer to the question as to which way is superior is easy, since existence is not knowing, but acting.

> Now when the arithmetical problem is this: on which side is there the most truth (and to be at one time equally on both sides is, as said, not granted to an exister, but is only the happy imagination of an imaginary I-I); on the side of one who objectively seeks the true God and the God-concept's approximate truth, or on the side of one who is infinitely concerned as to whether he in truth relates himself to God with the infinite passion of need: the answer cannot be doubtful for anyone who has not been totally muddled with the help of knowledge. If one, who lives in the midst of Christianity, goes into God's house, into the house of the true God, with the true concept of God in his knowledge, and now prays, but prays in untruth; and when another lives in a heathen land but prays with the whole passion of infinity, though his eyes rest on the image of an idol: where is there then the most truth? The one prays in truth to God, though

he worships an idol; the other prays in untruth to the true God, and therefore truly worships an idol (VII, 168; pp. 179-180).

It is important to notice that this question is about which kind of *life* can best be described as true; *it has no bearing on the question of propositional truth*. Climacus is not asserting the absurd thesis that someone can make a false proposition true if only he believes it in the right way. If a person believes that 3 plus 3 is 5, his belief is still false no matter how passionately he believes it. Climacus' question is not about objective propositional truth at all, but about existential truth. He is saying that a person does not exist true-ly merely by knowing what is objectively true. It is possible for a person to apprehend objective truth (though it must be remembered that on Climacus' view this is possible only in an approximative or abstract way) without allowing that truth to penetrate his existence. Such a person's beliefs are true, but his existence is not. Conversely, if the individual's relationship to what he apprehends as true is such that his existence has been transformed and permeated in the proper manner, than the *existence* of that individual may be described as true. He is himself true, or "in the truth," even if his beliefs are objectively false.

The thesis that a person could himself achieve "salvation," morally and religiously be "in the truth," even if his cognitive beliefs are false, is not obviously true, but it is certainly not absurd and does not involve any commitment to irrationalism or epistemological subjectivism. With regard to the sphere of morality, Climacus' view has a great deal of support. Most people would agree that it is possible for a person with confused or even mistaken ideas about morality to personally act morally. Thus, even the strictest moral deontologist can recognize that a hedonist like Epicurus can live a very moral life in spite of his (to the deontologist) wrong ideas. Contrariwise, it is possible for a person to understand objectively true moral principles and yet personally be a moral reprobate.

Many religious believers would disagree with such a thesis with respect to religion, at least, by claiming that salvation is dependent upon intellectual assent to certain doctrines or creeds. But even here the religious believer usually goes a long way toward Climacus' view by minimizing the amount of correct doctrine that must be assented to for salvation and emphasizing the necessity for those doctrines to be acted on.

Even such a noted defender of doctrinal Christian orthodoxy as C. S. Lewis seems to agree with Climacus in the final volume of the *Narnia* series, *The Last Battle*. There Lewis tells of a young warrior, Emeth,[5] who has sincerely worshipped and served Tash, a false deity, all of his life. In the final chapter Emeth tells of his encounter with Aslan, the great lion (who represents the true God.)

> The Glorious One bent down his golden head and touched my forehead with his tongue and said, Son thou art welcome. But I said, Alas, Lord, I am no son of Thine but the servant of Tash. He answered, Child, all the service thou has done to Tash, I account as service done to me. Then. . .I overcame my fear and questioned the Glorious One and said, Lord, is it then true. . .that thou and Tash are one. The Lion growled so that the earth shook. . .and said, It is false. Not because he and I are one, but because we are opposites, I take to me the services which thou hast done to him, for I and he are of such different kinds that no service which is vile can be done to me, and none which is not vile can be done to him. Therefore, if any man swear by Tash and keep his oath for the oath's sake, it is by me that he has truly sworn, though he know it not, and it is I who reward him. And if any man do a cruelty in my name, then though he says the name Aslan, it is Tash whom he serves.[6]

Here we have in literary form a striking illustration of what Climacus means when he says "If only the relation's 'how' is in the truth, then the individual is in the truth, even if he thereby relates himself to what is not true" (VII, 166; p. 178). An individual who is attempting to serve God "true-ly" is serving God if his service is true service, even if he has the wrong idea about God. Notice that for Lewis, too, this view in no way involves a commitment to relativizing objective truth. It is not because Tash and Aslan are the *same*—so that all beliefs, even contradictory ones, become true—that Emeth is saved, but because of the totally distinct characteristics of objective truth and falsehood. The objective religious truth is here seen as having the quality of only being truly realized by human beings when it is rightly acted upon. In Climacus' terms it is essentially related to existence.

5. *Does Subjective Truth Exclude Objective Truth?*

One question that is almost certain to arise here is why there must be an either-or between the subjective and the objective. Why cannot the importance of subjective appropriation be conceded, but the importance of objective truth be conceded as well? Granted, it is important *how* the individual believes what she believes. But isn't it important *what* she believes as well?

I believe that Climacus does admit the importance of objective content, though there are some passages that might appear to contradict this. The following answer to this challenge is completely consistent with what Climacus says. "Of course what a person believes *can* be important. That is, a person who has a superior conception of God *may* act differently than a person who has an inferior understanding. But the changed life never results from having the objectively true idea alone, but from being willing to act in accordance with the idea. Without the subjective appropriation, then, the objective truth is existentially worthless." To steal a phrase from St. James, intellectual faith without works is dead, since the devils also believe in God and even tremble. Hence proper objective beliefs without subjectivity are worthless, but one cannot say that a proper subjectivity without proper objective beliefs is worthless, since it is possible for a person to be better than his beliefs.

This is not inconsistent with recognizing the value of objectively true beliefs and conceding that, when connected with the proper subjectivity, true objective beliefs are valuable. Climacus himself seems to hint at this in his comparison of the pagan praying true-ly to an idol and the one in Christendom who prays falsely to the true God. Climacus does not say that the pagan has completely realized the truth but asks, "Where is there *more* truth?" — in the pagan or the "Christian." If one must choose between true subjectivity and objectivity, subjectivity must be preferred. But this does not entail that objectivity has no importance at all.

> Exactly equally important as the truth, and if one of the two must be preferred still more important, is the manner in which the truth is received: it would help only a little if someone got millions to receive the truth, if these receivers precisely by their manner of reception were transformed into untruth (VII, 208; p. 221).

But why must one of the two be preferred? The answer is that the objective route to morality and religion is a chimera, not a real option at all, according to Climacus. What is implied by the objective route is that a person, apart from any subjective commitment or appropriation on his part, could discover the truth about God (i.e., whether God exists, what God is like).

> The exister who chooses the objective way enters now into the whole approximating reflection-process, which wishes to bring God to light objectively, which cannot be achieved in all eternity, because

> God is a subject, and therefore is only for subjectivity in inwardness
> (VII, 167, p. 178).

Here is the heart of Climacus' concern. He is not saying that objective
truth is unimportant or that the individual should not care whether there
really is a God, should not care whether there really is such a thing as
immortality. He is rather arguing that the truth about such questions is
gained, not through detached theoretical inquiry, but through the process
of existing itself. "Believing the right things" may be important; but one
cannot say with respect to moral and religious truth that getting the right
beliefs is the primary task, with action to follow, since getting the right
beliefs is a product of how one lives. Finding the object of the search
depends upon how one searches. "For he who in quiet inward reflection,
honestly before God is concerned for himself, — he is saved by the God
from error. Even if he is ever so simple, God leads him in the suffering of
inwardness to the truth" (VII, 536; pp. 543-544).

One cannot "mediate" between the objective and subjective approaches as Climacus has defined them (the objective approach being *purely*
objective), since they are logically distinct, and an exister cannot choose
incompatible options simultaneously. That is like "being at two places at
the same time." "Neither can an exister be two places at one time, be
'subject-object.' He is nearest to being two places at one time when he is in
passion, but passion is only momentary, and passion is precisely the
highest degree of subjectivity" (VII, 167; p. 178). There is a hint here that
the route to whatever objective truth man can realize lies through
subjectivity. Climacus' primary quarrel with the objective approach is
simply its assumption that the objective truth can be achieved apart from
any personal appropriation on the part of the truth-seeker. As he sees it,
the objective way holds that the acquisition of correct objective belief is
man's primary task in life, and that living truthfully follows from having the
right objective beliefs as a matter of course. Climacus' counterthesis is
that living truthfully is man's primary task in life, and that having the right
beliefs follows from this as a matter of course. The recognition of the value
of objective content is not a repudiation of Climacus' attack on objectivity
as a detached, disinterested attitude towards existence. Since the
objective truth is a product of subjective commitment, the individual can
never transcend subjectivity and move on to the "higher" realm of
disinterested contemplation. He is and remains an exister.

This thesis that objective truth is the outcome of subjective truth is held
by Kierkegaard as well as Climacus, and it illuminates a great deal in the
authorship. At least in the case of Kierkegaard what underlies this view is a

faith in divine providence:

> But truly, just as little as God lets a species of fish remain in a particular sea unless the plant also grows there which is its nutriment, just so little shall God leave in ignorance of what he must believe the man who was truly concerned. . . The thing sought is in the seeking which seeks it, faith in the concern at not having faith; love, in the concern at not loving. . . . The need brings with it the nutriment. . . not by itself. . . but by virtue of God's ordinance.[7]

It is probably Climacus' thesis — subjective truth leads to objective truth — that lies behind Kierkegaard's own comment about the "objectivity" in Climacus. This applies particularly to the subjectivity of Christian faith, which both Climacus and Kierkegaard see as demanding a quite definite content.

> In all the usual talk that Johannes Climacus is mere subjectivity, etc., it has been completely overlooked that in addition to all his other concretions he points out in one of the last sections that the remarkable thing is that there is a "How" with the characteristic that when the "How" is scrupulously rendered the "What" is also given, that this is the How of "faith." Right here, at its very maximum, inwardness is shown to be objectivity. And this, then, is a turning point of the subjectivity-principle which, as far as I know, has never been carried through or accomplished in this way (*J. and P.* IV, 4550).

But what Kierkegaard notices here about faith is true of other stages of subjectivity in Climacus as well. His claim that truth is subjectivity does not imply that the "what," or content, is completely unimportant, but that the "how," or process of appropriation, is all-important. For suppose a person believed that he was an animal who should live to satisfy his physical needs? A wild passion to realize this truth would hardly be regarded by Climacus as the highest thing possible for a man, since such a life would be a low version of the aesthetic life. (However, an energetic attempt to live such a life might lead to seeing its falseness.) Climacus is not saying that a person's ideas about life and himself are unimportant; he is rather claiming that a person cannot be brought merely by disinterested logical thought to see the inadequacy of his ideas. The truth must be and can be realized through existence itself and through subjective reflection on existence. Climacus is asserting that when an exister seeks *God,* or "the infinite," or "the absolute," or the essential truth, the important thing is not the initial correctness of his intellectual understanding, but the way he seeks. He may have an inadequate conception of what he is seeking, but the right kind of passion will lead to a more adequate conception and exclude inadequate ones. In any case he will be traveling the right road, and his *existence* will thus be true. Hence his definition of subjective truth:

> *The objective uncertainty, held fast in the most passionate appropriation of inwardness, is the truth,* the highest truth there is for an exister. . . .The truth is precisely the venture which chooses the objective uncertainty with the passion of infinity (VII, 170; p. 182).

From the viewpoint of pure objectivity moral and religious questions can never be decided with certainty. The person who pursues religious truth subjectively, however, finds it immediately in his life if not in his ideas.

> The exister who chooses the subjective way in the same instant grasps the whole dialectical difficulty of having to use some time, perhaps a long time, in order to find God objectively; he grasps this dialectical difficulty in all its painfulness, because that same instant he must make use of God, because every moment is wasted in which he does not have God. That same instant he has God, not by virtue of any objective reflection, but by virtue of the infinite passion of inwardness (VII, 167; pp. 178-179).

6. *Truth as a Function of Passion*

The mention of passion in this context is of course hardly surprising, since passion is the content of inwardness or subjectivity. It is passion that provides both continuity and impetus to the exister's life. It is by passion that the exister ceases merely to reflect on or imagine the possibilities and truths that are available to her; by passion the exister "closes" the reflective process by identifying herself with one of these possibilities in action. If this process of reduplication is to be described as true, then it is logical that its truth will be a function of the quality of the passion, since passion is the ultimate source of the actions.

Actually, insofar as one is concerned with the truth about existence, passion plays a key role in all human realization of the truth, even approximative empirical truth, which can be realized intellectually. This is made clear in "The Interlude" in the *Fragments*. Climacus, like many empiricist philosophers, holds that all existing events are contingent; anything that "comes into existence" thus proves it is not logically necessary. All human cognition of existence, therefore, apart from what is immediately perceived, which Climacus sees as certain, involves cognitive uncertainty. This means that historical knowledge and other knowledge of matters of fact is never grounded purely in objectivity; the data from which the historian works always includes an element of uncertainty which the historian must herself negate. This uncertainty is negated by faith or belief *(tro),* understood as a passion[8] (IV, 244-245; pp. 100-101).

This kind of faith is not faith in any distinctively religious sense; it is faith in a "direct and ordinary sense." Even in the direct and ordinary sense, faith is a "passion." This can be seen by contrasting faith or belief in this sense with its opposite passion, doubt.

> Belief and doubt are not two forms of knowledge, which let themselves be determined in continuity with one another, for neither of them is an act of knowing; they are opposite passions. Belief is a sense for coming into existence, and doubt is a protest against every conclusion that wishes to transcend immediate sensation and immediate knowledge (IV, 248; p. 105).

Climacus thinks this is best seen in the Greek skeptics; such a skepticism is grounded in the will and can never be overcome merely by argument (IV, 245-247; pp. 101-103). This is why in Climacus' view the program of finding truth via a universal doubt cannot succeed. Such a doubt is in fact existentially impossible to realize, and if it were possible, it could not possibly be overcome, least of all "by itself," as Climacus thinks the Hegelian rationalists claimed.

Therefore, even the approximative truth sought by objective historical science is regarded by Climacus as grounded in subjectivity. And it is clear that he would draw the same conclusions with respect to the other social sciences and the natural sciences, insofar as these provide conclusions that transcend "the immediate conclusions of sensation." Actually Climacus' views here have a distinctively contemporary ring about them. His claims about the role of subjectivity in objective knowledge bear a striking resemblance to the philosophy of science developed by such thinkers as T. S. Kuhn, Stephen Toulmin, and Michael Polanyi, who emphasize the role of subjective commitments and values in making objective science possible. Climacus' claim that "universal doubt" is unrealizable — and, if it could be realized, would lead to skepticism rather than absolutely certain truth — can be seen as an early version of the twentieth-century attack on the epistemology of foundationalism, which holds that truth can be gained through pure, neutral reflection, which avoids all commitments except those justified by an impartial reason.

It must be emphasized, however, that such epistemological questions are not Climacus' primary concern. He emphasizes the significance of personal passion in objective reflection merely to "bar the door" to those who would attempt to escape from subjectivity through an impossible jump to "pure objectivity." For though subjective commitment plays a significant role in theoretical inquiry, it plays an absolutely decisive role in *action*. And it is, it must be constantly recalled, truth as realized in a life that Climacus is primarily concerned with.

The reader who recognizes the gulf between ideal being and existence and understands existence as a passionate, persistent striving to unite the temporal and the eternal can hardly be surprised by the thesis that existing truth is subjectivity. Of course ideal truth remains ideal truth; propositions are true or false as they are regardless of what any exister thinks, feels, or does. But true propositions as ideal realities do not *exist* in Climacus' sense. Even if an exister grasps such truths, she may grasp them by "abstracting" from existence. It is only when she passionately appropriates such truth that it can penetrate her life and thus truly be said to exist.

7. Subjectivity as Untruth: The Christian Perspective

Before concluding our consideration of Climacus' discussion of truth and subjectivity, it is important to notice a second view of the relation between truth and subjectivity; the thesis that subjectivity is *un*truth.

> Therefore subjectivity, inwardness is the truth; can there now be given a *more inward* expression for this? Yes, if the statement 'subjectivity, inwardness is the truth' begins like this: 'subjectivity is untruth' (VII, 174; p. 185).

The thesis that subjectivity is the truth lies within the sphere of immanence; that is, Climacus does not see anything distinctively Christian about it. It is a thesis that lies within the realm mastered by Socrates. The chapter entitled "Truth Is Subjectivity" is in a sense a repetition of the *Philosophical Fragments*. As in the *Fragments*, Climacus first tries to describe what seems to him to be the highest position possible through human thought and effort. For him this is the thesis that existential truth consists in being rightly related to the truth, rather than simply being related to the right truth. Having explained this thesis, Climacus then goes on to ask if there is a view that is distinctively different, a view that requires still more inwardness. This he finds in the thesis that subjectivity is untruth, the assumption that the individual is *not* capable of doing the truth or being in the truth, but must acquire the capability. This was the assumption that governed the literary conceit in the *Fragments*, where Christianity was "invented" as an alternative to the Socratic view.

In one sense the Christian principle that subjectivity is untruth contradicts the Socratic principle. This is the case if the Socratic principle is taken descriptively as applying to the individual's actual subjectivity. However, taken in a different sense, the two principles do not contradict each other. If the thesis that "subjectivity is the truth" is taken as an *ideal* rather than a descriptive statement, and the statement that "subjectivity is untruth" is taken as a descriptive statement, then the two theses are not contradictory at all. In fact, the Christian view requires *both* statements: Subjectivity is ideally the truth but is actually untruth. This is why Climacus says that the "higher" expression of "subjectivity is the truth" *begins* by regarding subjectivity as untruth. Both statements are necessary for the Christian view to emerge, since the heightened inwardness is the product of the contrast between the actual situation and the situation that ought to hold.

Hence the Christian principle that subjectivity is untruth in one sense contradicts the highest result of immanence, but in another sense it presupposes and builds on what immanence accomplishes. This double relationship is actually characteristic of the way Climacus views the relation between "the human" and "the Christian." Christianity always requires a transcendence which breaks with immanence by negating all human claims to self-sufficiency. This secures Christianity against any reduction to the category of "the merely human." But in a deeper sense his view is similar to Thomas Aquinas: "grace presupposes nature and perfects it." The truth that is accessible to immanence is true. When immanence is shorn of its self-sufficient pretensions, it becomes not only "incorporated" into the Christian, but actually forms the essential place of departure for the jump to Christianity, which, however, always remains a jump. The Christian principle that subjectivity is untruth, when combined with the claim that subjectivity is the truth, provides a "higher" view, Climacus thinks. But it is higher because it affords a deeper *subjectivity*, so in a sense it takes over and deepens the immanent principle.

It is even likely that Climacus' whole discussion of truth and subjectivity is implicitly a commentary on John 14:6: "I am the way, the truth, and the life." There Jesus did not merely claim to bring men the truth, but to *be* the truth. And Jesus is the truth by being the way, by being life ("existence"). Climacus' reflections on truth as subjectivity can be read as an attempt to elucidate the concept of truth in such a way that Jesus' claim becomes coherent. Climacus of course cannot and does not wish to argue that Jesus' claim is itself true. But he has given us a discussion of truth that at least makes sense of Jesus' claim by helping us to understand what it means to regard a life as true. If we may for a moment go behind the pseudonym, it is at least very probable that Kierkegaard's own reason for having Climacus discuss this issue bears on Christ's statement in John. For Kierkegaard continually reflected on the meaning and significance of this claim.[9] He was struck by the idea that what is distinctive about Christianity is that the founder claims to *be* the truth, while in all other religions the founder merely brings the truth or witnesses to it.

[1] W. T. Jones, *Kant to Wittgenstein and Sartre*, 2nd ed. (New York: Harcourt, Brace, 1969), p. 228.

[2] *Kierkegaard: A Kind of Poet* (Philadelphia: University of Pennsylvania Press, 1971), p. 192.

[3] *The Problems of Philosophy* (Oxford: Oxford University Press, 1946), p. 160.

[4] *Ibid*, p. 161.

[5] Interestingly enough, this is the Hebrew term for truth.

[6] C. S. Lewis, *The Last Battle* (New York: Collier Books 1970), pp. 164-165.

[7] *Christian Discourses* (X, 242-243; pp. 248-249).

[8] See chapter 12 for a fuller discussion of the nature of this faith.

[9] For an elucidation of this see Gregor Malantschuk, *Kierkegaard's Thought*, (Princeton: Princeton University Press, 1971), pp. 93-100.

Chapter VIII

IMMANENT RELIGION (1)
GOD AND AN ETERNAL HAPPINESS

1. *Philosophical Reflection on the Religious Life*

In the *Concluding Unscientific Postscript* Johannes Climacus distinguishes between two types of religiousness, referred to as A and B respectively. Religion A is supposed to be possible for any human being in virtue of his human abilities, while religiousness B, identified with Christianity, is supposed to be dependent upon a transcendent, authoritative, though paradoxical revelation. We shall refer to religiousness A as religion per se, or religion in general, or simply as religion. Johannes Climacus' reflections on religion per se constitute one of the most interesting and provocative sections of the whole Kierkegaard literature. Yet this actually has not been given a great deal of attention. The reasons for this are probably that theologians interested in Kierkegaard have tended to focus their attention on the discussions of "the absolute paradox" and concepts that have a direct relationship to Christianity, while philosophers have tended to focus their attention on such nonreligious concepts as the nature of existence, choice, and ethics.

Actually, it is fairly clear that Climacus' discussion of "religion" does have an essential relation to Christianity in its context in the *Postscript*; that is, Climacus discusses religion in general because he thinks it sheds light on his fundamental problem, the nature of Christianity and its relation to speculative thought. But it is also clear that Climacus' discussion of religion in general is philosophical. He is giving us the results of critical reflection on a dimension of human activity — religion. These critical reflections in no way appeal to, or purport to depend on, any religious authority, revelation, or particular religious tradition. Of course Climacus' discussions do show that he is most familiar with Christianity; his illustrations tend to be taken from the Christian tradition. But however limited or culturally narrow those reflections are, the intention of Climacus seems to be to analyze religion per se, not as an institution or cultural entity, but as a universal form of human existence.

Climacus' reflections can profitably be viewed in two ways, both comprehensible to contemporary philosophers. One is to examine his thought as an attempt to analyze a set of key concepts which, he believes, in their mutural interrelationships define the religious life. These concepts include the concepts of "God" and "the absolute *telos*," "an eternal happiness," "suffering," and "guilt." For each of these concepts Climacus attempts to analyze its special sense for the religious life by distinguishing its religious usage from others. In every case the concepts are understood primarily by focusing on their function within the religious life. From this angle Climacus' views can most profitably be compared with the post-Wittgensteinian discussions of religious language and its meaning in the context of forms of life.

The other way of looking at Climacus' discussion is as an attempt at a genuine phenomenology of religion. From this viewpoint Climacus is offering a description of forms of consciousness of the religious life and their significance. If this approach is used, his reflections can most profitably be compared with such thinkers as Schleiermacher, Otto, and William James. It would even be proper to say that Climacus is here giving an analysis of religious experience, if the term "experience" is understood in a particular way. Unfortunately, many writers in England and the U.S.A., influenced by British empiricism, tend to understand religious experience solely on the model of subjective sensation, the most discussed type of sensation being mystical experiences. If, however, experience is understood as Hegel and Dewey understood it, as the funded product of the interaction between a self and its environment, then Climacus is indeed giving an analysis of religious experience. In the following discussion I shall employ both of these approaches, at times looking at Climacus' analyses of key concepts and at times focusing on his descriptions of religious experience. The two types of approaches cannot actually be separated in his case, since his descriptions of religious experience are shaped by a distinct set of categories, but those categories are in turn illumined by attending to concrete human existence. We shall focus primarily on the concepts of God, an eternal happiness, and an absolute *telos* in this chapter, leaving the concepts of resignation, suffering, and guilt to the next.

2. Religion and Ethics

The starting place for Climacus' discussion of religion must be the relationship between religion and ethics. Climacus holds the relationship between ethics and religion to be very close. His whole discussion is couched in terms of his by-now-familiar distinction between the three spheres of existence: the aesthetic, the ethical, and the religious. In this schema, ethical life, which he understands as a progressive attempt to become one's true self through commitment to absolutely binding duties, forms the starting place of the religious life and remains as an essential element of the religious life. Without the presence of the ethical the religious life is reduced to, and confused with, the aesthetic life. The religious life, though not reducible to the ethical life, is nevertheless inseparable from it. Religious existence is impossible without ethical existence, though ethical existence of a sort is possible apart from a religious existence.

In actuality the distinction between the ethical and the religious life in Climacus' view of the spheres of existence is not drawn in the way that one might expect. One might naturally think that the religious life would be distinguished from the ethical by the inclusion in the religious life of a relationship to God, and by its omission in the ethical life. Such a relationship is not usually seen by contemporary ethical theorists as essential to an ethical life; thus it is a plausible candidate as a criterion for a distinctively religious way of existence. However, Climacus does not share this view that the ethical life involves no God-relation, and he does not distinguish between the ethical and the religious life on the basis of the lack or presence of a God-relationship. He thinks that the ethical life at its deepest level always implies such a relationship (VII, 205 206; pp. 218-219), since ethical duties understood as absolute and eternal also must be understood as divine in origin. Climacus' ethic is a thoroughly religious one.[1] The distinction between the ethical and the religious life is drawn on the basis of the *nature* of the God-relationship. The difference lies in the individual's attitude toward himself and God. The ethical individual sees himself as self-sufficient, at least partially or potentially. His existential task is to relate himself to God by positively actualizing his duty. It is apparent from this that some world religions and even some versions of Christianity would be classified by Climacus as falling under the category of ethical views of life. Such views are not thereby disparaged, since nothing about the truth or value of such a view has been established. Climacus merely wishes to distinguish between such life-views and those that are religious in a different sense. It may well be that advocates of ethical types of religiosity would object to Climacus' usage in restricting the term "religious" to the other type of religiousness. I believe their complaint might be just and would require a modification of Climacus' terminology. The distinctions he wishes to draw are unaffected by this, however, and no great harm will be done in this context if we employ his terminology, so long as we are careful to keep his special usage in mind.

In Climacus' sense the religious life is distinguished from the ethical by a discovery about the self. Though the religious person is committed to the same ideals as the ethical person, she believes that those ideals are incapable of fulfillment, not because of external barriers but because of her own inner condition. Her relation to God therefore consists primarily not in self-confident action but in repentance. Her task is not primarily to achieve a God-relationship herself by positively realizing her moral duty, but to achieve a state of inward obedience to God by allowing God to transform her character. This is well illustrated by *Fear and Trembling*, where Johannes de Silentio claims that "an ethic which ignores sin is an absolutely idle science, but if it acknowledges sin, then it *eo ipso* transcends itself" (III, 146; p. 108). The reason for this is given in a footnote attached to the same paragraph: "As soon as sin appears, ethics perishes, precisely because of repentance; for repentance is the highest ethical expression, but precisely as such the deepest ethical self-contradiction" (III, 146n; p. 108n).

The process of being transformed by God is a painful one, requiring the death of certain aspects of the current self. We therefore see immediately that the religious life in the distinctive sense is seen by Climacus as essentially related to the concepts of guilt and suffering. This relationship we will examine more closely in the next chapter.

It should be noticed in passing that the distinction Climacus draws between the ethical and the religious, while clear enough logically, does not imply a sharp divorce between these two spheres. One can easily imagine intermediate cases in real life that could not be clearly put in either category. One can therefore see why Kierkegaard in other writings conflates the two, calling them together the "ethico-religious." At least from the perspective of the religious view one could argue that the ethical position is not really abandoned in the religious view, since the ethical ideals are preserved. The change concerns the manner in which those ideals are to be fulfilled — via self-confident action on the part of the self or via allowing oneself to be transformed by God.

3. *An Eternal Happiness and the Absolute* Telos

The key concept by which Climacus introduces his discussion of religion is the concept of an eternal happiness, which he identified with the "highest good" or "absolute *telos*," a familiar concept in classical ethical theory. (Compare with Kant's discussion of the *summum bonum*, for example.) It is this concept that provides the link between the eternal and religious spheres for Climacus, but it also presents us with a problem. It is certainly true that a concern for immortality is a paramount human concern, and one can plausibly argue its centrality in an account of mankind's general religious experience. But can this religious concept be argued to be the highest good which the person who seeks to realize his *ethical* duty is attempting to realize?

It would seem that the answer is no, at least according to many ethical theorists. Kant probably would provide the clearest example. From a Kantian view the essence of duty is that it is done for the sake of duty, with no thought of reward. A person who makes her eternal happiness her chief concern in life would, on the contrary, appear to have a selfish or at least self-centered concern. She is not doing her duty because it is her duty but because of her hope for an eternal happiness.

What makes this problem really interesting is that Climacus seems to hold to the same type of ethical view as does Kant.[2] That is, he agrees with Kant that morality cannot be grounded in prudential considerations and that utilitarian views fail to capture what is distinctive about morality, which is a willingness to do one's duty regardless of the consequences (VII, 350; p. 361). Hence if the thesis that an eternal happiness is the highest good is inconsistent with the view that duty must be done for its own sake then there is an inconsistency within Climacus' own view.[3]

Climacus is quite aware of this danger. In his terminology it amounts to the question as to whether the religious life does not involve a reversion to the aesthetic categories of happiness/unhappiness (*lykke/ulykke*) rather than being an advance on the ethical life which preserves the ethical ideals. To meet the difficulty he makes an energetic attempt to carefully define (or perhaps to redefine) the concept of an eternal happiness.

A close look at the Danish term employed by Climacus lessens the problem, though it does not solve it. The expression employed for an eternal happiness is *en evig Salighed*. The term *Salighed* implies happiness, but it is the distinctive kind of happiness experienced by the saint, who has been beatifically transformed. It is very different from the term Climacus generally employs to describe the aesthetic life, *lykke*, which can mean happiness also but in the sense of good fortune or good luck. The person who is *lykkelig* is happy because she has received more than her share — or at least a fair share — of health, wealth, fame, or other goods, which are said by Climacus to be subject to the "dialectic of inequality" (VII, 340; p. 351).

This helps but does not really solve the problem. For it will still be claimed that an absolute concern for one's own blessedness is incompatible with doing one's duty for the sake of one's duty. Is a concern for salvation in this sense a quest for a reward, which inevitably taints the attempt to become ethically pure?

Climacus' answer is, "Not necessarily. It depends on how the state of blessedness is understood." It is clear that if an eternal happiness is defined in terms Climacus would classify as aesthetic, then one could not consistently also argue that duty is to be done for the sake of duty. At best one could hold to a type of religious utilitarianism in which the ultimate prudential sanction was the possibility of gaining an eternal happiness. For example, if eternal happiness is defined as a state of intense and varied physical pleasure, that is granted as a reward for moral action, then one could hardly say that a person whose primary aim in life was achieving such an eternal happiness was seeking to do her duty for duty's sake. In such a case the connection between duty and an eternal happiness would be, so to speak, an external one.

This is not, however, the only way an eternal happiness can be conceived, and it is not the way Climacus conceives it. His comments on an eternal happiness are initially puzzling, but I believe they begin to make sense if they are understood as an attempt to define an eternal happiness as the goal of moral action in such a way that it is internally related to moral duty.

Let me try to explain the notion of an internal relation between duty and reward.[4] If one considers the field of music, one can conceive of two very different types of reasons for wishing to learn to play a musical instrument or to play such an instrument well. Someone who acquires great skill on a musical instrument can sometimes (too rarely, perhaps) receive fame and wealth as a result. One can imagine individuals for whom this fact would become a reason for wishing to become virtuoso musicians. They wish to become musicians for the sake of the possible reward. Also, individuals who learn to play an instrument with great skill often receive great joy from the accomplishment itself. There is a deep satisfaction to the lover of music in the very act of making music. This satisfaction may also be viewed as a type of reward, and there are individuals for whom this reward may become a reason for seeking to become musically proficient.

These two types of rewards seem to be rather different. Perhaps musicians are usually motivated by both types of rewards simultaneously, or perhaps those who seek only the first type of reward are unlikely to become fine musicians and are thus unlikely to achieve their material aims. But the difference between the two types of rewards remains. I suspect that most people would find something superior about the quest for the second type of reward, which is the type that I would say is internally connected with the activity it rewards. The quest for the first type of reward may not be judged wrong or immoral, but there is nevertheless a purity about the second type of quest that the first one lacks. This might well be asserted by claiming that in the first case the person seeks to become a musician for the sake of some other goal, while in the second case the person is committed to music for its own sake.

Now, why should one want to say this about the second type of musician? Isn't the second type of quest, like the first, a quest for a reward? It seems to me that the difference lies in the nature of the reward and its relation to the activity in question. The second kind of reward is much more closely related to the activity than the first kind. The relation between being a musician and the satisfaction gained from creating music is far closer. I am not quite sure how to characterize this closeness, but I find the suggestion that the activity and the reward are in this case homogeneous in type to be a fruitful one.[5] The activity and the good that is the outcome of the activity are more than conventionally or causally connected, since they belong to the same family. Perhaps this could be expressed in the following way: Though the making of music and the satisfaction attained from making music can be logically distinguished, they nevertheless appear on reflection as forming a natural unity, such that the person who seeks this satisfaction is still making music for the sake of music. This concept of a reward that is homogeneous with the activity of which it is the outcome can be discerned in many human activities: exercising, courting, and even philosophizing. In each of these cases it is possible to distinguish a type of reward that can be sought without destroying the purity of one's devotion to the activity from a type of ulterior reward that, when sought, reduces the activity to a mere means. Think, for example, of the young man who truly loves a girl and courts her for the sake of the pleasure he gets from her company, and think of the man who hopes to make his fortune by marrying the daughter of a rich man. In each example the "pure" reward seems to be one that is homogeneous with the activity. These rewards are internally related to the activities they are the result of.

It seems to me that Climacus is attempting to describe an eternal happiness in very similar terms. An eternal happiness is viewed by Climacus as a reward. It is thus an end or goal that individuals can seek. But he insists that the true concept of an eternal happiness is internally related to the ethical striving of which it is supposed to be the reward (VII, 338; p. 349).

This is, I think the point of Climacus' strenuous attempt to maintain the necessity of the ethical as the starting point for the religious life. The person who conceives of an eternal happiness in terms of an external reward utilizes his imagination to construct various types of "happy outcomes." Such a person, who does not conceive of an eternal happiness in ethical terms itself, is said by Climacus to be a "poet."

> If one, however, wants to ethically establish a poetic relationship to reality, then this is a misunderstanding and a backward step. Here as everywhere the different spheres must by kept clearly distinct, and one must respect the qualitative dialectic, the jerk of decision that changes everything so that what was highest in one sphere in another sphere becomes absolutely inadmissible. If one considers the religious, then it is a requirement that it has passed through the ethical (VII, 336; p. 347).

Of course Climacus is not denying that forms of this "aesthetic" religiosity actually exist and that most people call this "religiousness." He is simply distinguishing such a religiousness from the distinctive kind he wishes to analyze, which does involve an essential relation to the ethical.

> When a so-called religious personality with all the enchantments of the imagination is pleased to picture an eternal happiness it means that he is a poet who has run away from the sphere of the aesthetic, who claims the privilege of native citizenship in the religious realm without being able to speak its mother tongue (VII, 338; p. 349).

That mother tongue is of course the ethical.

Climacus' point is simply that a truly ethically developed person will be more concerned about doing his duty than anything else. For him the finest "reward" he can conceive would simply be a state where he perfectly and purely fulfills his ethical duty by achieving a pure moral character. And just as with our musician it is possible to take satisfaction from doing one's duty and even to seek such satisfaction without abandoning the respect for duty itself. To a truly ethical person no happier state can be imagined than a state in which one eternally fulfills one's ethical requirements. Yet this in no way violates the purity of ethics, since if a person does not wish to do his duty for pure reasons, he cannot obtain this satisfaction, any more than a person can gain intrinsic satisfaction by making music without a love for music in itself. Thus for Climacus an eternal happiness can be both a state of happiness, earnestly sought by the individual, and at the same be the highest ethical goal, without violating the principle that the ethical life involves a concern for duty for its own sake.

Climacus presents three criteria by which the ethically pure concept of an eternal happiness can be distinguished. The first is the negative criterion that an eternal happiness cannot be aesthetically defined. Here Climacus would find it quite in order that some great religions, notably Christianity, have left the nature of the after life fairly undefined, and that an aesthetic person, who lacks ethical religious pathos, should actually find such a conception unappealing.

> It has been said wittily and correctly (aesthetically understood), that the angels are the most boring of all creatures, that eternity is the longest and most boring of all days, even a Sunday being sufficiently boring; and that an eternal happiness is an everlasting monotony, so that even the unhappiness [of the damned] is to be preferred (VII, 340-341; p. 352).

The second criterion is the formal requirement that an eternal happiness must be conceived as the absolute *telos* (VII, 341-342; pp. 352-353). This criterion is also partially negative, since it rules out any finite good — that is, any good that could logically be willed at one time but not at another.

> But it is a contradiction to will something finite absolutely, since the finite (*det Endelige*) must have an end (*en Ende*), so that there must come a time when it can no longer be willed. But to will absolutely is to will the infinite, and to will an eternal happiness is to will absolutely, because it must be able to be willed every moment (VII, 341; p. 353).

This entails that an eternal happiness is "not a particular something" and explains why it is such an abstract and aesthetically poor conception. Positively an eternal happiness can only be "the infinite," by which term Climacus means the ethical requirement itself.

There is a strong parallel here to Kant's ethical theory. Kant also says that the only thing that can be conceived of as absolutely good is a "good will" itself. The absolute moral principle can only be the formal, defining principle of duty itself, rather than any "material maxim." The ultimate *end* of moral action is the achievement of the state in which one acts morally. Kant does not derive morality from this end; he first defines the supreme principle of morality and from it defines the end of moral obligation. The difference is that Kant does not say happiness is identical with the highest good, but only a component of it.

In a similar way to Kant Climacus asserts that "an eternal happiness, as the absolute good, has the remarkable trait *that it defines itself solely in terms of its mode of acquisition*" (VII, 370; p. 382). This is the third criterion he presents to demarcate the concept of an eternal happiness. Since the mode of acquisition is ethical action, this is the clearest statement yet that an eternal happiness is not to be defined as an eternal reward for morality, but in essentially moral terms itself. An eternal happiness for an ethically developed person must be understood as the opportunity to perfectly fulfill his moral duty itself. The only thing I can seek *absolutely* is to do my duty. The only thing I can desire absolutely, if I am absolutely committed to my duty, is the realization of the state in which I can perfectly realize my duty. But to such an individual this will be a state of happiness, because this is the ethical individual's highest desire. It must be conceived as eternal because the individual who truly wills to realize this condition absolutely cannot will its realization for only a finite period. He cannot help but desire other opportunities to go on and on in his expression of these ideals.

Though there is a strong similarity to Kant here, there is also one significant difference, which concerns the nature of happiness and the relationship of the individual to happiness. Kant attempts to include happiness in his concept of the highest good by linking it with virtue. However, virtue and happiness are always distinct for him, since happiness is conceived as the sum total of the natural goods it is possible to realize. From Climacus' point of view Kant is still employing an aesthetic concept of happiness. Many people have argued that Kant's inclusion of happiness in the highest good and his claim that happiness is the appropriate reward for virtue is a desertion of the principle of duty for duty's sake. I do not myself agree with this criticism, but in any case it is easy to see that Climacus' view escapes the criticism altogether. Climacus does not merely link happiness with virtue in a synthetic concept, as Kant did. He defines (or redefines) happiness in terms of virtue. Happiness is the intrinsically satisfied state of the person who fulfills his moral duty.

This connection between virtue and happiness, this ultimate tie between duty and desire and between ethical obligation and man's highest religious aspirations, though it presents problems, is also one of the strengths of Climacus' account. We must not forget that many nonhedonists and nonutilitarian thinkers, such as Plato, Socrates, Augustine, and Aquinas, have held that in some sense happiness is the ultimate end of moral action.

In attempting to show that there is some plausibility to Climacus' linking of ethics and religion by his identification of the concepts of the highest good and an eternal happiness, we have not of course solved all the problems. In particular, the thesis is very dependent on Climacus' understanding of ethics as the task of "soul-making." The type of ethical theory we referred to as "society-transforming" will certainly not find the thesis plausible. But to the person who agrees with Climacus that the primary ethical task is "becoming a self," it can be plausibly argued that the highest ethical end is religious and that it can with reason be called an eternal happiness without violating the purity of the ethical.

4. *An Eternal Happiness as a God-Relationship*

There is one other significant element in Climacus' concept of an eternal happiness: the thesis that the possession of an eternal happiness is also identical with a God-relationship. If it seemed dubious to identify the ethical concept of the highest good with the religious concept of an eternal happiness, it may seem even more dubious to argue that these two identified concepts are the same as yet a third. Yet a little reflection shows that from Climacus' perspective it makes sense to do so. We must remember that Climacus is attempting to analyze religion in general and that the concept of God here cannot be identified with the God of any particular religious tradition, particularly not with a God who reveals himself in particular historical acts. A religion that knows God through particular historical acts would be a "transcendent" type of religion, but Climacus is attempting to analyze the possibility of a religion of "immanence."

These terms "immanence" and "transcendence" actually are not used by Climacus precisely as one might expect. In describing religion in general as immanent, Climacus is not denying that man's natural religious consciousness can form the idea of God as a transcendent being. He is quite aware that natural religion can be theistic as well as pantheistic. The terms "immanent" and "transcendent" do not primarily refer to the ontological status of God as the ultimate religious object but to the mode whereby man knows and relates to God. Climacus accepts the thesis that there is such a thing as a natural knowledge of God which is possible to all human beings. (More about this later.) Such a knowledge presupposes only what is common to, or "immanent" in, man's general consciousness. It belongs in the category of what theologians have traditionally called "general" or "natural" revelation. Any religion that is grounded in mankind's immanent ideas apart from any special revelation Climacus classes within immanence. Such a religious consciousness is achievable by man himself, with only the help from God which is offered to all human beings in virtue of their participation in the race. However, the God known in this way may be regarded as transcendent in the traditional theological sense of that word.

A transcendent religion, on the other hand, is one in which God is known "outside" man's general religious consciousness. In such a religion God is claimed to have objectified himself (or better, to have *subjectified* himself) by entering history in a definite and particular way. Only in such a way could man acquire a knowledge of God that challenges and corrects his natural religious consciousness.

The assertion that for Climacus a natural knowledge of God is possible may be surprising to some. The usual picture of Kierkegaard (taken largely from Climacus' writings) is that belief in God requires a leap of faith and is an embracement of the absurd.[6] This picture is, however, completely false to the natural religiousness Climacus describes. The concepts of the absolute paradox and the absurd are contained in his analysis of religiousness B (Christianity), not religiousness A at all. Though Climacus would (and Kierkegaard does) admit that faith of a sort is required to know God,[7] it is not the distinctive kind of faith Christianity involves, which Climacus calls faith in the "eminent sense" (IV, 250; p. 108). Rather, Climacus constantly assumes that the individual can be aware of God's reality and even possess a *kind* of personal certainty about it.

The strongest argument against the thesis that Climacus accepts the idea of a natural knowledge of God would be an appeal to his discussion of natural religious knowledge in the chapter on "The Absolute Paradox" in the *Fragments*. There Climacus identifies God with "the unknown" (IV, 207; p. 49) and seems to deny the possibility of any sort of natural theology. One might argue from this that there is an inconsistency between the *Fragments*, which denies the possibility of any natural religious knowledge, and the *Postscript*, which in many places assumes and asserts that the individual who is existing in an immanent religious consciousness knows and relates himself to God.

I do not think there is any inconsistency here. In the process of seeing why this is so the reason for Climacus' identification of an eternal happiness with a God-relationship will become clear as well. In the *Fragments* Climacus is not denying the possibility that human individuals can have an awareness of God's reality. He is denying the possibility of a speculative knowledge of God that is obtained purely through objective, rational thought. He is not denying the possibility of a natural *knowledge* of God (unless knowledge is defined in a quasi-scientific way), but of speculative, natural *theology*. The whole chapter focuses on *reason* as an objective, neutral faculty and examines the attempt of speculation by logical argument to arrive at a knowledge of God as factually real. His conclusion is that such logical arguments have value only as explicating our concepts about God; they do not bring us into contact with God as actual unless they are themselves permeated by faith (IV, 208-211; pp. 50-54). For example, the convincingness of the teleological argument is claimed to be a function of an ideal interpretation of nature which discounts evil and suffering. This interpretation, Climacus claims, is equivalent to faith in God itself, so that personal faith is not so much the outcome of the argument as the basis for it.

However, it is perfectly consistent with this denial of objective, speculative knowledge to admit the possibility of a subjective, existential knowledge of God. (Unless, again, one simply defines knowledge in terms of objective speculation, in which case one will need another word for what Climacus is describing.) After all, human beings are not disinterested, rational speculators (at least Climacus argues they cannot be *purely* that), but interested existers. It actually would be difficult and implausible to argue that this fact has no relevance to what human beings may know, since we have in the last quarter-century been forcefullly reminded of the role subjective commitments play even in such nonreligious areas as science.[8]

That Climacus really does hold that an immanent knowledge of God is possible is shown by the whole description of religiousness A, where the individual is constantly described as relating himself to God. However, citing a few specific passages may not only confirm this thesis but also give us a clue as to *how* God is said to be known. First, even in the negative discussion in the *Fragments* there is a hint that there is a way of knowing God if one does not fool oneself by relying on a "proof" that God can be known.

And how does the God's existence come out of the proof? Does it follow so very straightforwardly? Is the case not similar to the Cartesian dolls? As soon as I let go of the doll it stands on its head. As soon as I let it go — I must therefore let it go. So also with the proof. As long as I keep my hold on the proof [i.e., continue to be the prover], the existence does not come out, just because I am engaged in proving it; but when I let the proof go, the existence is there (IV, 210; p. 53).

What is interesting here is not the doll (which Climacus evidently misnamed), but the thought. Climacus seems to be asserting, not that man cannot know God's reality, but that he cannot know it by proof. He even seems to imply that the proof is a hindrance to the knowledge; with the proof out of the way the knowledge of God's reality is present.

I think what lies behind this is Climacus' view of logical argument itself. On his analysis logical argument can only "develop the consequences of a concept" (IV, 207; p. 49) or, to expand on this slightly, tell us what propositions are entailed by, consistent with, or inconsistent with other propositions. Whether a logical argument has any relevance to reality depends upon which propositions are true, but that is (at least ultimately) not a matter for logical argument to decide. Hence, even if there are sound arguments for God's existence (valid arguments with true premises), the individual's *acceptance* of the conclusion is ultimately dependent not so much on the argument's *logical* validity as upon the individual's acceptance of the truth of the premises. But *that* is not a matter of logic ultimately, since if premises cannot be known in some other way than by logical arguments, no logical arguments can be known to be sound. So even if there are sound arguments for God's existence, Climacus says that the individual's *acceptance* of the conclusion is still not *ultimately* a function of the argument, but of something else, which does not consist of logical argument, that something else being the way one knows the premises of the argument to be true. Hence, if "God's existence is to emerge from the proof" for the individual, he must "let go of the proof," which means he must recognize that his personal conclusion is rooted in more than the argument alone. This something more is simply his own personal knowledge, which is dependent upon his own personal experiences and achievements.

In a footnote to the subject of proving God's existence which appears in the next paragraph, Climacus describes the whole project of proving God's existence as a subject for a lunatic comedy. What he has in mind by this is illuminated in a longer version of this footnote, which was in the final draft but was shortened prior to printing.[9] In this longer version it is claimed that there has never been a genuine atheist or a person who didn't believe in immortality, only people who didn't want to "let what they knew, that God existed, get power over their minds." The person who attempts to prove God's existence thereby makes it appear that there might be some doubt about this question and therefore plays into the hands of the person who wishes to be an atheist.

Of course this astounding claim (which was removed before printing) cannot be taken in the straightforward sense that everyone consciously assents to God's existence. It must be understood analogously with the sort of claim a depth psychologist makes. Not everyone actually knows God's reality, but everyone has the potentiality to do so, a potential that the individual himself senses obscurely but can willfully block.

This altered version of the footnote accords quite well with some of Climacus' statements in the *Postscript*. When discussing the idea of proving God's existence, Climacus again argues that the problem with the proof is that it makes something that should be certain appear to be doubtful:

> For to demonstrate the existence (*Tilvær*) of one who is present (*er til*, exists) is the most shameless affront, since it is an attempt to make him ridiculous; . . . How could it occur to one to demonstrate that he exists (*er til*), unless it is because one has first permitted oneself to ignore him; and now one makes the matter still more crazy by demonstrating his existence (*Tilværelse*) before his very nose? A King's existence (*Tilværelse*) or his presence (*Tilstedeværelse*) generally has its own characteristic expression of subjection and submission; what if one in his sublime presence (*Nærværelse*) wanted to prove that he existed (*var til*)? Would one then prove it? No, one makes a fool of him, for his presence (*Tilstedeværelse*) is demonstrated by an expression of submission. . . and thus one also demonstrates God's existence (*Tilværelse*) by worship — not by proofs (VII, 475-476; p. 485).

It would be ludicrous to think that Climacus is saying that worship is a logical proof of God's existence or that it constitutes objective evidence for it. Rather, his point is that nothing like objective proof or evidence is necessary because God can be *present* to the individual. The individual acknowledges this reality through appropriate behavior, which is therefore an indicator in an outward way of God's reality, though not objective evidence.

In what sense can God be present to the individual? Climacus denies
that God could be sensuously present to a person, at least in a direct way.
The idea that God could be directly experienced Climacus characterizes
as paganism. "All paganism consists in this, that God relates himself
directly to man as the obviously extraordinary to the astonished
observer" (VII, 206; p. 219). Climacus satirizes the idea that a person
could directly experience God in this way by imagining a social conformist
who has never really had an awareness of God, who might be able to see
God if God were to take the form of "a very rare and tremendously large
green bird, with a red beak, sitting in a tree on the mound, and perhaps
even whistling in an unheard of manner" (VII, 206; p. 219). God as invisible
is not present directly or immediately in his creation.

This by no means entails that Climacus holds that God is not present in
the creation at all or that he cannot be known to be present. What it means
is that "the spiritual relationship to God in truth, that is, in inwardness, is
precisely conditioned by a prior irruption of inwardness, which
corresponds to the divine elusiveness" (VII, 206; p. 219). Though God is
not directly present in nature, "within the individual person there is a
potentiality (man is potentially spirit) which is awakened in inwardness to a
God-relationship, and then it becomes possible to see God everywhere"
(VII, 207; pp. 220-221).

What Climacus seems to be saying is this: God's reality can be known,
but not just by anybody and not just in any old way. To know God the
individual must first develop that capacity or set of capacities that
Climacus calls "inwardness." Of course some may find this thesis
suspicious. One might think this an attempt to evade the criterion of
intersubjective verification that we reasonably require of other personal
knowledge claims. For if some individual fails to discover God and thereby
"verify" his reality, the religious individual seems to have an "out." He can
always say that the failure to make the discovery was due to a lack of
spiritual development on the part of the individual.

However, though this may sound suspiciously easy, one must ask two
questions: (1) Is this not the sort of situation one would expect if there
were a God ? and (2) Does this differ much from other areas of human
knowledge? To the first question Climacus argues a strenuous yes. Since
God is himself spirit, it is logical that he can only be known in a spiritual
(inwardly developed) relationship. If there were anything externally
obvious about God (as there would be if he took the form of the large bird),
one simply would not discover God's true character. Climacus' thesis is
that the very nature of God demands that the individual personally must
develop himself to know God truly (VII, 207; p. 220). That this is so is also

an expression of God's love, since it means that the process in which one gets to know God is one that is upbuilding to the individual.

There is also the question of whether this really differs so much from other types of human knowledge (as Climacus tends to assume, I think mistakenly). For though we do demand that knowledge claims in other areas be "checkable," we do not assume that this can be done by anyone, on any occasion, in any manner.[10] The timber wolf can only be discovered by the trained naturalist or hunter, subatomic particles only by the trained physicist. In every case the nature of what is known seems to dictate the conditions under which it can be known and the capacities the knower must have. This is essentially what Climacus is claiming about knowing God.

What is known in this case, and what is the process of development that makes possible the knowledge? What is known is God as an essentially moral reality, the foundation of man's infinite moral obligation. The process whereby God is known is the process whereby the individual discovers the absoluteness and eternal character of the moral law, which is equivalent to its "divinity." The reason why this quest for an eternal happiness, conceived as the highest end of ethical striving, is identical with a God-relationship is that within the realm of immanence God is essentially known as the ground of moral obligation. Or, to make one important qualification, this is how God is known initially. One cannot ignore the "process" character of Climacus' thought, focusing as it does upon human existence. We shall see in the next chapter that in the course of her religious striving a person can develop a specifically religious kind of inwardness that makes possible a more specifically religious concept of God. However, God is known initially through moral obligation, and the conception of God within natural religion remains a moral conception. This is the focus of this chapter. Proceeding from this initial awareness of God, however, the person can gain a deeper awareness of God as she begins to acquire a specifically religious form of inwardness out of her moral inwardness. This process is the subject of the next chapter.

The "natural" knowledge of God that man can achieve falls within the realm of "recollection." Climacus uses this Platonic term again and again to describe the awareness of the eternal of which man is immanently capable. Recollection (*Erindring*) is distinguished from memory (*Hukommelse*) (VII, 471; pp. 480-481). Memory is a capacity that even the child possesses, but recollection is a capacity that, though immanently possible, must be acquired by the individual's actualization of it. To recollect is to come to an understanding of one's life which has eternal validity. Such an understanding employs what Climacus calls total categories — qualitative categories. Rather than understand oneself in relative and quantitative terms ("guilty to a certain degree," "more ethical than Joe Brown"), one comes to understand the essential character of one's life as a whole. Such recollection is ultimately equivalent to a person's ethical inwardness (VII, 479; p. 489).

Recollection is the term for the process that leads to "salvation," understood immanently. As such it contrasts with repetition (*Gjentagelse*), which is the equivalent Kierkegaardian term within the sphere of transcendent religion. The difference is that within immanence there is a fundamental kinship with the divine already present, which merely has to be "collected" (which may nonetheless be a strenuous process). Within the realm of transcendence the kinship with the eternal must be acquired; the self must be reformed. "*Gjentagelse*" literally means "again-taking." The self is not merely "taken" or assumed as already real; it must be "retaken."

In reviewing the possibility of recollection Climacus is reflecting on the Platonic tradition which holds that the eternal bears witness to itself within the self. Climacus therefore refers to the "lonely spring in every person where the God dwells, that spring in the deep quietness, when everything is silent" (VII, 152; p. 163). God's witness about himself in man is essentially man's awareness of the infinite moral ideal. Such moral knowledge is "interested knowledge," not speculative, disinterested knowledge. Though accessible to everyone, its acquisition is ultimately a function of the quality of one's moral passion or "degree of inwardness."

This view of Climacus that to be aware of moral obligation is to "hear the voice of God" is not a very popular one today, but that it is Climacus' view is undeniable.

> In the world-historical process, as it is seen by men, God does not play the role of Lord; as one does not see the ethical in it, therefore God is not seen either, for if one does not see him in the role of Lord, one does not see him (VII, 128-129; pp. 139-140).

God is only truly known as God when he is known as moral ruler, but man experiences God's commands only in his own personal awareness of morality. This moral awareness is realized only through its exercise, when the individual in self-concern begins to exercise his freedom in accordance with God's commands. Only in this way does God become for him a living reality: "Freedom is the wonderful lamp; when a person rubs it with ethical passion, God comes into being for him" (VII, 112; p. 124). Climacus' theses that the ethical task is to "become a self" and that God is the ground of morality lead him quite consistently to connect the process of "soul-building" with the gaining of a God-relationship. If a person avoids the straightforward acceptance of the moral customs of his society and seeks to discover the eternal, he discovers both God and himself. Such a person avoids the deceptive "direct relation to the truth, to the ethical, to God" (VII, 205-206; p. 219). He realizes the profound truth that a person cannot become an individual merely by imitating his culture; he must learn to act as an individual, which for Climacus is learning to stand before God with a consciousness of one's own responsibility. It is thereby that "the God-relationship makes a person a person" (VII, 206; p. 219).

Can this thesis that man's ethical awareness is an awareness of God be objectively defended? Ultimately I suspect Climacus would say no, since he is pointing to an awareness that rests on the individual's level of spiritual development and that therefore cannot be demonstrated "objectively." But I think a few things can be said in favor of the reasonableness of such "personal" knowledge.

First, it seems plausible that if there were a God of the sort Christians and Jews believe in, and if knowing about God were vital for human beings to attain fulfillment, then God would make himself knowable in the sort of way Climacus sketches. It is implausible to think that the knowledge of God would be dependent upon esoteric logical arguments or that the person's awareness of God would be conditioned by his degree of intellectual giftedness. Even the Scholastics recognized this. Thomas Aquinas, for example, takes pains to insist that in addition to speculative knowledge there is another kind of knowledge called "affective," "experiential," or "connatural" knowledge.[11] The latter type of knowledge is a more intimately personal type of knowledge which involves the whole man rather than just his intellect. One can know the virtues not only intellectually, speculatively, according to Aquinas, but also by *being virtuous*. The latter type of knowledge is attainable by anyone, not just by scholars. It is conditioned not by intellectual acuteness, but by the willingness of the individual to strive to realize the truth in action. Very similar notions to this can be found in other writers, such as Pascal, Newman, and William James, but it is easy to see that in important respects Aquinas' concept of "connatural knowledge" is similar to Climacus' concept of "subjectivity" or "inwardness." Such a view of religious knowledge makes the knowledge of God in principle accessible to all, limited only by the individual's failure to develop his specifically moral and religious qualities. This view accords well with our intuition of how God *should* be knowable, and it is at least consistent with the observed sociological situation, since the great majority of ordinary human beings in almost every culture believe in God, even though a large number of intelligent and highly educated people find God's existence questionable. It should be noticed that the great majority of those people who believe in God connect their belief and their concept of God with their moral experience in the way Climacus does.

It should be noticed that the sort of knowledge of God that Climacus thinks is possible in this way is a somewhat undefined knowledge. Since our knowledge of God is a knowledge of God through morality, the content of that knowledge is simply God understood as the reality disclosed in moral obligation. This is well illustrated by another pseudonym, who writes from within the perspective of religious "immanence." In *Fear and Trembling* Johannes de Silentio describes the limits of the sort of religious knowledge we have been discussing. If God is known only as the author of the moral law, then one does not know God as a particular, distinct reality capable of communicating particular "nonmoral" commands to an individual.

> The ethical is the universal and as such again the divine. One is therefore right to say that every duty is ultimately a duty toward God; but if one cannot say more, then one also says that I actually have no duty toward God. The duty becomes duty by being referred to God, but in the duty itself I do not step into a relationship with God. . . If I say in this connection, that it is my duty to love God, then I actually only utter a tautology insofar as "God" is here taken in an absolutely abstract sense as "the divine," or "the universal," or "duty" (III, 117; p. 78).

There is a difference of emphasis here, since Johannes de Silentio is primarily concerned with understanding Abraham as the "knight of faith," the representative of transcendent religiousness, and he therefore concentrates on the limitations of immanent religion. However, I do not think that his statements here are inconsistent with Climacus' view. The crucial question concerns the nature of God as he is known immanently. Is he known personally?

Climacus himself certainly conceives of God in personal terms, and I believe that he thinks God is *best* conceived immanently in this way. (We will discuss why in a moment.) However, I do not think he holds that God must be conceived in such a form or that he is only known in this way. What is essentially known is the absoluteness, infinite demand, and eternal character of the moral law itself. God is essentially these characteristics. Anyone who understands morality in this way essentially understands God. Therefore Climacus can treat Plato and Socrates, who at times lean toward personal conceptions of God but hardly could be said to be full exponents of traditional theism, as model examples of human beings who had attained the natural knowledge of God which is possible. It is probably for the same reason that Climacus frequently uses impersonal terms such as "the divine" and "the eternal" synonymously with the more personal terms "God" and "the God."

Having recognized the "range" of the concept God, we must also recognize that for Climacus the highest and best understanding of God does seem to be distinctly personal in character, and it is recognizably similar to the traditional theism found in the Judeo-Christian tradition and in other great world religions. I believe the reason for this is that Climacus finds the most natural interpretation of moral obligation to be that moral obligation is a relation between persons. He himself experiences the moral "ought" as a command, which therefore stems from a law-giver and judge; God is the being to whom I am *responsible*. This knowledge of God as personal is also linked to the awareness of moral guilt, which we shall discuss in the next chapter. The experience of guilt is a specific form of the consciousness of one's moral responsibility. This is the deeper, "higher" knowledge of God we referred to earlier,[12] which is a knowledge that can be acquired as the individual begins to acquire the specifically religious forms of inwardness.

Within this personal conception Climacus includes the traditional and overwhelmingly significant conception of God as creator. The ultimacy and absoluteness of morality and the individual's own sense of absolute responsibility toward God lead the individual to conceive of God as his creator and as the ruler of the universe. Though God is not directly present in nature, he is present there, and the individual who has acquired the requisite spiritual development can "see God everywhere" (VII, 207-208; p. 221). Socrates, the reputed inventor of the teleological argument, is credited with a similar procedure. Having "made sure of the God," he attempts to "interpenetrate nature with the idea of purpose" (IV, 211; p. 54). Hence the ontological characteristics of God are (epistemologically) grounded in his moral characteristics. The individual who is morally developed refashions his understanding of himself and the universe in which he finds himself in accordance with his moral insight. He sees the universe as a moral universe.

It should be noted that Climacus' linking of moral obligation with God is not dependent upon the merits of the "divine-command theory" of moral obligation. This theory, at least in most forms, holds that it is the fact that God commands an action to be done which makes it right. Climacus is only committed to the weaker theses that God does command us to do what is morally right and that men actually experience and become aware of moral obligations as divine commands. Neither of these two theses entails or presupposes a traditional divine-command theory, though both of them might follow from such a theory. So Climacus' view is not at all affected by the criticisms usually addressed against the divine-command theory.

It is also worth noticing that Climacus' views on knowing God are in very close accord with those expressed by Kierkegaard, especially in the *Up-building Discourses* or *Edifying Discourses*, which Climacus discusses as examples of a type of immanent religiousness. One striking illustration of this is found in the discourse, "Man's Need of God Constitutes His Greatest Perfection."[13] Here Kierkegaard emphasizes that true knowledge of God is obtained through the development of inwardness in which the person truly becomes a self and learns to know himself. The discourse outlines the possibility that knowing God's existence can become clear to a person "with a certainty of a very different order, and with a decisiveness that leaves no room for vagueness."[14] Here Kierkegaard is referring to the more specific kind of inwardness that makes possible a more specifically religious understanding of God. But it is still true that in the *Up-Building Discourses* God is initially known in and through the experience of moral obligation.

---

[1] This is true of all of Kierkegaard' authorship. Thus Judge William, who is supposed to portray the ethical life in *Either-Or* and the *Stages on Life's Way*, is religious in a rather deep way.

[2] S. K. does also; see the comments on "the reward disease" in "An Occasional Discourse" (part I of *Up-Building Discourses in Various Spirits*), published in English as *Purity of Heart Is to Will One Thing* (VIII, 144-151; pp. 68-78).

[3] There is an analogous problem for Kant, of course, who includes happiness as a part of the highest good, which is necessarily sought by the ethical agent.

[4] I am heavily indebted to Jeremy Walker, "The Idea of Reward in Morality" (*Kierkegaardiana* VIII, pp. 30-52), for both the ideas and examples employed here. Walker develops these ideas in the context of Kierkegaard's *Purity of Heart*, but I believe they are equally relevant to Climacus. The distinction between an intrinsic and extrinsic reward is, however, not original with Walker. Aristotle gives a recognizable version of this distinction, and H. P. Owen employs it in his *The Moral Argument for Christian Theism* (London: Allen and Unwin, 1965), pp. 40-41.

5 See Jeremy Walker, *op. cit.*, pp. 33-34.

6 See, for example, Camus, "An Absurd Reasoning," in *The Myth of Sisyphus and Other Essays*, (New York: Vintage Books, 1955), pp. 28-31.

7 See the important footnote in the *Postscript* (VII, 172-173n; pp. 184-185n), where Climacus explains that Socratic inwardness is a type of analogue to Christian inwardness, and thus "there is nothing to prevent talk about the paradoxical and faith in relation to Socrates," even though the difference is "infinite" and therefore the analogy is not strictly proper. Thus Socrates has faith, though not faith in the "eminent sense."

8 See Nicholas Wolterstorff, *Reason Within the Bounds of Religion* (Grand Rapids, Michigan: William B. Eerdmans, 1976), for an analysis of the reasons for rejecting epistemological foundationalism.

9 *J. and P.*, III, 3606 (*Papirer* V B 40:11).

10 See George Mavrodes, *Belief in God*, (New York: Random House, 1970), pp. 73-80.

11 This comparison was suggested by George S. Stengren in "Connatural Knowledge in Aquinas and Kierkegaardian Subjectivity," in *Kierkegaardiana* X, where it is developed more fully. Stengren cites Aquinas, *Summa Theologiae*, IIa-IIae, q. 45, art. 2 *corpus articuli*, and other passages.

12 See p. 153.

13 This is in *Four Up-Building Discourses of 1844* (V, 81-106). It can be found in English in *Edifying Discourses* (Minneapolis: Augsburg, 1962), pp. 120-160.

14 V, 102; p. 155.

Chapter IX

IMMANENT RELIGION (2)
RESIGNATION, SUFFERING AND GUILT

1. *The Religious Life as a Process*

In the last chapter we discussed the formative or structural elements of natural religion. In this chapter we shall look at the more personal, existential content of religion by examining the content of the religious life itself. Climacus' views in this area are responsible in large measure for the popular picture of Kierkegaard as a "gloomy existentialist," for he holds that the essential and decisive characteristics of religion are suffering and guilt, respectively. Of course those who regard Kierkegaard as gloomy (or worse) on these grounds fail to recognize the immanent religion Climacus describes does not necessarily represent Kierkegaard's own personal standpoint, at least not in the final period of his life. But Kierkegaard himself was deeply interested in the meaning and significance of suffering, and he, too, consistently connects religious development and suffering, though he considers kinds of suffering that Climacus does not touch on. Climacus' views on this subject, as on so many others, are worthy of consideration in their own right, however, and we shall proceed to consider them in that fashion.

In general Climacus describes the religious life as a progressive deepening of the individual's commitment to the absolute *telos*, quest for an eternal happiness, or God-relationship. (As we saw in the last chapter, he uses these terms to describe the same process.) Climacus describes three aspects in this process, which he refers to as the "initial, essential, and decisive" expressions of religiousness. The key concepts used in describing the aspects are resignation, suffering, and guilt, respectively. We shall examine his discussion of each of these in turn, attempting to make clear what Climacus means, seeing what can be said in favor of such a view, and determining whether it can rightly be said to be gloomy and pessimistic.

2. Negativity

The "negative" character of the religious life as Climacus describes it is what is likely to strike most readers initially. Resignation, suffering, and guilt are all fundamentally negative in their orientation. This must be understood in the light of the structure of existence itself, as discussed in chapter 4. Existence for Climacus is an unfinished process, a progressive but never final synthesis of time and eternity.

The contrast between Hegel and Kierkegaard is illuminating on this point. For Hegel it is also true that the negative is the moving force in history. Unless Spirit becomes what it is *not* by negating the status quo (itself as it is), Spirit cannot become itself in truth (itself as it will be). For Hegel, however, at least as Climacus interprets him, this negative moment must be finally overcome by a new positivity. It is this element in the Hegelian dialectic that Climacus rejects. For him this is equivalent to saying that existence is complete and finished. It is treating existence as complete and finished that gives Hegel the luxury of making systematic contemplation the highest human task, for "system" and "completeness" are equivalent terms (VII, 87; p. 98). For the individual in existence, however, existence is never finished and a system is impossible; therefore he can never become purely positive. The gap between his existential reality and his ideals always remains, a gap that demands a constant negation of the status quo.

Climacus' attitude toward the self here parallels the position of the left-wing Hegelians with respect to society. These "young Hegelians" believed that Hegel had betrayed his own principle by apotheosizing the political status quo. They took seriously the Hegelian principle that progress comes through negativity and called for a continual and "relentless criticism of everything existing."[1] This attitude can be seen later in Marx's call for a "perpetual revolution,"[2] a call echoed much later in the cultural revolution of Mao's China. In a similar way Climacus' attitude toward the self could be described as a sort of "perpetual revolution." The individual can never fully realize the ideal in existence; hence he must continually "negate the status quo." Existentially, *positive* development and growth are recognizable by the negative. This characteristic of existence comes through in Climacus' discussion of the existing individual which focuses on Lessing. But this negativity is even more characteristic of the religious sphere, where the "positive is the sign of the negative."

> Revelation is recognizable by mystery, happiness (*Saligheden*) by suffering, faith's certainty by uncertainty, ease by difficulty, truth by absurdity; if this is not maintained, then the aesthetic and religious run together in a common confusion (VII, 375n; p. 387 n).

The danger here arises from the fact that religiousness, according to Climacus, does involve a type of positivity, a new or higher "immediacy." This religious immediacy must be distinguished from aesthetic immediacy by the fact that it is permeated with, or conditioned by, negativity. The religious individual like the aesthetic individual, experiences joy and sadness. But the religious individual rejoices over her *sufferings*, sorrows over her *guilt*.

3. The Initial Task: Resignation and "the Absolute Commitment to the Absolute"

Climacus initially describes the religious life as the task of existentially realizing an absolute commitment to the absolute *telos* simultaneously with a relative commitment to the relative ends to which the individual finds himself related (VII, 359; p. 371). This description builds on the concepts we examined in the last chapter. If there is an absolute *telos*, then one's ethical obligation toward that telos must also be absolute in character. And we have seen that for Climacus this ethical task is simultaneously religious, since the attempt to realize the highest ethical good is equivalent to self-realization, religiously understood, which in turn can be described as the attempt to achieve an eternal happiness and a God-relationship.

What does it mean to be "absolutely committed to the absolute, relatively committed to the relative?" For Climacus it means that with respect to the relative the individual is *resigned*. The decisive criterion for an absolute relation to the absolute is that one is willing to give up the relative whenever the relative conflicts with the absolute (VII, 341; p. 353). If the individual is not willing to do this, then it is clear that his commitment to the absolute end is not absolute in character. Climacus' argument here is abstract and is valid even if someone understands the absolute *telos* differently than he does. This state of being willing to give up any and every finite good for the sake of the infinite Climacus calls resignation.

Some commentators on Climacus use resignation and suffering as synonyms, but I believe Climacus distinguishes them in the following way: Resignation is the state in which the individual is willing to sacrifice any finite good for the sake of the absolute. Suffering is the condition of the individual who is attempting to realize this condition but has not fully done so, thus experiencing the pain of "dying to self." Resignation, therefore, is simply another way of describing the task of being absolutely committed to the absolute and relatively to the relative.

Resignation is the opposite of mediation, a concept to which Climacus devotes quite a bit of attention. In the *Postscript* he discusses two types of mediation. There is first the attempt to mediate between existence and thought, in which the individual seeks to evade the responsibility that comes from existing. This sort of mediation blurs the distinction Climacus insists on between thought and existence. It is essentially an illusion. From the perspective of thought one can "mediate" (which in this context means, I think, to synthesize, reconcile, or resolve differences) between thought and existence, but in that case one deals not with existence but with existence as thought. Insofar as the individual exists, on the other hand, he cannot get "outside" his existence to a detached standpoint from which he can view his own existence as simply something to contemplate (VII, 346; pp. 357-358.)

The second type of mediation concerns the ethical life. With respect to this sphere, which is our concern at present, mediation is the process of "giving to Caesar what is Caesar's." That is, it is the process of reconciling relative goods to each other by ranking them and assigning to each its proper share of attention, energy, and time. Mediation therefore assumes a qualitative similarity among its objects and attempts to evaluate them quantitatively. Climacus by no means assumes that this process is easy, nor does he denigrate it. With respect to all relative goods — such as food, shelter, career satisfaction, familial bliss, and so on — such a process is unavoidable and appropriate (VII, 346; p. 355). The relative is the proper sphere of "both-and," and the well-rounded person is the one who has broad interests, but nevertheless keeps his responsibilities in proper perspective.

What Climacus attacks is the attempt to regard the *absolute telos* as one good among others. This attitude is characteristic, he thinks, of middle-class life in Protestant Denmark. The individual wants to be alderman, crack rifle shot, lovable father, *and* to have an eternal happiness. It is in this sense that "mediation . . . is a rebellion of the relative ends against the majesty of the absolute, which is supposed to be dragged down to the level of everything else, and against the dignity of man, seeking to make man a mere servant of relative ends" (VII, 363-364; p. 375). To regard the absolute *telos* as one more thing one would like to have "in addition to" is precisely not to regard it as absolute.

The only protection against such a devaluation of the human task is resignation. One might be tempted to ask here: Why does Climacus assume that the absolute must conflict with the relative? The answer to this is that he does not assume that they must conflict. Resignation is described in hypothetical terms; it is a willingness to give up the relative *if* it should conflict with the absolute. There is no necessity for an actual conflict, but the possibility of such a conflict provides the test of whether an individual's commitment to the absolute is truly absolute.

Why does Climacus assume the possibility of such a conflict? Such a possibility is inherent in taking the notion of an absolute *telos* seriously. If the absolute *telos* cannot conflict with relative goods, then either it is being understood as a relative good, which demands only its proper share of the pie, or it is understood to exhaust itself in the concrete ends, in which case the "absolute good' becomes contentless, a concept with no definite meaning. In either case the result is mediation.

> The principle of mediation either lets the relationship to the absolute *telos* be mediated into the relative ends, whereby it itself becomes relative, or else lets it as something abstract exhaust itself in the relative ends as its predicates, whereby the majesty of the absolute relationship becomes an empty phrase, a showy introduction to life which yet remains outside it, a title-page not bound with the book (VII, 351; p. 363).

Climacus does not deny that the relationship to the absolute *telos* can become concrete in practical action for relative goals. What he denies is that the absolute *telos* can ever exhaust itself in such goods. Climacus' view here has experiential support as well. It is characteristic of individuals who have been absolutely committed to "becoming themselves" and "finding God" that they have been willing to sacrifice many of the relative values, such as comfort and security, that most of us build our lives around.

This discussion of mediation and resignation is illuminated by Climacus' discussion of the medieval monastic movement, which can here be seen as a representative of general religious monasticism, which plays such a large role in mankind's religious experience. Climacus first offers a critical evaluation of such a withdrawal from the world. Monasticism represents an attempt to express one's absolute commitment to the absolute by a specific external mode of life. Such a peculiar external mode of existence cannot ultimately be a true expression of the absolute commitment, since though peculiar, the monastic way of life is ultimately equivalent to a distinctive type of finite life style (VII, 355; p. 366). The medieval "did not have complete confidence in its inwardness until this became an outwardness" (VII, 358; p. 370). "The inwardness of the Middle Ages was a suspicious inwardness, and therefore wanted to see the outward expression. . . . The Middle Ages believed of God that He was jealous to see the outward expression" (VII, 359; p. 370). Climacus offers as the ideal "hidden inwardness," which "demands no outward sign at all." Here "the passion of infinity is in the exercise of the absolute distinction, but it wants to remain an inwardness, without jealousy, without envy, without suspicion. . ." (VII, 359; p. 370).

Though he presents such a hidden inwardness as the ideal, it is worth noting that Climacus has some reservations about its realization.[3] He sees how easily such a hidden inwardness can become a mask for a total lack of inwardness, while the person actually practices mediation. This qualifies his criticism of the monastic movement severely. If one cannot remain in the finite while simultaneously practicing resignation and thereby maintaining an absolute relation to the absolute, then

> analogies to the monastic movement are unconditionally to be preferred, whether one hisses or sings, whether this assertion is met with tears or with laughter in the speculative nineteenth century. In the monastic movement there was at any rate passion, and a respect for the absolute *telos* (VII, 359; p. 371).

In the present situation, Climacus says, there is "really no very great reason for warning people against the cloister" (VII, 360; p. 372). So long as the candidate for the cloister humbly confesses that it is weakness and not superior holiness that compels him to withdraw from the world, then his choice is justified. Climacus says that the main reason he could not have entered a cloister in the Middle Ages was that if he had done so, people would have regarded him as a holy man. That, however, is scarcely a danger any more in Protestant Denmark, since a candidate for the cloister would very likely be regarded as insane (VII, 360; p. 372). So Climacus urges "honor, as is fitting, for the monastic movement of the Middle Ages" (VII, 361; p. 373), which compares rather well with the philistinism of Climacus' contemporaries, I believe Climacus would have made the same judgment about any number of other supposedly Christian lands in the twentieth century.

Many will certainly find Climacus' description of the religious task too "otherworldly" for their taste, and as evidence they may well cite Climacus' positive attitude toward monasticism. It must be admitted that Climacus' religious perspective, which rests on his soul-making ethic, discussed in chapter 5, is "other-worldly" in a certain sense. He presupposes that the individual's absolute concern is with his own eternal happiness and that every concrete human good may have to be sacrificed for the sake of this. There is an abyss that separates such an ethico-religious perspective from the mindset of much contemporary thought, including religious thought. However, truth is not decided by "the crowd," and Climacus would claim that this rejection of his view simply shows how spiritually underdeveloped the mass of people are today.

Climacus' view is not *completely* otherworldly, however. He says that resignation does not mean indifference toward the finite (VII, 358; p. 370).

> An older man can very well wholeheartedly share in the play of children, be the person who really brings life into the play, but he does not play as a child: thus the person who grasps as his task to practice the absolute distinction relates himself to finitude (VII, 359; p. 370).

Climacus here claims that the individual who has an absolute commitment to his own salvation can be "relatively committed to the relative." He can be genuinely concerned about social progress, health reforms, better conditions for families. He may even be the one responsible for bringing "life" into these activities. But he nonetheless does not regard the success or failure of such schemes as infinitely significant, since the absolute task, for him as well as other human beings, never becomes identified with such programs and can be carried on whether they succeed or fail.

It must be recognized that Climacus here is not attempting to describe a distinctively Christian understanding of existence; he is analyzing a religion of immanence, though it is clear that Climacus himself thought Christianity presupposed and built on the sort of hidden inwardness he talks about. I have some criticisms of Climacus' hidden inwardness myself, focusing on the way he conceives the relation between the relative and the absolute, which I shall develop in the last chapter on objectivity and subjectivity. These criticisms are in part those advanced against Climacus by Kierkegaard himself and by Anti-Climacus.[4] (But my criticisms apply in part to Kierkegaard, too.) However, my criticisms should be distinguished from those of a thinker who does not recognize such a thing as an absolute *telos*. I believe that Climacus' criticisms of mediation are sound and that he is right in maintaining the distinctness of the absolute *telos* and consequent possibility for conflict with the relative. Thus I am essentially in agreement with him that resignation is an intrinsic part of a viable religious perspective.

4. Suffering

Resignation is the existential expression for the religious task as initially and ideally comprehended. Resignation is the willingness to sacrifice any and every finite good for the sake of the absolute. As such, it functions as a test the individual can apply to himself to see if his commitment to the absolute is absolute.

Since the task is existential, however, it is not enough to describe it ideally. Until the individual has passed the test of resignation, he is always immediate, and insofar "is involved absolutely in relative ends" (VII, 375; pp. 386-387). Since the individual in this situation is always to a certain extent "caught" by relative ends — such as health, career, family, money, etc. — to achieve the state of resignation he must begin by "dying to immediacy," by *suffering*. Clearly Climacus thinks this situation is generally present in human religious life. Thus he claims that "religious action is recognizable by suffering," that "the religious address has essentially the task of *uplifting through suffering*," and that suffering is therefore the "total category" of the religious life (VII, 375, 378-379; pp. 387, 390).

Before one can evaluate these claims, one must first understand what Climacus means by suffering (*Lidelse*). He goes to great pains to distinguish the religious concept of suffering from the corresponding aesthetic concept, just as he did with the concept of an eternal happiness. Religious suffering is not to be identified with the suffering that comes about through misfortune (*Ulykke*) any more than an eternal happiness is to be identified with the happiness that comes through good fortune (*Lykke*). Aesthetic suffering is accidental in the sense that some people are unfortunate and others fortunate with respect to it. Of course such suffering is pervasive in human existence, and it can have religious significance. But it gains its religious significance from the way the individual receives and appropriates the suffering. Ordinary suffering can shock and destroy an individual's illusory happiness; it can awaken her to the shallowness of her essentially aesthetic life. And ordinary human sufferings can enrich the religious life for those who accept these sufferings from God's hand and learn to benefit from them. But it is the manner of reception that makes such sufferings religious.

The nonreligious sufferer tends to respond to suffering in one of two ways. Either he consoles himself with the help of what Climacus calls the probability of "worldly wisdom," or he seeks solace in the world of the poetic. Worldly wisdom "comforts" by assuring the sufferer that things are not really so bad as they seem, that in all probability things will soon take a turn for the better, etc. Such calculating worldly wisdom Climacus finds repugnant in the strongest sense. He calls it "comical" and "stupid" whether it calculates correctly or incorrectly, since "all its calculation is an illusion, a business which rests inside the chimerical idea that there is something certain in the world of finitude" (VII, 398; p. 409). At bottom such finite wisdom is still a form of the aesthetic life, though a degenerate one, since the significance of life still consists in this case in being lucky enough to slip through unscathed by fate. The comical aspect and the stupidity lie in the fact that the individual believes he can assure himself by his own finite common sense of being able to do this, oblivious to the power of existence to mock "the best laid plans of mice and men."

The poetic response to suffering Climacus treats more kindly. The poetic response is to seek repose through the imagination, through the arts. Climacus calls this an illusion, but nonetheless a beautiful illusion (VII, 397; p. 409). It is an illusion because it is really an escape from existence. The poet discovers eternity, but it is an illusory eternity, an eternity of the imagination that lies outside his existence and does not penetrate and transform that existence.

The religious exister, on the other hand, understands suffering as essential to existence. Suffering is not something to withdraw from into the world of imagination, nor is it an accidental characteristic that attaches itself to some people (the unfortunate) but not to others. It is something that persists as essential to the religious life (VII, 389; p. 400). From the religious perspective the categories of the fortunate and the unfortunate can only be used in a jesting way, since all people are essentially sufferers — or ought to be so (VII, 380; p. 392). Religious suffering cannot therefore be straightforwardly identified with illness, pain, poverty, and the like. Even the most outwardly fortunate individual can be a religious sufferer in the most decisive sense.

What is this religious suffering if it is not suffering in the ordinary sense? It is precisely the process of "dying away from immediacy" which is necessitated by the individual's absolute commitment to relative ends. It is the establishment or reestablishment of a proper relation to God. (Climacus' thesis that an absolute relation to the absolute is identical with a God-relationship must be kept in mind.) This dying away from immediacy is a "self-annihilation" that is "the essential form for the God-relationship." This self-annihilation is "to express existentially the principle that the individual can do absolutely nothing of himself, but is as nothing before God" (VII, 401; p. 412). This principle becomes the formula that describes religious suffering. In tracing the progression from resignation to suffering, Climacus also goes from an abstract, ethical description of the religious life (to be related absolutely to the absolute and relatively to the relative) to a more concrete and distinctly religious description (to recognize that without God an individual is nothing and can do nothing, along with its corollary, "with God the individual can do something").

The link between these two is the concept of "dying away from" or "self-annihilation." Because the individual is trapped in the relative, she must die to immediacy. But one dies to immediacy precisely by coming to understand the nothingness of one's immediacy. The person who stands before God with a consciousness of her own nothingness has died to immediacy. She no longer rests secure in what Climacus calls the sensory-illusion that she can do this or that; she is conscious that apart from God she is nothing and can do nothing.

We can now understand why this religious suffering is, or ought to be, universal. For the consciousness of her nothingness that the religious individual seeks to realize is simply the literal truth about the condition of every human being as finite creature, if indeed there is a God. If God is the creator, not merely in the sense of the one who began things at a point in time, but in the decisive sense that everything that exists does so from moment to moment because God wills it, then it is quite literally true that apart from God a created object is nothing. Because of God man is something; he is in fact a noble something, created for eternal life with God. But his nobility lies precisely in his ability freely to recognize or fail to recognize his dependence on God. This freedom means that man is to an extent independent of God. But even this independence is itself dependent upon God's creative power, most properly used when man recognizes — freely — his dependence.

> And this is the miracle of creation, not the bringing forth of something which is nothing over against the Creator, but the bringing forth of something which is something, and which in true service of God can itself use this something in order to become nothing before God (VII, 207; p. 220).

This recognition of the true relation between creature and creator is another expression for *worship* (VII, 358; p. 369). For Climacus this is the true aim of religious suffering, and it is the reason why he regards suffering as the essential category that attaches itself to the whole of religion. For what could be more fundamental to religion than the acknowledgment by creatures of their relation to their creator in worship?

Why is this process of rightly worshipping one's creator called *suffering*, however? The answer is in part that it simply is a painful thing for human beings to recognize and existentially express their dependence on God. Human beings are self-assertive and prideful. The true religious life consists of purging away this deceitful independence and learning to live by a conscious, continual dependence on God. Climacus illustrates this by his example of the well-to-do man who wishes to take an outing in the Deer Park. This seemingly trivial amusement is only accomplished by the religious individual at great cost, because that individual takes quite literally the thought that he "can do nothing of himself." Even an outing in the park he can do only with God's help and only after having conquered the temptation to think that this is an act that can be done by the individual himself without any thought of his dependence on God and responsibility to God.

Climacus' designation of the existential religious task as suffering makes still more sense if we examine the Danish term he employs (*Lidelse*), which comes from the verb *at lide*, just as the English term "suffering" comes from the verb "to suffer." The English verb "to suffer" originally had a double meaning, which it has almost but not completely lost. To suffer meant not merely to feel pain; its primary meaning was originally "to let, to allow, to undergo, or take up a passive relation toward something." Thus, in the King James Bible Jesus says, "Suffer the little children to come unto me." The Danish verb *at lide* still maintains this double meaning, which we can dimly discern in the corresponding English term, and Climacus uses *Lidelse* in a way that reflects this ambiguity.[5] Religious suffering is the *action* of becoming *passive* over against God, of allowing God to direct and govern one's life.

In the *Fragments* Climacus describes the nature of created contingent objects, which he distinguishes from eternal logical entities, which are properly spoken of as necessary. "All coming into existence is a *suffering* (*Liden*) and the necessary cannot suffer (*lide*) the suffering (*Lidelse*) of actuality. . ." (IV, 237; p. 91). Here Climacus describes the distinctive characteristic of all created objects (including man) as having *suffered* the change of coming into existence, a change that is effected by God understood as the ultimate freely effecting cause (IV, 239; p. 93). It is the existential realization of this "suffering" in the consciousness of the individual that constitutes the religious task. And because of the pride and self-assertiveness of human beings this process of suffering turns out to be a suffering in the ordinary English (and Danish) sense as well. Dying to immediacy is painful as well as passive.

Climacus' emphasis on this religious suffering as the activity of acquiring a properly *passive* relation toward God (rather than simply experiencing pain) is well illustrated by another passage.

> To act (*at handle*) could now appear to be just the opposite of to suffer (*at lide*) and insofar it seems strange to say that the existential pathos' (which is active) essential expression is suffering. However, it is only apparently so, and this shows again here what is characteristic of the religious sphere, that the positive is recognizable by the negative (VII, 375; p. 387).

The most strenuous action the individual can achieve is won through the religious pathos in which the individual wins through to the recognition of his own passivity over against God, his continual dependence on God as the one without whom he could do nothing.

We can now easily see that Climacus is justified when he claims that the suffering of the religious life is not masochistic.

> Suffering as dying away from immediacy is therefore not flagellations and the like; it is not *self-torture*. The self-torturer does not by any means express the fact that he can do nothing before God, for he thinks the self-torture to be something (VII, 403; p. 414).

It is worth noting that this is true not only of physical self-torture but of psychological self-punishment as well. The suffering Climacus is referring to has nothing in common with the masochistic self-punishment one might picture as the heart of his conception of the religious life prior to a careful reading of the text. Melancholy is as far from religion as frivolity.

It is also worth noting that Climacus rejects a quietistic interpretation of his thesis. Learning to recognize that one can do nothing apart from God does not entail that the individual ceases to do anything (VII, 440; p. 452). The goal of the religious life is not cessation of outward activity but learning to perform such activities in continual dependence on God. The religious individual who takes his outing to the Deer Park faces two difficulties: First he must "annul the illusion" and come to comprehend that he can do nothing of himself. Second, having conquered this difficulty, he must "with God be able to do it" (VII, 422-423; pp. 434-435). And the individual is pictured by Climacus not only as taking his outing, but actually enjoying it.

> Our religious individual chooses the way to the Deer Park,. . . "But he does not enjoy himself," someone perhaps says. Oh, yes, he certainly does. And why does he enjoy himself? Because it is the humblest expression for his God-relationship to confess his humanity, and because it is human to enjoy onself (VII, 428; pp. 440-441).

The end result of religious suffering is therefore not a negation but a reaffirmation of man's created humanness.

5. *"Spiritual Trial" and the Transcending of the Ethical Stage*

The individual who experiences this religious suffering has a distinctive and essentially religious element in her life. Her life is still ethically colored; she by no means has rejected or abandoned the ethical. But her life can no longer be described as merely ethical. It is helpful here to distinguish two uses of the term "the ethical": as a stage or existence-sphere and as a component in human existence. A person whose highest existential categories are ethical exists in the ethical *sphere*, which, as we have seen, involves a God-relation, but one in which the individual sees herself as self-sufficient. The religious individual does not cease to attempt to realize her ethical task; thus the ethical remains as a *component* of her life. But for her ethical striving is an element in another project, the achievement of a God-relationship. Or, to put things more correctly, she no longer attempts to achieve a God-relationship simply through ethical action. (The ethical life in its highest form is also an attempt to achieve a God-relation, but one that limits itself to ethical action.)

Climacus is maintaining that the religious life, though it has its origins in the ethical and always contains an essential ethical dimension, is not reducible to the ethical life. As the religious life develops, God, who is first discovered through ethical striving, becomes in the consciousness of the religious believer a distinct reality who can be related to in a direct way (though God is still here known immanently — that is, via universally accessible immanent ideas, rather than through special revelations and experiences). This relationship between the ethical and the religious is illustrated by a passing Climacus remark in which he says that though the ethical comes into the religious life regulatively and takes command, it still "is always somewhat removed from the absolute God-relationship" (VII, 424; p. 436). The same point is illustrated by another pseudonym, Johannes de Silentio, in *Fear and Trembling*, when he speaks of the fact that the individual, who by his guilt has gone outside the universal (the ethical), can only return to the universal through "an absolute relation to the absolute [God]" (III, 145; p. 108).

Climacus' thesis that religious life is irreducible to ethical life is significant, since it cuts against the view of many of his contemporaries, who had accepted Kant's thesis in *Religion Within the Limits of Reason Alone* that the essence of true religion in "good life conduct."[6] The tendency to reduce the religious life to some type of ethical life is illustrated also by Strauss' *Life of Jesus*, and it is a tendency present to a greater or lesser extent in all of classical liberal theology. Climacus wishes to maintain that the religious life is distinctively religious in character, and he therefore focuses on worship, a distinctively religious practice, as the essence of the religious life. (As we have seen, however, he interprets worship somewhat novelly in terms of his concept of suffering.) The grounds for his thesis that the religious life has its own unique character lie in the existential discovery that moves the individual into this religious suffering. This discovery is that the individual is "caught in immediacy" and unable to relate himself straightforwardly to God and God's creation in the proper way and thereby to fulfill his ethical duty. First, the individual must secure a proper relation to God (an absolute relation to the absolute) by dying to immediacy. And this is a distinctively religious task. Thus the discovery of God's reality and the necessity for the individual to relate himself to God comes about through the individual's awareness of his own insufficiency.

This distinction between the religious and the ethical life comes to the fore in the concept of spiritual trial (*Anfægtelse*), a concept that is to English readers more mysterious than it needs to be. This is the term that is translated by the German *Anfechtung* in the Lowrie-Swenson translation of the *Postscript* and "trial of temptation" by Lowrie elsewhere. Howard and Edna Hong's choice of "spiritual trial" as a translation is considerably more helpful to the English reader. Climacus says that a spiritual trial "originates first in the characteristically religious sphere, and occurs there only in the final state, increasing quite properly with the degree of religiousness. . . "(VII, 399; p. 410). It is important therefore to try to gain a clear idea of what this *Anfægtelse*, or spiritual trial, really is.

Spiritual trial is described as being "in the sphere of the God-relationship what temptation is in the sphere of the ethical relation." The individual is said to be innocent in a spiritual trial, yet it is described as a fearful suffering. What tempts the individual in a spiritual trial is "the higher" and it is described as a "repellant" temptation (VII, 399-400; pp. 410-411).

The basic contrast between spiritual trial(*Anfægtelse*) and temptation (*Fristelse*) seems clear enough. In temptation the individual's weakness tempts him to indulge himself and succumb to a "lower" vice. In a spiritual trial, on the other hand, the individual is pressing on toward a relationship to "the higher," God himself. As a person recognizes the strenuousness and suffering he is reaching toward, he is frightened or repelled. He is tempted — or rather, tested — by "the higher." This may be confusing to those readers who are accustomed to think only about the lower kind of temptation (*Fristelse*), the kind one gives in to if one *seeks* the object that is the source of the temptation. In a spiritual trial, on the other hand, the individual is tempted to refrain from going on to realize the higher, and he gives in to the temptation by *failing to seek* the source of the temptation (which therefore should not really be called the *object* of temptation.) In this case "the ethical" could be said to be what the person is tempted *to*, since he is tempted to slip back from the strenuousness of the religious life into the more comfortable categories of the ethical.

Climacus himself gives one illustration of what he means by spiritual trial. In his discussion of the religious individual who is reflecting on whether he should take an outing to the Deer Park, he mentions that such a person must make sure he is not being prompted by a "momentary craving" or "whim of his immediacy," but rather by a genuine human need (VII, 430, p. 443). In such a situation the individual will "distrust himself" and ask whether he could not do without his diversion a little longer. The problem is "to find the right, the boundary which is so difficult to find between indolence and the limitations of finitude." This difficulty can easily awaken in the individual "the human irritability which rightly feels the sting of being dependent in this way, thus constantly having to understand that a man can do nothing of himself" (VII, 431; p. 443). This irritability tries to make the individual think that the God-relationship does not need to be brought into play on such an insignificant matter, and this Climacus diagnoses as a case of spiritual trial.

It could be clearer just what this temptation consists in, perhaps. But it does illustrate Climacus' main points about spiritual trial. It is a situation in which the individual has a well-developed God-relationship. In confronting the strenuousness and anxiety of this relationship the individual is tempted to slide back onto a more comfortable mode of existence, in which he is not confronted by the necessity to constantly relate his every action to God.

Another illustration of a spiritual trial might be taken from Silentio's *Fear and Trembling*. In this work Abraham's test in being called to sacrifice his son Isaac is discussed as an example of a spiritual trial. Abraham is tempted by the thought that sacrificing his son is repugnant from an ethical point of view, and he anxiously must decide whether God has really asked him to do such a thing. Here again the individual is repelled by the fearful uncertainty of the religious life and tempted to take comfort in the security of the ethical. We cannot be sure, of course, that Climacus would approve of every feature of this example, but it does seem to fit his description of the concept.[7]

Climacus also says that the individual in a spiritual trial is innocent, as would not be the case in an ordinary kind of temptation (VII, 400; p. 411). This may be a little puzzling since Climacus certainly does not think the individual who fails to pass a spiritual trial is innocent, and one might think the individual who does not succumb to ordinary temptation is also innocent. What, then, is different about the two situations? I believe this can be explained as follows. A person who is confronted by a "lower" temptation is frequently already somewhat guilty in that she may have opened the door to the temptation. In any case the fact that she is really tempted is a sign that her character is somewhat weak and therefore shows her lack of innocence. It is at least not praiseworthy. The occurrence of spiritual trial, on the other hand, does not reflect badly about the individual's character, since it is only the more religiously developed individual who ever discovers such a conflict. In a way, then, one might say the occurrence of spiritual trial is a healthy sign in a person's moral and religious development, in a way that is not true of moral temptation. (It is of course not healthy to yield to the temptation.)

6. Guilt

Climacus' exposition of religiousness has, as he himself says, a "backward" direction. He begins with an ideal description of the religious task, which is to relate oneself absolutely to the absolute and relatively to the relative, the test for which is resignation. To accomplish this task the individual discovers that he must first "die to immediacy," as he is absolutely committed to the relative. Thus suffering, understood as the existential realization of the creature's total dependence on the creator, which is acknowledged in religious worship, is described as the essential form of religiousness. Next Climacus analyzes the existential status of the person who has embarked upon this task, and he finds another failure. The person who fails to adequately realize the proper attitude toward God is guilty before God; hence the decisive expression of religiousness is guilt, along with its corollary, repentance. Here Climacus' exposition is clearly phenomenological. He says that "this is the way it goes in existence and the investigation seeks to repeat it [the process]."[8] But this backward movement is precisely a forward one in the existential sense, since it means a deeper plunge into existence (VII, 459; p. 469).

It is not surprising that Climacus views guilt as the decisive expression of religiousness, since the point that distinguished the religious life from the ethical life was the individual's awareness of his lack of self-sufficiency. Thus we can easily see why guilt is described as the "decisive" expression for the religious life. The religious life that grows out of the ethical life here takes on a decisively religious color. But not every type of human failing can properly be described religiously as guilt, not even every type of religious failing. Hence it is essential for Climacus to give a careful analysis of this concept, distinguishing it from similar concepts and removing possible misinterpretations.

For Climacus guilt is in one sense not a gloomy concept, since it is a measure of existential progress:

> So the essential consciousness of guilt is the deepest possible plunge into existence, and at the same time it is the expression for the fact that an exister is related to an eternal happiness. . . it is the expression for the relationship by reason of the fact that it expresses the incompatibility or disrelationship (VII, 464; p. 473).

The theme that "the positive is recognizable by the negative" is a familiar one for an exister who is always in the process of striving to realize an ideal that can never be perfectly realized in existence (VII, 465; p. 474). Thus it is not surprising for Climacus to affirm that the highest relation an existing individual can maintain to an eternal happiness takes the form of a disrelation in which the individual realizes how far removed from such an eternal happiness he is. And here it must be remembered that an eternal happiness is defined in terms of the realization of a pure moral and religious character on the part of the individual. Climacus is affirming that the moral and religious individual who stands highest is the one who despite, or perhaps because of, all his striving recognizes how far from the ideal he is. And one can also understand why Climacus affirms that guilt in this sense is the "deepest possible plunge into existence," since the individual who recognizes himself as guilty takes full responsibility for becoming what he has become. He exists in the fullest sense.

There is a great temptation, however, when guilt is so closely connected with existence, to transform guilt into innocence by seeking to "put the blame onto existence." In this way guilt is transformed from a moral quality into an ontological quality. All men are "guilty" because of the very nature of the conditions of existence. Climacus himself almost suggests such a view by tying guilt very closely to the nature of temporality:

> Thus things go backward: the task is brought to the individual in existence, and just as he wants without further ado to make a big splash and wants to begin, it is discovered that a second beginning is necessary, the beginning upon the immense detour of dying from immediacy; and just when the beginning is about to be made here, it is discovered that there, since time has meanwhile been passing, an ill beginning has been made, and that the beginning must be made by becoming guilty and from that moment increasing the total guilt which is decisive with new guilt (VII, 459; p. 469).

Such passages have led some commentators to think that for Climacus guilt is primarily ontological rather than moral.

Climacus makes it perfectly clear, however, that he does not view guilt as ontological, although he sees how strong the temptation is to regard it as such.

> The difficulty is really a different one; from the fact that guilt is explained by existing it appears that the exister is made innocent; it appears that he may be able to throw the guilt over on the one who has brought him into existence or upon existence itself (VII, 460-461; p. 470).[9]

What Climacus says here is not that guilt is explained by existence (as in the Lowrie-Swenson translation), but by *existing*, i.e., by the individual's manner of existing. This makes it *appear* that the guilt can be thrown off on God or upon existence itself, but Climacus says explicitly that this is not the case. If guilt could be blamed on existence, then properly there would be no such thing as human guilt; the "consciousness of guilt would be nothing else but a new expression for the suffering of existence" (VII, 461; p. 470), which does have its ground in finitude.

Though Climacus distinguishes very carefully between guilt, which is an immanent concept, and the specifically Christian concept of sin, it is noteworthy that what he wishes to say about guilt is very much like what orthodox Christians wish to say about sin. For he claims, as Christians do in their doctrine of original sin, that guilt is both a universal condition and yet something for which the individual is responsible. It is not surprising that Climacus' interpreters have found such a view difficult and that they are tempted to convert it into an ontological thesis, just as many theologians have either wanted to push the Christian concept toward Pelagianism, affirming the possible innocence of some individuals, or likewise toward an ontological doctrine that does not imply a moral failing on the part of the individual. We will see in chapter 12 how Climacus deals with the concept of sin. But there are significant parallels between sin and guilt.

His argument that guilt does imply a moral failing on the part of the individual is existential and not theoretical. That is, Climacus does not try theoretically to explain how man can be universally guilty yet individually responsible. Rather, he argues that these are the existential facts that the honest individual discovers and must therefore accept, however poorly they comport with his a priori theories. Climacus' primary argument is that the very attempt to "throw off guilt" and "excuse oneself" is itself a demonstration of the individual's responsibility. "He who is essentially innocent can never hit upon the idea of casting guilt away from him; for the innocent person has nothing at all to do with the quality we call guilt" (VII, 416; pp. 470-471).

> It is true of guilt, if it is of any other quality, that there is a catch to it; its dialectic is so crafty that he who justifies himself totally precisely denounces himself, and he who justifies himself partially denounces himself totally (VII, 461; p. 471).

Climacus is not here making the absurd claim that a person can never justifiably claim that he is innocent with respect to some particular matter. And his point is not that a person who is too anxious to proclaim his innocence thereby may make himself suspicious in the eyes of others, who rightly see such anxiety as a sign of guilt. This is the point of the proverb *"qui s'excuse s'accuse."* His argument rests on the assumption that a *totally* innocent person simply would have no acquaintance with guilt at all. Hence a person who argues that he is not guilty, either partially or totally, reveals an acquaintance with guilt, which shows that guilt is not a stranger to him. However innocent he may be in some particular respect, his life as a whole is one in which guilt plays a role.

It is important to understand that in speaking of guilt Climacus is not using the term quantitatively but qualitatively. Such qualitative concepts are described as "total predicates" — that is, the term "guilt" here is not being used to characterize some elements in a person's life and not others, but to describe the character of a person's existence taken as a whole.

One might ask how such a "total predicate" gets its meaning, since such concepts as guilt are contrast terms that only have meaning in relation to their opposites. Thus we normally describe a person as guilty in this or that respect, to a greater or lesser degree, which is properly contrasted with being innocent in this or that respect or innocent to a greater or lesser degree. Such contrasts drop out when the term "guilt" is used as Climacus uses it, since he is certainly not claiming that individuals are totally guilty in this comparative, quantitiative sense, which would be an absurd empirical claim. The contrast term for Climacus must be a state in which the individual is totally or essentially innocent. In such a state, which would be analogous to that of Adam and Eve prior to the Fall, man would be essentially innocent and therefore would not even be aware of such a thing as guilt. The person who has acquired "the knowledge of good and evil" by doing evil thereby betrays himself through his very awareness of guilt. Though he may be in many cases comparatively and quantitatively innocent, his life as a whole falls under the category of guilt.

I believe that the existential backing for the claim that the individual is aware of guilt lies in Climacus' discussion of "the boundary between finitude and selfishness," which we discussed in connection with spiritual trial. No doubt many human failings are due to finitude; no one can continuously worship God as he ideally should. His very temporality makes it impossible to maintain the proper reverence *always*. And many other failings can no doubt be traced to the hereditary and environmental factors that have shaped the particular quality of the individual's finitude. Despite these excuses Climacus is asserting that no individual can say with good conscience that "he has done all he could." A person might be tempted to say that he has done as much as the next fellow, but that is quite a different matter. Each person is aware of failings that are distinctively his own. Even if he were tempted to affirm his innocence, the impossibility of determining precisely the boundary between finitude and selfishness would prevent him from knowing this with any assurance.

For Climacus such a qualitative concept of guilt is not a sum to be determined empirically. Rather, this concept of guilt comes into being "when the individual puts his guilt. . . together with the relation to an eternal happiness" (VII, 462; p. 471). It does not matter if the guilt be "a single one, even if it was the most insignificant of all" (VII, 462; pp. 471-472). Alternatively, Climacus says that the seriousness of the individual's guilt is recognized when the individual puts the conception of

God together with the conception of guilt (VII, 462; p. 472). These alternative formulations are of course equivalent, since an eternal happiness for Climacus consists in the proper realization of the individual's relation to God. What he means by these formulations is that the individual's assessment of his guilt is a function of the standard he uses to measure himself. For Climacus, man is intended to be a pure, moral being who freely relates himself to God for all eternity. This is the standard, and man's failure must be understood in relation to such a standard. From this it can be seen that Climacus' assertion that guilt is the decisive expression of religiousness is not rooted in misanthropy or a gloomy, pessimistic view of man. On the contrary, it is grounded in an elevated, uplifting view of man as an eternal creature, intended to relate freely to God and to realize an eternal happiness.

There are of course other possible standards by which an individual may measure his life. With his theory of various existence spheres Climacus is quite aware of this. Different standards produce different conceptions of guilt, and Climacus reviews a series of such conceptions so as to distinguish the religious conception of guilt from all others. Corresponding to every lower conception of guilt there is a corresponding satisfaction for guilt, and these can be used to categorize the conception of guilt as well. All of these "lower" conceptions are distinguished by the fact that they make guilt "comparative and momentary."

One of the lower conceptions of guilt is the civil[10] conception of guilt. Here the standard is obviously that of being a respectable, law-abiding citizen (VII, 472; p. 482). Another "low" conception is "the aesthetic-metaphysical conception of nemesis" (VII, 472; p. 482). Here Climacus seems to have in mind the view of guilt present in Greek tragedy, which treats guilt as a finite fault that can be satisfied by temporal suffering.

The most interesting "lower" conception of guilt is that contained in the concept of penance. It is here that Climacus chooses to analyze the widespread phenomenon of religious asceticism. As in the case of monasticism, Climacus' chief example is taken from the Middle Ages, and once more his attitude is ambivalent. On the one hand he clearly criticizes the notion of penance because it "finitizes guilt by making it commensurable." Penance, however, does have the merit that it sincerely discovers "guilt which eludes the attention not only of the police but of nemesis" (VII, 473; p. 482). In comparison with the spiritual deadness of the nineteenth century, which, like the twentieth, took a basically complacent attitude towards guilt, the Middle Ages deserve praise.

Honor for the Middle Age's penance. It is at least a childlike and spirited endeavor in the great and he must have lost all imagination and by much understanding have become as good as completely stupid, who cannot put himself back into the Middle Ages and can actually praise forgetfulness and thoughtlessness and "just look at my neighbor" as something truer (VII, 473; p. 482).

Ultimately the medieval practice of penance and other such ascetic practices whose aim is satisfaction for guilt, contain a faulty "childlike" view of God. But such a view is infinitely preferable to one that "leaves God out of the game entirely" (VII, 473; p. 483). A maiden who believes she has offended her lover may hit upon a ludicrous device to make her lover favorable to her again, but "does not her love hallow the ludicrous?"

> And so it is also: the religious man who goes astray in his authenticity — the passion of his authenticity casts a kindly light over him in comparison with the religious man who, on the street, from the newspapers, and at the club, has learned all about how to manage God, knowing how the other Christians do it (VII, 474; p. 484)[11]

Thus Climacus' final definition of religiousnesss is that it is "the totality of guilt-consciousness in the particular individual before God in relation to an eternal happiness" (VII, 483; p. 492). This guilt-consciousness "accepts no satisfaction for guilt" (VII, 472; p. 481) and insofar might be thought to end in despair. Climacus claims that this is not so, however: "But the hidden inwardness' eternal recollection of guilt is not despair either, for despair is continuously the infinite, the eternal, the total in the moment of impatience, and all despair is a type of bad temper" (VII, 484; p. 492). Guilt has, it seems, both a positive and a negative side; it both "assuages and rankles" (VII, 466; p. 475). The fact that the individual recognizes his guilt is a sign that he does indeed have a relation to an eternal happiness. His joy over this cannot transcend or eliminate his sorrow over his guilt, though, anymore than it can eliminate his condition as a sufferer, since if it did, it would also eliminate the grounds for his happiness (VII, 394; p. 406).[12] However, though such religiousness refuses to accept any satisfaction of guilt, it still rests on "an obscurely sensed possibility" of such a thing (VII, 472; p. 481). Man must be at least capable of *hoping* that guilt can be resolved. In this hope immanent religion rests in the final analysis on "recollection," the belief that the eternal is man's possession. The religious individual does not, however, make use of recollection to speculate theoretically, but energetically attempts to *exist* in his eternal recollection. It is at this point that the religious life became dangerously close to the view that Climacus calls humor, to be discussed in the next chapter.

Climacus' whole description of religiousness is in many important ways similar to the type of religion described by Kant in *Religion Within the Limits of Reason Alone*, though, as we have noted, there are important differences as well. Climacus' description of the "obscurely sensed possibility" of a satisfaction for guilt sounds like Kant's statements on the possibility of an atonement for sin.[13] Man can never know that there is such a thing, according to Kant, and therefore it cannot be transformed into a principle of action. It is a possibility for which man hopes, however, and by means of which he protects himself against the moral despair that threatens when he honestly measures himself by the supreme standard. As such a possiblity it is significant. For both Climacus and Kant this is the final word of immanent religion, religion within the bounds of human thought.

[1] See Marx's letter to Arnold Ruge, printed as "For a Ruthless Criticism of Everything Existing" in Robert Tucker, ed., the *Marx-Engels Reader*, 2nd ed. (New York: Norton, 1978), pp. 12-15.

[2] The phrase "The Revolution in Permanence" is used by Marx in the "Address of the Central Committee to the Communist League," *Ibid.*, p. 511.

[3] This suspicion of Climacus becomes outright rejection by Kierkegaard himself and his Christian pseudonym, Anti-Climacus. See *Attack on Christendom* and *Practice in Christianity (Training in Christianity)*.

[4] See chapter 13.

[5] The Danish term *lidelse* does not ordinarily carry this double meaning, even though *at lide* does.

[6] *"Whatever, over and above good life-conduct, man fancies that he can do to become well-pleasing to God is mere religious illusion and pseudo-service."* (New York: Harper & Row), p. 158. This is not the whole story to Kant's view of religion, however. See pp. 182-183.

[7] Climacus does discuss Silentio's example as an example of a spiritual trial, but he cautiously warns that the picture given of the religious life in *Fear and Trembling* is not complete because sin is not really brought into the picture. If sin is considered, then "the teleological suspension of the ethical must be given a more definitely religious expression" (VII, 226; p. 238). This "more definitely religious expression" sounds something like the theological concept of the atonement and has as a consequence that the "trial" is not an occasional, irregular happening, as it was for Abraham, but the whole of life.

[8] This sentence is omitted in the Lowrie-Swenson translation.

[9] This passage is badly translated in the Lowrie-Swenson edition. There it reads "for the fact that guilt is accounted for by existence." The Danish word translated "existence" here is the infinitive form of the verb *at existere,* which refers to the *activity* of existing, not the noun *Existentsen,* which is used later in the passage to refer to that which one is tempted to throw the blame on.

[10] Significantly the word for "civil" here also can mean "bourgeois" or "middle-class."

[11] Though he is discussing immanent religion, Climacus frequently takes examples from Christianity, since even in Christianity religiousness A can be the religion of "everyone who is not decisively Christian."

[12] Climacus' argument here concerns suffering, but the parallel with guilt is obvious.

[13] See *Religion Within the Limits of Reason Alone,* p. 134.

Chapter X

IRONY AND HUMOR:
SOME BOUNDARY SITUATIONS

1. Irony and Humor as Existential Transition Zones

One of the most fascinating and yet mysterious aspects of Climacus' writings concerns irony and humor. Not only does Climacus use irony and humor extensively, he also writes about them copiously. His reflections on irony and humor, besides being significant in themselves, are elements in his existential reflection; they also cast a great deal of light on Climacus himself as an author and on certain otherwise puzzling features of the *Fragments* and *Postscript*.

Climacus' reader is almost bound to be puzzled by what Climacus says about irony and humor. The unsuspecting reader is likely to bring with him his previous understanding of irony and humor, which has probably been shaped by high school literature classes and television comedies. But it is a little difficult to understand the connection between irony as a literary device employed by Jane Austen, or humor as exhibited in a situation comedy, and Climacus' discussion of these concepts. If one were to guess as to the relation between irony and humor and Climacus' thought, one might initially hazard the view that humor at least would be an element in the aesthetic life. Climacus, however, treats irony and humor as existential zones or spheres in their own right. And humor is specifically asserted to be the boundary zone of the religious life, higher even than the ethical, far removed from the aesthetic.

In speaking of irony and humor as existential spheres or "ways of life," Climacus is obviously not employing the terms as most people do today. But his usage is not totally removed from ordinary usage either. He has taken what appears to be the distinguishing characteristics of irony and humor as found in literature and life and used these to designate and illuminate two whole ways of life. As we did with the concept of the ethical, we must here distinguish between irony and humor as components in existence and irony and humor as the names for existence-spheres, existence possibilities in which these components are dominant. Thus irony and humor are existence-spheres, but they may also be elements in the lives of existers who are not "ironists" or "humorists," but ethicists or even Christians.

The best starting place for a discussion of Climacus' use of irony and humor is the theory of the spheres of existence.

> There are three existence-spheres: the aesthetic, the ethical, the religious. To these correspond two boundary-zones: irony is the boundary-zone between the aesthetic and the ethical; humor the boundary-zone between the ethical and the religious (VII, 436; p. 448).

Irony and humor are essentially existential transition points, definable only in relation to the other existential spheres. However, since existential transitions for Climacus are the result of freedom and are consequently never necessary, two other comments must be made.

First, irony and humor are transitional in the sense that they make *possible* the jump from the aesthetic to the ethical and from the ethical to the religious. However, they do not cause or effectuate the transition. For this reason it is possible for the existing individual to become suspended at the transition point itself, which therefore becomes a type of zone or sphere.

Second, irony and humor are not zones or spheres in the same sense in which the aesthetic or ethical are said to be spheres. Hence Climacus talks only of three spheres. The reason for this, as we shall see, is that irony and humor are not *universal* existential possibilities, as are the aesthetic, ethical, and religious spheres, which are essentially realizable by all human beings. Irony and humor presuppose a specific level of intellectual and cultural development.

2. Contradiction and Negativity in Life

The key concept in Climacus' explanation of irony and humor is the concept of "contradiction." Leaving aside irony for the moment, let us examine his analysis of humor. Humor is the sphere of existence that "has the comical *within* itself" (VII, 455; p. 465). The comical is in turn defined, along with the tragic, in terms of "the contradiction." "The tragic and the comic are the same, insofar as both are contradiction; but *the tragic is the suffering contradiction, the comical the painless contradiction*" (VII, 447; p. 459). What follows is a long footnote in which Climacus presents a potpourri of examples designated to show that what people commonly regard as comical situations do indeed contain a "contradiction" in which "one is justified in overlooking the pain, because it is inessential" (VII, 447n, p. 459n).

A look at some of these illustrations of the comical gives some idea of what Climacus means by "contradiction." The situation of a woman who seeks permission to establish herself as a public prostitute is said to be comical, whether she is refused or permitted. If she is refused, the case is comical because "one thinks correctly that it is difficult to become something respectable, . . . but to be refused permission to become something contemptible, is a contradiction." If on the other hand she is given permission there is also a contradiction between the "impotence and power" of the legal authority. This authority has the power to give permission but yet cannot make the activity permissible (presumably in a moral sense) (VII, 448-449n; p. 460n). A baker who turns away a poor person without giving him anything by explaining that he cannot give to everybody — "there was another here recently who did not get anything either" — is comical since "he seems to reach the sum and total — all by subtraction" (VII, 448n; p. 460n). A caricature is said to be comical because of the contradiction between likeness and unlikeness that it contains.

In some of these cases, such as the prostitute, if the example were taken from real life, one might very well find the situation tragic rather than comical. This is not really surprising, however, since he claims that the very same circumstance can be both tragic and funny. Whether it is funny or tragic depends on our perspective and degree of involvement, which in turn determines whether we can "look away from the pain" that the situation contains. Almost everyone has experienced this at some time. The public embarrassment at inadvertently going into a restroom of the opposite sex, so painful at the time, can seem hilarious to oneself and others when recollected at leisure. When the event is past, the pain can safely be "looked away from."

For these examples it should be plain that Climacus is not talking about a logical contradiction when he speaks of contradiction. The contradictions he focuses on are not logical but existential. He is discussing the incongruity, tension, or contrast between one state of affairs and another. In the case of the prostitute there is a tension between the ordinary concept of legal permission as a certification of respectability and the actual case. In the case of the baker the individual cites his inability to give to everyone as a reason for failing to give to anyone, which may seem comical in itself, and then cites his failure to give to another person as support, a case of nonactivity that existentially runs counter to the energetic striving implied by not being able to give to *everybody*. As other examples of "contradiction" Climacus cites the incongruity between a facial gesture and a hand movement, between a person's future expectations and reality, or between the mixture in an account of fantasy and realism. In every case the contradiction is between clashing or incongruous realities. Understanding this use of "contradiction" is crucial, not only to understand irony and humor, but also to grasp later on what Climacus means by the "contradiction" that the religious "absolute paradox" contains.

If humor is grounded in such contradictions, it is not surprising that Climacus regards humor as more than an insignificant diversion of human life. For "wherever there is life there is contradiction" (VII, 447; p. 459), and existence itself is said by Climacus to be a contradiction in just this sense.

> Existence itself. . .is a striving, and is just as pathetic [in the sense of being pathos-filled] as comical; pathetic, because the striving is infinite, or directed toward the infinite, is infinitizing, which is the highest pathos; comical, because the striving is a self-contradiction (VII, 72; p. 84).

Existence is for Climacus, as we have noted countless times, a synthesis of contrasting or opposing elements. But since existence is never finished so long as one is existing, the synthesis always remains incomplete, hence can equally well be described as (in his sense) a contradiction. The failure to fully realize the ideal elements is the contradiction between actuality and ideality. As a result Climacus is continually led to emphasize the significance of the negative in human life as the condition for existential growth. For only the negation of the established order makes change possible. As we shall see, *irony and humor are at bottom seen by Climacus as forms of this existential negativity, forms which make possible the development and growth of the individual.*

The contradiction that lies at the heart of irony and humor when these are regarded as existential spheres is the fundamental contradiction within existence itself. "What lies at the basis of both the comic and the pathetic in this connection is the misrelationship: the contradiction between the infinite and the finite, the eternal and that which becomes" (VII, 70; pp. 82-83). This is the tension between the infinite, eternal, and absolute ideals that a person ought to realize and the finite, temporal, and relative conditions she actually lives in. Irony and humor as absolute qualities represent a fundamental "seeing through" or negation of the relative and temporal, which is necessary if the eternal and absolute are to be discovered. The difference between irony and humor depends upon the existential depth with which the individual apprehends the eternal and her own situation with respect to the finite.

The same type of negativity that is present in irony and humor as existential life-possibilities is present in ordinary irony and humor. This ordinary irony and humor is irony and humor as an element or component in existence rather than as a sphere or zone of existence. Its distinguishing mark is relativity. A man who from a superior position looks ironically on others, such as a city sophisticate who ironically undermines the values held dear by a group of uneducated rurals, is engaged in negating what he regards as lower on the basis of his presumed higher position. All such irony Climacus designates as relative irony, which everyone has a little of, since everyone finds someone to feel superior to. This relative irony, since it is possessed by everyone, is not the distinguishing mark of Climacus' ironist, who does not merely dissolve one relativity on the basis of a higher relativity, but dissolves "every relativity" through his discovery of the absolute (VII, 436-437; pp. 448-449). It is this sort of absolute quality that demarcates the life of the ironist or humorist in Climacus' special sense of the term. This sort of absolute irony is only legitimate when the individual preserves a relation to the eternal, which provides the higher viewpoint that justifies the negativity. The individual who lacks the positive relation to the eternal but nevertheless turns against the relative values of life is described as in despair, and his activity leads to nihilism. It is ironical that much of what is described as existentialism fits this category and certainly would have been so regarded by Climacus.

3. *Culture and Reflection: Is the Theory of Existence-Spheres Universal or Applicable Only to an Elite?*·

One of the characteristics of irony and humor is that they presuppose a certain level of intellectual development on the part of an individual. For example, Climacus says that irony is the union of ethical passion. . . and of culture (*Dannelse*) (VII, 437; p. 449). With respect to humor the same type of relation holds. Climacus distinguishes between a simple religious individual who does what he does directly and a simple, educated religious individual who can only accomplish via humor what the simple individual does directly (VII, 149; p. 159). It is noteworthy that on this point Climacus' views seem to be in harmony with Kierkegaard himself, who wrote so much about irony, beginning with his doctoral dissertation. In the *Point of View for My Work as an Author* Kierkegaard says that irony presupposes "a very specific degree of intellectual culture, such as is very rare in any generation" (XIII, 550; p. 54).

The difficulty that this raises appears when irony and humor are brought into connection with the spheres of existence. Since irony and humor are the transition zones between the spheres, does this imply that the process of existential development Climacus sketches is only relevant to cultured, educated people? The answer to this question gives us some important insights into the meaning and value of the spheres.

Climacus certainly regards the aesthetic, ethical, and religious spheres as universal possibilities, which do not presuppose any particular degree of intellectual gifts or development. This is the main thrust of his humanistic demand that the ethical and religious be equally attainable by all men. The most insignificant human being is capable of forming a resolution before God, which is an act the mightiest ruler of a nation cannot surpass. In speaking of the religious person, though Climacus restricts humor to the sophisticated person, he just as plainly asserts the existence of a simple religiousness. The more knowledgeable religious individual has no advantage over the simple believer; if anything, it is the other way around. The same theme occurs frequently in comparing the "simple man" with the simple, wise man. The wise man "feels himself gripped by a profound humanity, which reconciles him with the whole of life" (VII, 132; p. 143). This humanity is grounded in his understanding of his equality with the simple man:

> The difference between the wise man and the simplest human being is merely this vanishing little distinction, that the *simple man knows the essential*, the wise man little by little comes to *know that* he

> knows it, or comes to *know that* he does not know it. But what they
> both know is the same (VII, 132; p. 143).

If the spheres of existence are thus universally achievable, why are irony and humor, which are not, regarded as boundary zones of the spheres? The answer is that there are two ways of realizing oneself. The ethical and religious passion that makes a human being a self is achievable by the simple person in a direct or straightforward way. There are also people, however, who because of talent and education become intellectually reflective about life to a special degree. Climacus believes that these people have essentially the same task as the simple and that they have no real advantage over the simple in carrying out that task. But the way they accomplish the task is different. It is this latter group for whom irony and humor form transition zones in their existential development. And since it is this group for whom Climacus is writing, it is natural for him to include irony and humor in his account of the spheres, without thereby making them spheres in their own right.

The distinction between these two classes of people is not a sharp one, and probably in our day of practically universal education it has to a certain extent been erased, at least in the economically advanced countries. But one can still recognize a difference between the factory worker or farm laborer who lives his life on the basis of values and beliefs that are firmly rooted in his personality but who can perhaps not give a clear intellectual account of them, and the sophisticated intellectual who has read Hume and Kant, doubts the existence of God, and wonders whether all moral values are the product of cultural conditioning. Climacus is not implying that the simple person is totally unreflective or unconscious about his beliefs. The difference is not between a person who thinks and one who does not. What distinguishes the intellectual is the primacy given to thought in his life, which leads to the danger that critical thought will paralyze his practical life or even that thought will become a substitute for living.

Climacus is not, however, demeaning the intellectual life. The cultured individual who shows due respect for the simple ethical and religious truths that compose the "universal human" finds genuine value in his reflective efforts. "When he [the wise man] enthusiastically honors this [the simple] as the highest, it honors him in return, for it is like it becomes something different for him, despite remaining the same" (VII, 132; p. 143).[1]

The connection between irony and humor and reflection allows us to get a sharper understanding of these concepts. *Irony and humor are boundary zones in which the individual has acquired an intellectual understanding of a truth that he has not yet existentially realized.* This understanding is sufficient to undermine the relativities of the individual's past and present existence, but it does not in itself make an existential advance to the next sphere a reality. Being essentially reflective, humor and irony are only achievable by reflective individuals. The intellectual understanding that is their content makes *possible* the existential jump to a higher sphere. But since there is always a gap between thought and action, it follows that the possession of such an understanding by no means guarantees that the individual's intellectual understanding will become concretized in her life. Hence irony and humor are not only transition points, but existential zones in their own right, the sphere of a cultured individual whose understanding is more advanced than her existence.

4. *Irony*

Irony is the boundary zone between the aesthetic and the ethical spheres. The intellectual understanding that makes irony possible is therefore ethical understanding. Irony is the attitude of the individual who has hitherto lived only for the relative but has discovered the infinite ethical demand to become a self. "Irony arises by constantly placing the details of the finite together with the infinite ethical demand and letting the contradiction come into existence" (VII, 436; p. 448).

Generally people simply accept initially the relativities of life, the values handed to them by culture, in an unthinking and automatic way. When the reflective adolescent begins to question the established order and arrive at values that are "true for him," he is close to being an ironist. His critical reflection, as it were, destroys or negates the former certainties of his life and thereby opens up the possibility of a higher mode of existence. Whether such an individual actually becomes an ironist in Climacus' sense depends upon two conditions. First, he must not simply unreflectively replace the values of one social group with those of another. The individual who has reached a more sophisticated cultural level and, as part of a new avant-garde stratum of society, looks with contempt on his old "middle-class" values is merely what Climacus calls a relative ironist. His ironical attitude toward his former values is itself ironical since he is essentially the same as he was then, a creature who simply goes along with "the crowd." The individual's irony must apply to all such relative values.

The second condition for true irony is that the irony must be based on a positive relation to the absolute, eternal values that man can discover. It is possible for the individual to discover his superiority as the individual over the relative cultural patterns handed down to him, which is at bottom the discovery of man's eternal character and destiny, and then to misuse this self-understanding. The individual can assume a purely negative role with no positive standpoint to justify the critical "shaking of the foundations." In this case the individual's spiritual development turns in the direction of what Climacus calls "the demonic," and the irony becomes nihilism.

Since the ironist has this positive relation to the eternal, he is very close to being an ethicist himself. He understands the absolute obligation of the individual to become a self. In fact, the ethical individual's life contains irony, which he employs as his "incognito." (More about that later.) But the ironist in the final analysis fails to act on the basis of his understanding; he does not inwardly commit himself by identifying with the task that he intellectually understands to be necessary (VII, 437; p. 449). Irony is "an existential determination." But it is an existential form in which the individual's existence is bound up with his reflective *understanding*. That understanding enables the individual to negate the previous order but does not itself realize a higher order. One can see why irony (and humor) are said to be boundaries, since in a real sense they are decision points. The ironist cannot return to his "innocent" immediacy; if he advances, he must go on either to the ethical or the demonic.

Socrates is a key figure in Climacus' account of irony, though Socrates is portrayed not merely as an ironist but as an ethicist using irony as his incognito (VII, 437; p. 449). Socrates seems to represent to the history of the race the breakthrough to individuality that we earlier described as a phenomenon in the individual's life, who in that way has to repeat the history of the race. Socrates "saw through" the relativities of his culture. His critical negativity is expressed in his questioning his supposedly wise contemporaries. The justification for Socrates' ironical attack on the establishment is his discovery of the eternal ethical truth that is in every man's possession. This discovery is properly expressed through the Socratic practice of the maieutic method.

Socrates, however, is not only an ironist but an ethicist. From him we therefore discover the role of irony in the ethical life, for irony is the ethicist's "incognito," or outward disguise. Outwardly Socrates appears to be an ironist, and the external observer cannot detect the difference. The reason the ethicist must use irony as his incognito is that it preserves his inwardness and isolation, ensuring that he seriously is attempting to become a self and not merely to appear to be a self in other people's eyes. He also thereby frees other people from dependent relationships that would hinder their own spiritual development. And finally the ethicist understands that he can never adequately express his ethical commitment in the relativities of the external life. He does attempt to do this; it is a misunderstanding to see the ethical life as a withdrawal from the world. The ethicist who has found his eternal self attempts to express his commitment in his actual life. But he sees that he may outwardly resemble someone from whom he may be radically different. There is a discrepancy between his inner life and his outer life. His life always contains more than can be seen, and he therefore views his outward efforts ironically.

> But why does the ethicist use irony as his incognito? Because he grasps the contradiction between the way in which he exists in his most inward being, and his inability to express it in his outwardness. For the ethicist indeed becomes revealed, insofar as he empties himself into the factual tasks of actuality; but the immediate individual does that too, and what makes him an ethicist is the movement by which he sets his outward life inwardly together with the infinite requirement of the ethical and this can not be seen directly (VII, 438-439; p. 450).

The ethicist, like the immediate man, may be a devoted father, citizen, and loyal worker. But for him these tasks are concrete expressions of his absolute commitment to the demands of eternity. However, there is an incommensurability between these demands and his finite achievements. Because of this the ethicist never allows his life to be fully identified with the outward tasks. He can never take his outward accomplishments as proof of his ethical character, as perhaps an observer might be tempted to do. Therefore, in the midst of the most strenuous activity he maintains a detached attitude toward the significance of these achievements.

Irony is, like the ethical itself, not destroyed but preserved as the individual progresses existentially. Hence Climacus, who describes himself as a humorist, employs irony in abundance and for much the same reasons as Socrates. He continually undermines the securities of bourgeois complacency (*spidsborgerlighed*), at the same time preserving his independence and regarding his own activity with a detached eye. Thus in his writings the security of the "alderman" who wishes to be a "crack rifle shot," the social activist who wishes to help mankind by the construction of railroads, and the man of learning who has discovered the marvels of astronomy and veterinary science are all viewed from the perspective of what is eternally significant, and thereby ironically undermined, insofar as such things claim to be the true content of an individual's life.

Irony represents the discovery of the self as distinct from a cultural ensemble. It therefore is described as separative; it is what separates what is distinctively "me" from what is not, the negation on the part of the individual of the cultural order so that the cultural order can become truly the possession of the individual. We can therefore understand Climacus' remark that irony is "teasing" and "divisive," in contrast to humor, which is "sympathetic" and "profound" (481-482n; pp. 490-491n).

Climacus says that irony and humor are only "relatively" different. They both are grounded in the final analysis in "recollection." "What is essential for irony: recollection's escape from temporality into the eternal, is again the essential for humor" (VII, 231; p. 242). The Platonic concept of recollection is used by Climacus to designate any view whereby man is regarded as immanently possessing a consciousness of the eternal. Since irony involves such a consciousness in the form of the individual's ethical consciousness, it falls within the category of immanence. The term "recollection" is particularly suited for irony and humor because it connotes man's ability to *intellectually* grasp the eternal. This intellectual consciousness provides a basis for "retirement out of the temporal." Instead of synthesizing the temporal and the eternal by allowing the eternal to transform the temporal, the individual rests in his intellectual consciousness of the eternal. He regards the eternal not as something to be achieved in time but as a secure possession. This is an apt description, not of the ethicist, but of the ironist, who understands what the ethicist understands but retreats from the task of expressing this understanding in existence. As we shall see, this concept of recollection is even more significant in understanding the humorist.

5. Rethinking the Existence-Spheres: Where to Place Humor in Relation to Religiousness

Before considering the specific character of humor, we must face one interpretive difficulty. On the surface, at least, it appears that Climacus could not quite make up his mind about the place of humor in his schema of existence spheres. The difficulty concerns the relationship of humor to immanent religiousness, "religiousness A." At times Climacus seems to make humor the stage that precedes religiousness A and that properly forms a boundary between the ethical and religious life. At other times, however, he seems to place humor beyond religiousness A as a transition zone between immanence, whose highest expression is religiousness A, and transcendence, the sort of religiousness exemplified by Christianity.

For example, Climacus says rather clearly in the middle of the

Postscript that humor is the boundary of Christianity (VII, 230-231; pp. 242-243). Though humor, lying within the region of immanence, is essentially different from Christianity, it can nonetheless acquire a *knowledge* of the Christian ideas.

> It [humor] can come deceptively close to what is Christian; but where decisiveness takes hold [*fanger*]; there where existence captures [*fanger*] the exister like a card already played [*ligesom Bordet fanger*],[2] so that he must remain in existence; while the bridge of immanence and recollection is burned behind him; . . .there humor does not follow (VII, 231; p. 243).

As in the relation between irony and ethical truth, humor is here represented as an intellectual understanding of Christian truth that has not been existentially realized by the individual. As such, humor "becomes the last *terminus a quo* in relation to determining what is Christian" (VII, 231; p. 243). A little later he says that humor is "the conclusion of the immanent within the immanent" and is therefore "the last stage in existential inwardness before faith" (VII, 249; p. 259).

However, later in the *Postscript*, in connection with the discussion of religiousness in general, humor seems to occupy a different place. The inward religiousness that focuses on suffering and guilt, which itself is clearly asserted to fall within the province of immanence, is described as higher than humor. Here humor is described as the boundary between the ethical and the religious life in the immanent sense (religiousness A).

The stages are ranked in this connection by Climacus according to their relation to "the contradiction" between the infinite and the finite which makes up the comical element in existence. The aesthetic or immediate consciousness "has the comical outside itself." This means that the aesthete is himself comical but is not conscious of this; hence the comical is "outside" his consciousness. The ironist and the ethicist both have the comical *within* themselves, though the ethicist does not dwell on this. Since he is an exister, he has no time for such contemplation, hence "only sees the comical as constantly vanishing." Humor also has the comical within itself and is "justified against everything which is not religiousness." The religious individual is higher still; by virtue of the passion in his God-relationship he is inaccessible to comic apprehension. Religiousness has the comical "within it as something lower," and thus it is "by means of the comical secured against the comical" (VII, 454-455; pp. 464-465).

The idea behind this ranking is that something is only legitimately comic for the one who has a higher perspective. (The same is true for irony.) The individual who exists in a contradiction does not experience it as comic but as tragic, which is why so many things appear funny only in retrospect. Since humor is "the painless contradiction," it must know a "way out." Therefore the individual who has transcended a contradiction alone has the right to smile at it.

It is on this basis that the immanent religious sphere is ranked higher than the humorous. The religious individual, in his passionate God-relationship, is living out contradictions the humorous man has never touched on, much less resolved. The immanent religious individual himself knows "no way out." His suffering and guilt are his ties to his eternal happiness, and he knows of no higher perspective from which to smile at those contradictions:

> If one were to say repentance is a contradiction, *ergo* it is comical, one would immediately see that this is nonsense. Repentance lies in the ethico-religious sphere, and therefore is so placed that it has only one higher sphere, namely, the religious in the strictest sense. But it was not this [strict religiousness] it was proposed to make use of in order to make repentance ridiculous; *ergo* it must have been something lower, in which case the comical is unjustified (VII, 453; p. 463).

Here humor seems to fall prior to religiousness A, which is clearly distinguished from religiousness B.

So where does humor really fall within the spheres? Is it the last stage of immanence, the boundary between immanence and transcendent religiousness? Or is it a stage within immanence, the boundary between the ethical life and the immanent religious life? There are several possible ways of resolving this difficulty.

First, one might simply conclude that Climacus is inconsistent, either unintentionally or intentionally. It seems highly unlikely that the first could be the case, since the contradiction is so obvious and since it concerns the fundamental schema that Climacus constantly relies on throughout the book. Some would no doubt take the contradiction as intentional, perhaps a trap laid for those who wish to take the book too seriously, a proof that Climacus, as a humorist, has no serious purpose. It seems clear to me, however, that Climacus would have regarded such a comment with contempt and that sort of "humor" as scarcely worthy of the name. Some of Climacus' most biting attacks focus on inconsistency, the inability of an individual to think a thought "whole" and to its most extreme conclusions. Sloppy, muddled thinking is hardly his answer to his opponents; still less does he repudiate thought altogether. The humorist, on the contrary, is first and last a type of thinker whose home is "the metaphysical sphere."

The other possible ways of resolving this difficulty require a rethinking of the existence-spheres themselves. One might take a clue from the fact that Climacus sometimes refers to immanent religiousness as ethical religiousness and understand the ethical stage as *including* religiousness A. If this is right, then one could understand "the religious sphere" as referring exclusively to religiousness B. This would entail that humor could be both the boundary between the ethical and the religious spheres and at the same time the last sphere prior to faith, since "faith," or the transcendent religiousness, would be identical with the religious sphere. This view is supported by the fact that the ethical life and the immanent kind of religiousness both lie within immanence, and the fact that immanent religion is, as we have seen, undeniably ethical in character. It also makes sense of Climacus' repeated assertions that there are only three spheres, since if immanent religion forms a sphere of its own, there would seem to be four.

There are, however, also rather serious objections to such a view. For one thing it is still inconsistent with Climacus' clear statement that humor falls below the *immanent* kind of religiousness. Making religiousness A an element in the ethical sphere also does not fit the classification of the stages Climacus gives, where he mentions the ethical stage as lower than humor, and "the religiousness of hidden inwardness" as higher, and also mentions a "strict kind of religiousness" that is higher yet (VII, 453-455; pp. 463-465). In any case the detailed elaboration of religiousness A is sufficient to make clear that though ethical, this form of religiousness is also distinctively religious and irreducible to the ethical life.

Yet a third way of resolving the problem of the position of humor opens up if we make religiousness A an element of religiousness B instead of "lowering" it to the ethical sphere. If religiousness A is a part of transcendent religion, then it could be higher than humor, and yet humor would still be "the last stage prior to faith." Again, humor could also legitimately be said to be the boundary between the ethical and the religious spheres, and again the four spheres would be reduced to three.

In support of this reading one could cite the fact that the whole discussion of religiousness A in the *Postscript* falls under the section "The Problem Itself," the problem being the problem of Christianity: "The Individual's Eternal Happiness Is Decided in Time Through the Relationship to Something Historical. . . " (VII, 333; p. 345). The problem of Christianity is here described as "pathetic-dialectic." The pathetic or pathos-filled element is treated first and separately, and this becomes what Climacus calls religiousness A. But he begs the reader not to forget that the difficulty of the problem lies ultimately in putting the two elements together (VII, 334; p. 346); that is, the religious passion described as religiousness A must be put together with the dialectical elements described as B, so as to form a new pathos (VII, 485; p. 493).

However, against this inclusion of religiousness A with B there are also some telling points. First, there are the many clear assertions by Climacus that religiousness A falls within the region of immanence.[3] And Climacus asserts just as clearly that religiousness A is not merely an aspect of B, but a religious life that can be lived in itself.

> Of religiousness A one may say that, even if it had not been in paganism, it could have been because it has only human nature in general as its presupposition (VII, 488; p. 496).

> Religiousness A can exist in paganism, and in Christianity it can be everyone's religiousness who is not decisively Christian, whether he be baptized or not (VII, 486; p. 495).

What one would like to do here is accept both of these two solutions (putting religiousness A with the ethical or with religiousness B) as good answers to the problem in certain contexts without requiring us to commit ourselves to either for all contexts. But how can we do this?

My conclusion is that this problem can only be resolved if we reconceive Climacus' view of the existence spheres. It is very tempting —almost irresistible, in fact — to read Climacus as if he were presenting a sort of "system," albeit an existential one, though those who treat Climacus in this way are usually careful to insist that Climacus' thought does not form a system. But he really is not giving us a system, even an existential one, unless we mean by "system" a set of coherent concepts that can be fruitfully employed in understanding existence. In any case the theory of existence-spheres or stages should not be treated as a system. By that I mean that it should not be treated as a fixed schema, an arrangement of positions that mutually exclude each other and through which the individual must progress in lockstep fashion. The spheres are rather to be understood as existential possibilities that can be helpfully reflected on with the help of certain defining categories. But being *existential* possibilities they are related in many complicated ways that any conceptual schema necessarily fails to do justice to.

Therefore it seems to me to be perfectly legitimate and in no way inconsistent to rethink and reclassify the spheres when different contexts and problems make it appropriate to do so. The ethical and immanent religious spheres have many links. We have seen how the religious life begins in and always preserves a relation to the ethical life. And even though the religious individual no longer understands the project of becoming a self to be possible through ethical striving (action and victory), but only sees it as achievable through religious suffering and guilt, there is still a similarity to the ethical life. Though the immanent religious person sees her transformation as effected by self-negation rather than self-affirmation, she still believes that she can *herself* realize this process of self-negation via her own religious consciousness and striving. This similarity Climacus highlights by saying that both the ethical life and the religious life are forms of immanence. At times, therefore, Climacus thinks of the immanent religious life as continuous with, or even as a part of, the ethical life. In these cases it is natural for him to situate humor, the boundary between the ethical and religious life, as the final stage prior to faith, or transcendent religiousness, which is in this case identified with the religious life.

In other contexts it is just as natural for Climacus to emphasize the connection between religiousness A and religiousness B. For although religiousness A is capable of an independent existence, it is also clear that it is a component, transfigured as are all the lower existential passions when they are taken up in something higher, of religiousness B.

> Religiousness A must first be present in the individual before there can be talk about becoming aware of the dialectical B. . . .One will therefore see how foolish it is when a man without pathos wants to relate himself to the Christian; for before there can be any talk at all of merely being in the situation for becoming aware of it, one must first exist in religiousness A (VII, 486; pp. 494-495).

Religiousness A is the pathetic element, and when "mixed with the dialectic to produce a new pathos," it produces Christianity.

It is therefore perfectly legitimate in certain contexts to emphasize the connection between religiousness A and religiousness B and to speak of the religious life simply as a unity. Again this makes humor the boundary between the ethical and the religious and at the same time the last stage prior to faith.

It may still appear that humor is being placed in two different spots in relation to religiousness A, both before and after, depending upon whether religiousness A is grouped with the ethical (which is legitimate when such a religious life is lived in its own right as within immanence) or with religiousness B (which is also legitimate when such religious passion is an element in the life of faith). This appearance is correct but not inconsistent. For humor is not a "slot" in a lock step of existential positions, but an existential possibility with a "range." Climacus says expressly that "the humoristic is very encompassing, precisely as constituting the boundary-zone of the religious" (VII, 392; p. 403).

What he means by this is very important. Humor is not merely a point that a person transcends when he "moves on" to the religious life. As the boundary of the religious life it is "very encompassing." This means that humor as an existential possibility is very close to the religious life. It is the boundary or limit of the religious life *throughout* the compass of the religious in the sense that it is always the jumping-off point for religious striving and also always remains present as the "escape" for the individual who finds the religious life too strenuous. For humor is simply the situation of the individual who understands religious truth but fails to passionately exist in that truth. As such, humor and the religious are really coextensive, mutually limiting concepts, since the religious person can always fail to existentially realize the truth he understands. Therefore it is perfectly proper to discover humor both at the beginning *and* at the end of religiousness A. It attaches itself to the religious life as a whole.

6. *Humor as Recollection and "Revoking"; Climacus as Humorist*

In actual life humor not only accompanies the religious life, it is mixed with it. Actual human beings never represent "pure" types, and it is in fact impossible to conceive of an individual who could continuously achieve and maintain the religious passions of suffering and guilt described by Climacus as true religiousness. Hence humor actually becomes an element in the religious life. Humor represents the moment in the religious life in which the individual takes refuge in an "eternal consciousness." Both humor and religiousness rest in recollection, which is the human capacity to know the eternal within the self. Religiously this consciousness of the eternal is expressed through action; humor seeks repose in the recollection itself.

What this means concretely is that humor is the "out" that the individual follows when she no longer can endure the existential contradictions of the religious life. "The totality of guilt-consciousness in the single individual is the religious. Humor reflects on this, but recalls[4] it again" (VII, 483; p. 492).

Climacus calls the highest form of religiousness "an eternal recollection of guilt which accepts no satisfaction." He says, however, that this eternal recollection has its being in an "underlying immanence" which contains an "obscurely sensed possibility" that there is such a satisfaction (VII, 472; p.

481). He later says that the eternal recollection of guilt is "the mark indicative of the relationship to an eternal happiness," a mark that is "enough to prevent the individual from leaping aside to despair" (VII, 484; pp. 492-493). In other words, the only way man can endure the burden of guilt is by means of the reflection that it is through bearing this burden that he can achieve his eternal happiness. The thought of an individual earning an eternal happiness is ultimately comic, since there is always an incommensurability between one's temporal efforts and the infinite goal. This contradiction is ultimately the same for all, because it is qualitative in nature, and the quantitative differences between one person's efforts and another's are therefore insignificant. The *pure* humorist recognizes this comical contradiction and "gives up," choosing instead to rest on his recollection of the eternal, which is at bottom to presuppose that all people possess the eternal already; it is not to be acquired in time. The religious individual, however, in the grip of his passion is always "departing from the comic" to energetically attempt to realize the eternal.

> The hidden inwardness of religiousness A must also discover the comic, not that the religious man is thereby different from all others, but in order that he, though most heavily burdened by bearing the eternal recollection of guilt, is like all others. He discovers the comic, but because he in his eternal recollection constantly relates himself to an eternal happiness, the comic is constantly disappearing (VII, 484; p. 493).

It is this connection between religiousness A and humor that makes intelligible Climacus' claim that his own existence is "within the boundary of religiousness A" (VII, 486; p. 495). Since he has told us time and time again that his own mode of existence is that of a humorist, this can only mean that humor is not only the boundary of religiousness, but can be a constituent of it.

This humor that is an element in the religious life is further illumined by looking at the "pure" humorist whom Climacus sketches, who is *not* a religious individual. The humorist's view of life is said to be "the backward perspective" (VII, 525; p. 533). "To exist is like walking down a road," but the remarkable thing about it from the humorist's perspective is that "the goal lies behind" (VII, 390-391; p. 402).

For Climacus this is characteristic of contemplative or detached reflection, since existence has a forward direction but understanding has a "backward" direction. The humorist's reflection takes him "out of time into eternity," since his life-view presupposes eternity as an eternal possession, not something to be won or lost in time. Because of this "backward," reflective quality the humorist is continually led back to childhood, which becomes a symbol of the innocence that is man's possession at bottom (VII, 524-525; pp. 532-533). The humorist sees the contradiction is not tragic but humorous. He knows "the way out." In fact, the whole business of existing is a jest, something to smile over, since it has no *eternal* significance. The humorist's smile is, however, "sympathetic." His humor is not teasing and divisive, as is irony, but reunites him with mankind, since all human beings in the final analysis "get equally far" (VII, 391; p. 403). Therefore, the humorist, though he strives as energetically as anyone else, always "recalls" his efforts.

All his temporal efforts in the final analysis must be treated as a jest, and this "lack of seriousness" is the "revocation." We must also note that the humorist's life is grounded in recollection, and so he is primarily a thinker of whom it can quite properly be said that he has his home in the "metaphysical" (VII, 102; p. 112).

All of these characteristics are well illustrated by Climacus himself. By understanding his concept of humor one gets a much better understanding of Climacus, and in the same way a close study of Climacus as an author and exister helps to clarify the concept of humor employed. For example, at the end of *Postscript* Climacus gives his own "recall" or "revocation."

> As is Catholic books, especially those of an earlier age, one finds at the end of the book a note which informs the reader that everything is to be understood in agreement with the teaching of the holy, universal mother-church — so what I write contains also a piece of information to the effect that everything is so to be understood in such a way as to be recalled [*tilbagekaldt*], the book has not only a Conclusion but in the bargain a recall [*Tilbagekaldelse*] (VII, 539; p. 547).

This "recall" not only secures the reader's independence; it is required if Climacus is to be consistent to his character. The humorist always recalls or revokes. Since the humorist views all human striving as a jest and eternity as the secure possession man has "behind" him, it would be a contradiction for Climacus to write a book in a serious tone, as if he believed his work could be decisive for anyone's eternal happiness. Hence both the *Fragments* and *Postscript* take on their humoristic flavor. Climacus says of himself frequently that he "lacks seriousness," and to make this lack obvious he even relates the distressingly frivolous events that precipitated his authorship. Of course Climacus' own attitude toward his work is in no way binding on his readers, who presumably will approach the book from their own existential perspectives. Climacus' "recall" must be taken as expressing his own attitude toward the book, not as an "objective" judgment that the book contains no serious content. A humorist will therefore read the book in the same spirit as it was written, a religious individual rather differently.

Since the humorist is essentially a thinker, we can also understand why Climacus is the pseudonymous author Kierkegaard creates to do battle with that speculative Hegelian thought that had transgressed the proper boundaries of thought. Contrary to what many commentators say, Climacus is by no means opposed to thought. He is himself a speculative thinker, though one whose reflection has existential significance.

> Honor be to speculation, praise to everyone who in truth occupies himself with it. To deny the value of speculation. . . would in my eyes be to prostitute one's self, and would be especially miserable of one, the most of whose life, according to its poor opportunities, is consecrated to its service, especially miserable of one who admires the Greeks (VII, 42; p. 54).

It is precisely because Climacus is himself a humorist within the metaphysical sphere that he can critically attack the "pure" speculation that makes contemplative thought, not a significant and valuable element in existence, but existence itself. Climacus himself warns that one cannot straightforwardly attack the "objective" view of life from an ethical or religious point of view:

> By immediately beginning with ethical categories in opposition to the objective tendency, one does it an injustice, and fails to hit it solidly, because one has nothing in common with what is under attack. But by remaining in the metaphysical sphere, one can use the comical, which also lies in the metaphysical sphere, so as to catch up with such a transfigured professor (VII, 102; p. 112).

It is also Climacus' status as a humorist that enables him to write about Christianity. Humor can gain a *knowledge* of the Christian concepts without commitment, since Climacus affirms that it is one thing to know what Christianity is, another to know what it is to be a Christian (VII, 231, 322; pp. 243, 332). Therefore, Climacus can mediate the dispute between Hegelianism and Christianity with insight into both parties' perspectives, while retaining an independent point of view.

There is one more point about humor that must be noted. We have treated humor as the boundary of the religious life and as a transitory moment within the religious life. But Climacus says that humor serves one more religious function: It is the religious person's incognito, just as irony was the ethicist's incognito. The reason is that the true religious individual does not wish to appear outwardly better than other men. He feels compelled "to set up a screen between people and himself, in order to protect and insure the inwardness of his suffering and God-relationship" (VII, 440; p. 452). It is not that the religious individual is inactive in the world or that he, like the humorist, revokes the significance of this activity. But the significance of this activity is that it is done unto God; he therefore does not seek any worldly "profit" from his religiousness by posing as the "awakened" individual who "has God in his pocket" and wishes the world to notice him. The religious person therefore preserves the humoristic as his outward appearance. It is the proper form of humility in an individual who honestly recognizes the incommensurability between God's ideals and his own religious strivings, particularly insofar as those strivings become expressed in outward action. The religious person who wishes to please God might recognize, for example, an ethical obligation to help feed the hungry people of the world. Perhaps he fasts once a week or even ten times a week. But he is less than ideally religious if he himself cannot see how short of the ideals his actions fall, ludicrous if he tries to portray himself outwardly as mankind's great benefactor. Humor is the religious individual's protection against pride. It prevents the overestimation of a man's religiosity, both on the part of the religious individual himself and on the part of others.

[1] Omitted from Lowrie-Swenson translation.

[2] A card-playing expression that literally translates "like the table captures."

[3] See for example the "Comment" on VII, 488-489; pp. 497-498, and also the discussion of guilt at VII, 464; p. 474.

[4] The term "recall" here is *tilbagekalder*, which means literally "to call back," but could be translated "revoke."

Chapter XI

TRANSCENDENT RELIGION (1)
REASON AND THE PARADOX

1. *Climacus and Christianity: Existence-Communication*

As we have constantly stressed, Johannes Climacus' authorship is designed chiefly to clarify and illuminate the nature of Christianity and to mediate the dispute between Christianity and man's intellectual speculation. Climacus sees Christianity as an "existence-communication" and thinks the misunderstandings of it are caused by "forgetting what it means to exist." Thus he gives an extensive treatment of existence, chiefly ethical existence, and also an extensive treatment of the kind of religious existence that can develop out of man's ethical striving. We have examined this analysis of the ethical and religious life as it is "naturally" possible for man (the realm of "immanence"). Now we must consider Christianity itself, which Climacus analyzes as the religion of "transcendence."[1]

As a philosopher or humorist Climacus does not of course give us a picture of Christianity as it appears to the believer. This does not mean that what he says is false or misleading; only that it represents an intellectual outsider's point of view rather than a view that is permeated by Christian experience and commitment. Hence we can expect Climacus to give a rather bloodless and abstract description of Christianity, employing philosophical categories such as "transcendence," and "paradox." Climacus corresponds precisely to his own description of the humorist as the one who has gained a knowledge of the Christian concepts but is not himself a Christian.

One might think initially that in his description of transcendent religion Climacus is merely giving us an abstract philosophical outline of a type or species of religion, as he did in the case of religion A, and that the value of his description might be independent of whether it corresponds to any particular historical religion such as Christianity. At least this appears to be the case in the *Fragments*, where he attempts first to define immanence by taking Socrates' principle of recollection as starting point, then experimentally attempts to deduce an alternative to the Socratic view. This alternative "happens" to resemble Christianity. This first impression of the book is not completely correct, however, because it does not take full account of the ironical and humorous form of the book that constitutes Climacus' "recall." For the content of the deduced "hypothesis" includes the thesis that the hypothesis (that the God came into being in time so that men might gain an eternal happines in time) "could not have originated in any human heart,"[2] but could only have come from the God (IV, 271; p. 138). Hence, if the hypothesis were merely Climacus' invention, it would not truly differ from the Socratic view. Climacus himself is conscious that he is not really the author of his "hypothesis," and he even cites this fact as evidence that his hypothesis has been framed correctly and thus does represent a genuine alternative to the Socratic view (IV, 191; p. 27). He himself says that if he writes a sequel, he will give the problem its right name, which is of course Christianity. In our discussion of the *Fragments* we shall, without ignoring the hypothetical, experimental form of the book, take notice of the fact that the book is intended to illuminate the problems connected with Christianity.

In the *Postscript,* which is of course the half-promised "sequel," the pretense that Climacus is inventing a religion is dropped, and the problem is given its "historical costume" and specifically called Christianity. Even here, however, Climacus focuses on what he calls the dialectical aspect of Christianity, the intellectual elements in Christian belief. This does not mean that Climacus thinks that Christianity is a set of doctrines to be intellectually accepted. He understands quite clearly that Christianity is a way of existence grounded in a definite kind of passion. Christian beliefs are never regarded by Christians as *merely* propositions for assent; they are believed by acting on them. Nevertheless, Climacus understands that distinctively Christian mode of existence as stemming from (or rather, as we shall see, identical with) an affirmation of an equally distinctive intellectual content. Naturally he is as a thinker chiefly interested in that content, though as a subjective thinker he is equally interested in the existential implications of that content.

It is in this light that Climacus' thesis that Christianity is "not a doctrine" or "teaching" but an "existential communication" must be understood (VII, 328; p. 339). This statement has led to great misunderstanding, though Climacus anticipated this and attempted to avoid it with a footnote attached to this statement. In this note he explains that "it is one thing to be a philosophical doctrine which wants to be intellectually grasped and speculatively understood, and quite another thing to be a doctrine that wants to be realized in existence" (VII, 328-329n; p. 339n). Christianity is the latter sort of doctrine, but since the nineteenth century is so "dreadfully speculative," Climacus is afraid that if he uses the term "doctrine" at all, it will be understood in the first sense. Hence he coins a new term, "existential communication." He is very far from denying that Christianity has intellectual content; in fact, he conceives it as his specific task to describe that content accurately, which because of its nature he refers to as "the dialectical." This dialectical content is the "absolute paradox" that is "the specific thing in Christianity." Only this content must not be understood as a task for thought, as though Christianity were a doctrine in the first sense above instead of an existence communication, but as "relating itself to the pathetic as an incitement to new pathos" (VII, 488; pp. 496-497). In other words Christianity contains a definite intellectual content, but the significance of that content is that it makes possible a new passion which expresses itself in a new mode of existence.

Climacus' view here is illuminated by comparing it with a common understanding of Christianity that appears to be similar but is nevertheless somewhat different. It is fairly standard for a theologian to say that it is not enough merely to believe the Christian doctrines; the individual must act on what she believes. Or it is sometimes said that the Christian must not merely believe in an intellectual way; how she believes is what is important. Climacus is not happy with such formulations (VII, 529-532; pp. 537-539), not because he does not think Christian belief has any content, but because he wants to establish a closer connection between that content and existence. The above-mentioned views still make the connection between belief and action external, according to Climacus. First the individual believes; then she must act on her belief. She must believe and act, but the believing and the acting are distinct. Climacus understands Christian belief as not merely accompanied by action but as essentially expressing itself in action. Because of this he attempts to rethink the nature of that belief in such a way that it does not exclude belief as an intellectual act but does exclude even the possibility of belief being *only* an intellectual act. This conception of Christian belief is itself demanded by the specific nature of the content of Christian belief.[3] In this way the "existential appropriation" that is Christianity and the content of Christianity, which is the absolute paradox, can be seen to correspond exactly to each other (VII, 532; p. 540). Both the content of Christianity and the appropriation of Christianity become "specifically different" from everything else.

It is in fact this content that protects Christianity against all speculative attempts at understanding and explaining. It is the fact that Christianity is rooted in the absolute paradox that reveals that it is not to become an object of speculation, but a communication to exist in. The paradox marks the boundary of theoretical thought, which, like Kant's antimony of reason, serves as a hint that one must turn to the practical life of action.[4] It is also the fact that Christianity is rooted in the absolute paradox that entails its transcendent character as something "which did not originate in any human heart." The paradox guarantees God's transcendence. At the same time it preserves man's humanness. It saves human equality by reducing to insignificance the intellectual differences between individuals, and it preserves man's freedom by making the appropriation of Christianity a spiritual activity which is conditioned by one's own development of subjectivity. All of these protective functions of the paradox must be developed and explained. But first we must try to understand the concept itself.

2. Can Faith Be Rationally Examined?

Nothing could be clearer in Climacus' writings than that he regards Christianity, from the viewpoint of its intellectual content, as a paradox —in fact, "the absolute paradox." Another expression he employs as the equivalent is "the absurd."

> What is the absurd? The absurd is, that the eternal truth has come into existence in time, that God has come into existence, has come into existence exactly as an individual person does, not distinguishable from other people (VII, 176; p. 188).

From this it is clear that the paradox revolves around the traditional Christian claim that the man Jesus was the incarnation of God. It is very difficult, however, to gain a clear understanding of why Climacus insists on calling this event the absolute paradox or the absurd, and what he means by doing so.

One might think that Climacus is attempting to "protect" Christianity by removing it from the arena of rational examination. On this view reason has its boundaries, which it must accept, and Christianity lies outside those boundaries. Thus Climacus is regarded by many as an irrationalist. Many have gotten this message from Climacus and attributed it to Kierkegaard, including both those who approve and those who reject this separation. And we shall see that there is a sense in which this view is correct. Climacus does hold that reason has limits and that Christianity lies outside those limits. Such a view may indeed be irrationalistic. Whether it is depends on how the limits of reason are drawn. Are the limits rational limits, limits to which reason itself can assent? Or are they arbitrarily drawn limits, imposed in an irrational way, by fiat, or by an authority that refuses to submit to rational examination?

The latter would indeed be irrationalism. But Climacus very clearly rejects any suggestion that reason must bow before an authority it has no right to examine or that religious faith (specifically Christianity) is exempt from the process of rational examination, his name for which is "dialectics." He criticizes severely as superstition the notion that faith should not be reflected on. For example, he rejects the idea that either the Bible or the Church provides an authority that exempts Christianity from rational reflection.

> In general one can recognize the infinite reflection, in which alone subjectivity can become concerned about its eternal happiness, by one thing: it has the dialectical present in it everywhere. Let it be a word, a sentence, a book, a man, a society, or whatever you please, as soon as it is proposed as a boundary, a boundary which is not itself dialectical, it is superstition and narrowness of spirit. There is always such a need, both lazy and anxious at the same time, in a man to get something really firm, which can exclude the dialectical, but this is cowardice and deceitfulness toward the divine (VII, 24n; p. 35n).

It is quite true that for Climacus Christianity ultimately turns out to be a mystery that human reason cannot fathom. But he recognizes that this claim itself must be subjected to rational examination. The reason this is so is that "a negative answer [which in our case would be to the question of whether Christianity can be rationally understood], a 'no,' dialectically requires just as much development to be determined as a positive answer, and only children and naive people are satisfied with a *'das weiss man nicht'"* [nobody knows that] (VII, 139; p. 150).

This does not mean of course that a simple, unreflective person cannot be a Christian. It may in fact be easier for such a person to be a true Christian, which is after all a way of existing. But it does mean that the questions of a person who is reflectively developed are legitimate and that he has a right to seek answers for them. In fact Climacus is quite confident that if those critical questions are honestly answered, no harm is done to faith whatsoever. Though it is certain that faith is never the product of rational thinking, it is also just as certain that rational thought can safeguard the *possibility* of faith: "For dialectics is in its truth a willing, helpful power, which discovers and helps to find where the absolute object of faith and worship is. . ." (VII, 426; p. 438). Dialectics is not an enemy of the religious; "along with everything else" it "serves and obeys the religious" (VII, 455; p. 465).

3. Logic and the Paradox: Is the Paradox a Formal Contradiction?

To many thinkers it appears that if reason does examine faith, the judgment drawn will inevitably be that faith is reprehensible, at least as Climacus describes faith. For faith centers on the paradox, and the paradox is described as a "contradiction." If this contradiction is taken to be a logical one, then it seems that reason must repudiate faith, since the logical principle of noncontradiction is the basis for all meaningful discourse and reflection. Even the person who denies the principle that a proposition and its contradictory cannot both be true employs it if he wishes his denial to be a meaningful statement. A proposal to abrogate this principle can hardly be expected to obtain rational support.

But does Climacus mean a logical, formal contradiction when he calls the paradox a contradiction? Does he think that "God" and "man" are contradictory predicates so that to affirm that something is man entails that it is not God? In that case to affirm that Jesus was both man and God would be clearly contradictory in a logical sense, since it would amount to the affirmation that Jesus both was and was not God.

There are some things in Climacus' account to suggest that this interpretation is correct. At times Climacus calls the paradox not merely a contradiction but a "self-contradiction," a term often used informally today to refer to a proposition that either is or entails a formal contradiction. He also says in many passages that to believe the paradox one must believe *against* the understanding (VII, 495; 504). He describes the paradox as " absolute" and claims that no human being can show that the contradiction is merely apparent or illusory. These considerations do not definitely establish that the paradox is a logical contradiction, but they can all be construed as pointing in that direction.

Climacus also says that the paradox is "the historical reality which can only have become historical in opposition to its own nature" (VII, 504; p. 512). One might reasonably translate the term "nature" here (*væsen*) as "essence," and take the paradox to be the assertion that God, whose essence (logically defining properties) is to be one sort of being, has nonetheless become something logically inconsistent with his essence. This would seem to imply that God, who is necessarily A, has nevertheless become not-A without ceasing to be God. The properties that are most plausibly substitutable for A and not-A are eternity and temporality, respectively. Climacus consistently seems to hold that God is by definition eternal, and he speaks as if temporality and eternity are incompatible properties. On this reading the paradox involves the contradiction that something essentially eternal has nevertheless become temporal, without ceasing to be what it is.

Despite these arguments I think one can show that Climacus does not mean a formal contradiction when he asserts that the paradox is a contradiction. Climacus in no way wishes to repudiate the principles of formal logic, nor does he think that the Christian believer must do so. At the most Climacus is chargeable with employing a terminology that is somewhat sloppy and misleading, especially to twentieth-century readers, and even more especially to readers in England and the U.S.A. This terminological imprecision is grounded in the polemical character of the books. Since the works are specifically aimed at the Hegelians, particularly the Danish Hegelians, it is only to be expected that the linguistic usage is shaped by the customary meanings in the Hegelian world of discourse. This by no means implies that Climacus slavishly accepts his language from the Hegelians; he generally takes this language and gives it his own special sense. But some of the Hegelian meaning usually still remains.

One of the terms that Hegel used differently than do twentieth-century philosophers is precisely the term "contradiction." For Hegel any relation of opposition can be described as a contradiction. For example, nature is referred to as an "unresolved contradiction," since it is a union of contingency and necessity, irregularity and unpredictability in the midst of regularity and predictability.[5] Hegel may sometimes use the term "contradiction" to designate a formal contradiction (or, rather, what a contemporary philosopher would call a formal contradiction), but he does not use the term only or even mainly in this sense. Contradictions are the creative oppositions that when mediated by thought, lead to higher realizations of spirit. They are thus found in every element of the Hegelian system, including logic, nature, and spirit itself. We must note that for Hegel logic is not merely formal logic but the dialectical process of thought itself. Thus for him contradictions can be "logical" without being formal.

It is this Hegelian usage that I think explains Climacus' designation of the paradox as a contradiction. The Hegelians were familiar with the concept of a contradiction as positing a task for thought. For Hegel all such contradictions are relative and can and must be "mediated" or resolved. On this view no boundaries can be set to reason, and rational thought can penetrate reality completely. Climacus wishes to explain a contrasting view that posits boundaries or limits to rational understanding. In Hegelian language this is simply the concept of a contradiction that cannot be mediated or resolved by thought. Such a contradiction would be "absolute" in comparison to the relative oppositions that thought is capable of resolving. But the opposition that resists mediation is not necessarily a formal contradiction in the contemporary sense.

We have already seen in our examination of humor how Climacus employs this nonformal sense of contradiction.[6] Humor is the awareness of a fundamental contradiction between the requirements of the eternal and man's temporal striving, a contradiction that is "recalled" by the humorist. The humorist knows a "way out" — namely, the way of taking the whole of existence as a jest, since eternity is man's eternal possession. But the contradiction he recalls is not a formal contradiction but an incongruity.

It should also be clear, both from our earlier discussion of humor as well as from the discussion of existence, that time and eternity are not logical contradictories but existential contraries or incongruities. The union of time and eternity is the union of what is experienced as conflicting and hence tension-filled, but not what is logically perceived as impossible because meaningless. If the notion of the union of time and eternity were meaningless, then existence itself would be a meaningless impossibility, since existence is a synthesis of temporality and eternity.

Many arguments can be given that the contradiction Climacus sees in the paradox is not a formal contradiction. For one thing, Climacus himself distinguishes between a formal contradiction and the kind he wishes to analyze. In discussing the question of the case of the man who becomes a disciple of the God through an historical report, he distinguishes between the sort of contradiction the paradox contains and the sort of contradiction that would vitiate the whole discussion of Christianity by making meaningful thought about it impossible. On Climacus' view, as we shall see more fully in the next chapter, every disciple is a "first-hand disciple" who receives the condition of faith directly from God. An historical report by the first believers can be the means for this encounter with God, but the faith comes not from the historical witness but from God himself. If the individual's faith were derived from the historical witness, then that historical witness would then be the God for the believer, since the original believer would be the source of the life-changing transformation in the later believer. Such a supposition is rejected by Climacus as a "meaningless one," which is unthinkable in a *different* sense than when it was said of the paradox itself that it was unthinkable.

> Our hypothetical assumption of this fact [the Paradox] and the individual's relation to the God contains no self-contradiction, and thought is free to occupy itself with it as the strangest of all proposals. That meaningless consequence [that later believers could receive faith from earlier believers], on the contrary, contains a self-contradiction, which is not content with positing something unreasonable, which is our hypothetical assumption, but inside this unreasonableness it brings forth a self-contradiction, that the God is the God for the contemporary believer, but the contemporary the God for the third party (IV, 263-264; p. 127).

The self-contradiction spoken of here seems formal, since the contemporary believer is asserted both to be God (to the third party) and not to be God (in his relation to the God). Climacus sees clearly that this sort of contradiction means the end of all reasonable consideration of anything, and thus he tries to distinguish between this sort of "limit" to thought and the kind of boundary he wishes to draw in presenting Christianity.

I believe the same point is made in the *Postscript* where Climacus distinguishes between "nonsense" and "the incomprehensible" (VII, 495; p. 504). At first glance this passage might appear irrationalist, since Climacus here asserts that faith is "against the understanding" and rejects the idea that any human being possesses a "higher understanding" for which the paradox can be intellectually resolved. We will discuss later what Climacus means by believing "against the understanding." What is important in this connection is to notice that he draws a distinction between "nonsense" and the "incomprehensible:"

It is easy enough to leap away from the toilsome task of developing
and sharpening the understanding, and so get a louder hurrah, and
to defend oneself against every accusation with the remark that it is a
higher understanding. Therefore the believing Christian both has
and uses his understanding, respects the universal-human, does not
explain it as lack of understanding if somebody does not become a
Christian; but in relation to Christianity he believes against the
understanding and here also uses the understanding — to make
sure that he believes against the understanding. Nonsense he
therefore cannot believe against the understanding, which is perhaps
what one would fear, for precisely the understanding will see
through that it is nonsense and will prevent him from believing it; but
he uses the understanding so much that he by it becomes aware of
the incomprehensible, and then he relates himself to this, believing
against the understanding (VII, 495; p. 504).

This lengthy quote is not an easy one to interpret, but several points can
be gleaned. Reason, or the understanding (*Forstand*), plays a vital role in
the believer's life. First, it evaluates certain things as "nonsense" and
thereby prevents the believer from accepting them. Second, it helps the
believer clarify a distinct and peculiar concept (the incomprehensible),
which is not nonsense but which must be believed "against the understanding." It is without doubt this passage that Kierkegaard himself is
thinking of when he comments that he developed the idea in the *Postscript*
that "not every absurdity is the absurd or the paradox. The activity of
reason is in a negative manner to distinguish the paradox, but then no
more" (*J. and P.* I, 7).

This same distinction is illustrated by other Kierkegaardian pseudonyms,
most clearly by Anti-Climacus, who is closely related to Climacus, the
major difference being that Anti-Climacus looks at Christianity from an
ideal, committed stance. Anti-Climacus discusses Christ as the "sign of
contradiction," a concept that, like Climacus' paradox, makes it impossible
for the individual to arrive at faith merely through rational inquiry. Anti-
Climacus, in discussing signs of contradiction, distinguishes between two
different sorts of contradictions, just as Climacus distinguishes between
nonsense and the incomprehensible. All contradictory signs for Anti-
Climacus involve two elements. There is one type of contradiction (clearly
a formal, logical type) where "the two things cancel each other in such a
way as to make the expression nothing" (XII, 117; pp. 124-145). Christ's
incarnation is *not*, however, this type of sign, nor is it "the opposite of a
sign, an unconditional hiddenness." It is rather the type of contradiction

one gets in a communication that is a "union of jest and seriousness" (XII, 117; p 125).

If the paradox is understood as a formal, logical contradiction, then it would completely fail to fulfill the functions Climacus thinks it does fulfill. For Climacus the paradox must be unique and "absolute"; it thereby makes Christianity unique by differentiating it from every other religion or philosophical system. If the paradox is simply a formal contradiction there would be nothing unique about it, since such contradictions can be endlessly multiplied. As formal contradictions all of these are formally similar with no uniqueness or "absoluteness" conceivable. On such a reading of the paradox one could not possibly distinguish between the absurd and absurdities and between nonsense and the incomprehensible.

A little reflection easily shows that a formal contradiction completely fails to perform another function of the paradox, which is to mark the boundary of reason. A formal contradiction, though irrational, falls completely within the boundaries of reason's competence. That an assertion is formally contradictory is precisely the sort of thing that logicians make it their business to discover. If a particular proposition can be known to be formally contradictory, then it follows that a clear understanding of the concepts involved is attainable. Otherwise the contradictory relationships would not be ascertainable.

Climacus, on the other hand, is clearly thinking of a concept that resists this sort of clear and distinct comprehension. The two "contradictory" elements in the paradox are divinity and humanity. To know that the "God-man" is a formally contradictory combination, one would have to have a clear understanding of the nature of God and the nature of man. Only if one had this knowledge could one positively assert that the two concepts were formally contradictory. Yet Climacus denies that any such speculative knowledge is possible, either with respect to God or to man (IV, 213; pp. 56-57).

It is true that in the *Fragments* Climacus defines God as the Unknown, which is absolutely unlike man. But the Unknown is really an unknown, a mystery to man, not a clearly understood negation of human nature as such. God and man are said to be "absolutely unlike," but the recognition of man's unlikeness to God is said to be something one first learns from the God's appearance (IV, 214; p. 58). The result of this discovery of the unlikeness between God and man is precisely to confirm that man's natural state is one in which he is ignorant of his own nature *and* of God's nature (IV, 213; p. 56). The nature of this unlikeness we will explore later in detail, since it is the key to understanding why the paradox is a paradox,[7] but it does not seem to be the unlikeness of formally contradictory qualities. It is at least hard to see how Climacus could know this in view of his thesis about man's lack of knowledge concerning the two concepts in question. Though it may *appear* or seem likely to a human being that God could not become a man, this is not something that Climacus would accept as knowledge. It is certainly not knowable a priori or analytically —that is, simply on the basis of one's understanding of the terms. Climacus therefore is in no position to affirm that the incarnation involves a formal, logical contradiction, and his own considered position is that no one else can know such a thing either.

Still more light is shed on this question by an examination of Climacus' views on logic. Some writers have assumed that Kierkegaard was influenced by Hegel's attack on the principle of contradiction and that his embracement of the paradox rests on the rejection of this logical principle. This is totally wrong. Climacus and Kierkegaard are completely together on this point, consistently defending the traditional Aristotelian logic and consistently attacking the Hegelians for what they interpret as a rejection of the principle of noncontradiction.[8] Climacus' whole polemic in the *Fragments* and *Postscript* takes the following form: Speculative thought has a definite character (immanence); Christianity has a logically distinct (in fact, logically opposite) character (transcendence). Hegel's thought is speculative, therefore it is not Christian. The conclusion is that Hegelianism may be true or false, but it is certainly false for the Hegelians to claim to be Christian.

This argument clearly rests upon holding tightly to the logical principle that A cannot be not-A. For this reason Climacus insists on the validity of the traditional logic and resists strenuously the importation of "movement" into logic (VII, 88-89; pp. 99-100). It may be true in existence that one thing can be transformed into its opposite; something hot can become cold. But in the conceptual order there is no "movement." "Cold" means cold, and "hot" means hot. Climacus holds that even in existence the principle of contradiction holds in one connection. Though it is possible for the same person to *be* both good and bad (obviously in different respects), it is impossible for a person to simultaneously *become* good and bad. By this I think Climacus means that one cannot simultaneously develop a habit of moral obedience and one of moral indiscipline. In the moment of choice the individual must choose between good and evil, and the principle of "either-or" comes into its own. The very concept of a choice implies that to accept A one must reject not-A; thus the ethical life is rooted in the principle of noncontradiction.

It is these formal logical principles that form the basis for Climacus' own "dialectics," or systematic reflection on concepts in their logical relations (especially including conflicting relations). Without the ability to make "the absolute distinction" between a quality and its opposite, no dialectic is possible.

> At bottom it is precisely unshakeableness in the absolute and the absolute distinctions that makes one to be a good dialectician, which is what our age has absolutely failed to see, by suspending and in suspending the principle of contradiction, without seeing what even Aristotle maintained, that this sentence, that the principle of contradiction is suspended, is based upon the principle of contradiction, since otherwise the opposite sentence, that it is not suspended, is just as true (IV, 270; pp. 136-137).

It is for this reason that Kierkegaard himself was attracted to King Lear's remark, "Yes and no at the same time, that is not good theology," as he noted in his *Journals and Papers* (IV, 4773), a remark Climacus echoes in the *Fragments* (IV, 219; p. 66).

It seems clear enough, then, that Climacus' description of the absolute paradox is not intended to imply a formal, logical contradiction. It still remains to be seen what he does mean by this term "contradiction" and why, if the paradox is not a formal contradiction, belief in it is said to go "against the understanding."

4. Is the Paradox an Apparent Contradiction?

The paradox is not to be understood as a formal, logical contradiction, but it nevertheless must be some sort of "contradiction" or incongruity that presents a difficulty for thought. A natural suggestion at this point would be to regard the paradox as an apparent contradiction. The notion of an apparent contradiction can perhaps be roughly defined as follows: An apparent contradiction is a purported fact or state of affairs that nevertheless appears counterintuitive or even impossible because attempts to describe the situation require the use of logically contradictory expressions. Imagine, for example, a culture that lacked the concept of "mist." One could easily imagine in such a culture attempting to describe the phenomenon of mist by a contradictory expression: "It's raining yet it's not raining." It is conceivable that if mist were unknown in such a culture, its very existence would seem paradoxical and difficult to accept.

The paradox in this sense is a well-known rhetorical and literary device. Because of the complexity of reality and the inelasticity of human concepts, a paradoxical description of a situation frequently rings "truer" than a nonparadoxical one. "It was the best of times, it was the worst of times."

The difficulty with this suggestion that the contradiction in the paradox is only apparent is that Climacus seems to repudiate the idea. He particularly rejects the suggestion that the paradox is only a metaphor or a rhetorical, attention-grabbing device (VII, 184; p. 197). He wishes to distinguish his paradox, which he calls absolute, from those relative paradoxes that reason can hope to dissolve (VII, 182-183; pp. 194-195).

I think there are two reasons for Climacus' unhappiness with the idea that the paradox is only apparent. The first is that this suggestion implies that the paradoxicalness of the paradox is temporary. Because our concepts are inadequate, the truth must be stated in paradoxical form. Or perhaps the value of the paradox is to make a striking impression and call attention to itself. In either case there is no reason why the paradoxical form cannot be finally replaced or "mediated" by a clearer, philosophical statement of the truth. The second reason for Climacus' unhappiness is that an apparent paradox seems to be a relative paradox, which may be paradoxical to some people but not to others. The simple believer may have to be content with "faith," but the learned can advance to the level of understanding. In this way the Hegelian project of rationalizing Christianity so as to make it acceptable to contemporary thought, which is, broadly understood, the project of many contemporary theologians today also, appears justified.

Against such a relativizing of the paradox Climacus maintains that the incomprehensibility of the paradox is not a function of the limited knowledge of ancient man or the difference between the learned and the uneducated man today (VII, 493-494; p. 502). What seems to draw his fire in the suggestion that the paradox is only apparent is the implication that some people can resolve the paradox and thereby know that it is only apparent.

The trouble arises because when we say that something is only *apparently* something else, we usually imply that there is a higher perspective from which the reality of the thing can be known. Suppose, however, that this were not so; at least suppose that there is at least one case where there is no human level at which something, which appears to be but cannot be known to be a paradox, could be understood in a nonparadoxical manner. The suggestion is that the paradox might be "apparent" in the literal sense that it *appears* to be a contradiction, but it is impossible to determine whether it really is. In this case asserting that the paradox is apparent would not imply that it actually is a contradiction which would require the believer to repudiate the law of noncontradiction, but it would not imply that it is not such a contradiction either. This would avoid the impression that there is some superior position for which the paradox is no longer a paradox.

If the paradox were an apparent contradiction in this sense, it would be believable — since it might in some circumstances be possible to exercise faith that the contradiction was not a genuine, formal contradiction — but it would not be knowable. And one can begin to see why faith in such a paradox might be described as going against the understanding, since even though it is not known to be a formal contradiction, it nevertheless appears to be one. This "appearing" could be explicated in various ways, but I think the most straightforward would be to say that when the individual attempts to understand the paradox rationally, he finds himself stumbling into logical contradictions or at least using self-contradictory expressions, though he is aware that these expressions do not do justice to what he is attempting to express. This would be quite in line with Kierkegaard's own comment about the limits of reason in relation to Christian dogma:

> How little the understanding can achieve in a speculative sense is best seen in this, that when it reaches the highest level it must explain the highest by using a *self-contradictory* expression. Numerous examples in the *Formula of Concord* serve as examples (*J. and P.* III, 3656)

Kierkegaard does not say here that the highest *is* something self-contradictory; it is, rather, something that causes man to employ self-contradictory *expressions*, no doubt becase of his lack of understanding.

I believe that this is precisely the way Climacus regards the "absolute paradox." What he wants to say about the incarnation is that it is an incomprehensible mystery that no human being can intellectually resolve. It *seems* or *appears* to man that it is a contradiction to say that an individual man could be God. This paradox may *only* be an apparent one, but its paradoxicality is, if relative to anything, relative to human nature as such, and therefore is not grounded in the differences between human beings. This is in fact just what Climacus says; whether the paradox is in itself a paradox he cannot say. What he does say is that from a human perspective the paradox appears to be a contradiction. "The paradox is essentially related to being human" (VII, 494; p. 502). I think, therefore, that the best initial description of what Climacus means by calling the incarnation the absolute paradox is that he means that the incarnation is an apparent contradiction, not in the sense that it appears to be a contradiction to some people but not to others, but in that it necessarily *appears* to existing human beings as a contradiction. The paradox in this interpretation could truly function as a boundary to human reason. A relative apparent paradox would fall within the province of reason since it can be penetrated by thought and its paradoxicality removed. A logical contradiction could similarly be analyzed and definitively disposed of by thought.

Calling the paradox the boundary of reason by no means implies that it is illegitimate for reason to *attempt* to understand it. It is precisely by attempting to understand the paradox that reason can discover that it is truly the paradox, not merely a relative paradox. There is thus no suggestion here of an alien, arbitrary, "undialectical" authority that is imposed on reason from the outside, but a limit that reason can test for itself. In the attempt to understand, reason discovers the inadequacy of its concepts also, and is thereby prevented from making a definitive judgment that the paradox is logical nonsense.

5. *The Paradox as the Boundary of Reason*

The concept of a boundary or limit to reason has intrigued many philosophers. Wittgenstein attempted to define the limits of reason in his *Tractatus Logico-Philosophicus.* There he encounters difficulty in discovering such a limit. How can reason discover a limit for itself, since it would seem that in order to know the limit reason would have to "think both sides of the limit" and hence exceed the limit? Wittgenstein attempted to deal with this problem by placing the limit in *language* — i.e., by clearly distinguishing between what can be said and what cannot be said.[9] Even this is paradoxical, since the language used to draw the limit runs the danger of exceeding the limit itself. Wittgenstein recognized this by claiming that his book must be understood as a ladder one draws up after it has been climbed.[10] "My propositions serve as elucidations in the following way: anyone who understands me eventually recognizes them as nonsensical.[11] It is interesting that Wittgenstein himself was by no means contemptuous of whatever lay beyond those limits. The arena of the "mystical" was for him the home of values and existential meaning.[12]

Kant's *Critique of Pure Reason* is another attempt to draw the boundaries of theoretical reason. For Kant reason is the faculty that seeks a unified understanding of phenomena. As such, no finite goal or limit to reason's quest can be imagined. For every condition presented to reason, an explanation must be sought in a further condition. This "infinite" striving is in reality a quest for a unified, ultimate explanation of everything, the "unconditioned condition," which provides the explanation for everything else while requiring no explanation itself. This concept is "the Idea of reason" (or Ideal, when conceived as personal), and Kant claims that this is the source of the concept of God as the Absolute Being upon which all things depend.[13] When applied to the self and the world, other Ideas of reason are derived.

What Kant says about this Idea is very interesting. He claims it is an Idea that reason must necessarily think, but can never know. As an ideal it has a valuable "regulative" function, always drawing man onward in his intellectual quest by preventing him from resting content with any finite explanation as ultimate.[14] Every state of affairs or principle that serves as an explanation can in its turn be made an object for explanation. However, this Idea of reason can never itself be the object of knowledge, which is limited to spatio-temporal objects. As an Idea it therefore marks the boundary of reason.

How can the status of the Idea as the transcendent boundary of human knowledge itself be recognized without exceeding the boundary by making the Idea something known? Kant answers this question, at least in part, by claiming that when reason attempts to exceed these limits, it falls into various intellectual difficulties. Among these are the paralogism of pure reason, fallacious theistic arguments, and most remarkably, "antimonies" that sound remarkably like Climacus' paradox. When reason attempts to exceed its boundaries by making an Idea of pure reason the object of knowledge, reason finds itself driven to making contradictory affirmations. For example, reason asserts that the world has a beginning in time and also no beginning, that there are simple substances and there are no simple substances.[15] Kant says that these difficulties are "the most fortunate perplexity into which reason could ever have become involved."[16] The failure of reason to gain satisfying answers in such areas is to be taken as a hint to turn from the speculative to the more profitable practical employment of reason.[17] The boundaries of reason are thus not known positively but negatively, by the fact that when reason reaches these limits it involves itself in apparently contradictory assertions.

Whether influenced by Kant or not, Climacus' discussion of the paradox is remarkably similar in form to Kant's discussion of the antimonies, though of course different in content. Like Kant he holds that reason contains a restless infinity. He says that it is the highest paradox of thought to "discover something which cannot itself be thought" (IV, 204; p. 46). Though this is a paradox, one "should not think ill of the paradox, for the paradox is thought's passion." The ultimate goal of thought, which thought is passionately seeking, is itself a paradox — namely, the concept of "that which cannot be thought." Climacus claims that this passion is "at bottom present in all thinking," though it is not usually noticed because of "custom" (IV, 204; p. 46).

Climacus does not argue for these assertions, but it is not too difficult to outline the thinking that lies behind them. The restlessness of reason, the fact that no fact or principle that reason can grasp is accepted by reason as final, Climacus interprets as in effect a quest for reason's limits. The fact that reason continually seeks to expand its bounds by testing every "temporary limit" can be viewed as a kind of quest for a Kantian Idea, a search for an ultimate limit, which, even if unachievable, nevertheless guides and orients thought, forcing it ever "onwards."

Man's quest for understanding is here regarded by Climacus as rooted, like all other human achievements, in a passion. This passion for understanding has, like other passions, an imperialistic quality, which turns out to be very significant in understanding the ways in which faith and reason can conflict. The limit that reason is seeking is in one sense reason's goal, but if such a limit were actually discovered, the result would be a "collision," since such a limit could not be known by reason and this would be reason's "downfall" (IV, 204; p.46).

This paradoxical object, which provides both the goal and limit to reason, Climacus designates the "unknown," and "just as a name" he designates this unknown "the God" (IV, 207; p.49). It is of course a rather significant name. Climacus here makes it plain that from a speculative point of view God is not positively knowable; if "knowable" at all, he is only knowable negatively. I think it would be clearer if Climacus were to say that "the God" is not knowable by speculative reason, though the concept of "the God" can be acquired by speculative reason. It is given negatively as the boundary of thought; that which thought cannot think.

> God is in this manner a highest concept. Such concepts do not let themselves be explained by anything else, but only are explained by deepening oneself in the conception itself; the highest principles for all thought only let themselves be demonstrated indirectly (negatively) (VII, 185; p.197).

It is vital to emphasize that the God who is "the unknown" and "the paradox" is the God in time. As was made clear in our examination of religion A, it may be possible for man to gain an understanding of God as eternal through "recollection." What is paradoxical is the assertion that the eternal God is knowable — indeed, only adequately knowable — as a particular historical entity.

We still must deal with the question of why this event is paradoxical by looking at the contradictions it appears to contain. But it is important to understand its formal character as the absolute paradox and what it implies. Otherwise hopeless confusions emerge later on. The paradox is for Climacus the limit which reason can discover and which it "at bottom" is seeking. The paradox reveals itself negatively to reason as the limit by involving reason in contradictions when it attempts to understand it. As such it signals the "downfall" or end to the speculative project of understanding ultimate reality, and it constitutes a signal to enter an existential relation with what is *believed* but cannot be known to be ultimate reality. The paradox in this sense is the key category of Christianity, which protects it against reduction to an "immanent" doctrine or theory.

> Insofar as thought lyrically seeks to transcend itself, it wills to discover the paradox. . . .on this point rests all the Christian categories. Outside of this point every dogmatic determination is a philosophical matter which has "originated in the human heart" and thinking is immanent. The last thing that human thought can will is to will to transcend itself in the paradox. And Christianity is precisely the paradox (VII, 84; p.95).

6. *The Perfect Synthesis of Time and Eternity: "The Strangest of All Things"*

We have argued that the paradox is not to be understood as a logical contradiction but as a logically odd notion that produces contradictory ideas when thought seeks to understand it. The paradox is thus an apparent contradiction, not in a relative sense, but in the absolute sense that it appears to be, but cannot be known to be, a contradiction. Such an absolute paradox is nevertheless precisely what reason itself, in its infinite quest to understand everything presented to it, is seeking: the limit of reason itself, that which cannot be mastered by thought. It still remains, however, to explore the content of this conception. Why is the paradox the absolute paradox? What sorts of contradictions does it engender for reason when reason attempts to understand it?

Climacus' whole concept is really a rather strange one, which probably explains why so many have interpreted his paradox as either a logical contradiction or as a merely relative paradox. The notion that some event is strange and difficult to understand is not problematic, nor is it difficult to see why such events are sometimes best described in paradoxical language. However, the notion of an event that is "absolutely" strange and difficult to understand (to human beings at least) and that is therefore absolutely paradoxical is rather unique. Yet this is precisely how Climacus describes the paradox. It is not a logical contradiction; thought is free to deal with it as "the strangest of all things" (IV, 263-264; p.127). The paradox is "the most improbable of all things" (IV, 218, p. 65).

Where exactly does the strangeness of the paradox lie? Climacus says again and again that the heart of the paradox, both in itself and in relation to the believer, lies in the conjunction of the historical or temporal with the eternal. The paradox has a double aspect. There is first the event itself, the "God in time," which is "the absurdity that the Eternal is the historical" (IV, 227; p. 76). The second element in the paradox concerns the believer's relation to the absolute historical fact. Here the paradox again concerns eternity and history, for the contradiction lies in the believer's *becoming* eternal in time through a relation to something historical. We shall in this chapter concern ourselves primarily with the first aspect of the paradox, leaving the paradox of the believer's relation to the incarnation to the next chapter, "Faith and History."

In trying to understand why Climacus regards this conjunction of temporality and eternity as paradoxical, it is important to remember that the concepts of temporality and eternity are not strange or new; they are precisely the elements of which existence itself is composed, and they have underlain Climacus' whole discussion of the ethical and religious life. Indeed, one could well argue that existence itself is a paradox, for Climacus, since it is said to be "that child begotten by the infinite and the finite, the eternal and the temporal" (VII, 73; p. 85). Existence has exactly the characteristic Climacus demands from a paradox; it cannot be thought and thus serves as a limit to thought (VII, 283-286; pp. 293-296). It is "something thought cannot think." Existence is itself a paradox, since "the fact that an eternal spirit exists is itself a contradiction" (VII, 189n; p. 202n).

This similarity between existence and the incarnation might suggest the possibility of an analogy between human existence per se and the absolute paradox. As a matter of fact, Climacus says there is such an analogy, though the difference is nevertheless "infinite" (VII, 172n-173n; pp. 184n-185n). As is so often the case, Socrates serves here as the paradigm of human existence. Socrates had an awareness of the eternal through recollection. His infinite merit in Climacus' eyes is that he did not employ this understanding speculatively, but used it to transform his existence. As an existing individual Socrates inwardly related himself to the eternal. This Socratic inwardness is therefore said to be "an analogue to faith," the difference being that in the Socratic paradox the eternal itself is not paradoxical; only the relationship between the eternal and an existing individual is (VII, 172n-173n; pp. 184n-

185n). The reason why Socrates shunned speculation in favor of existence would seem to be his discovery of the paradoxical nature of existence, which comes to the scene in Socrates' wonder as to whether "he was a stranger monster than Typhon, or a friendlier and simpler creature by nature partaking of something divine" (IV, 204; p. 46). "This seems to be a paradox," Climacus says lightly. For Socrates this was the paradox upon which the speculative project foundered and which therefore led him to the project of existing. The quest for virtue replaced the quest for scientific comprehension.

From Climacus' treatment of Socrates we learn that "paradox" is not merely an event to Climacus, but a category he applies to a number of things, among them human existence itself. He applies this category to sin, to the life of the believer in Christ, and to the forgiveness of sins, for example. But in every case the fundamental elements seem to be temporality and eternity. Why do these concepts refuse to "go together," so that when joined they produce a paradox? This is a question about which Climacus says surprisingly little, considering its importance. That temporality and eternity are contrasting, conflicting elements is something he takes as obvious. The reason for this, I think, is that since existence is itself a never-completed synthesis of these two elements, he assumes that every exister is himself aware of their nature and the difficulty in joining them.

Eternity for Climacus represents perfection. The eternal is that which is full and complete. The temporal, on the contrary, is that which is incomplete and "on the way." The problem of the relation of time and eternity reflects itself in the Platonic problem of participation. Changing particular objects as particulars imitate or participate in perfect, eternal forms, the universal realities that are the source of all being. It is well known that Plato never adequately explained the notion of participation, and in a sense this problem is Climacus' also: How can the eternal exist? How can what exists realize the eternal? It is a problem that reflects itself in epistemology and logic, which we touched on in our examination of Climacus' account of truth. How can a human thought or belief, understood as a temporal moment or segment of an individual's psychological history, be eternally true? Or to put it another way, how can a timelessly true proposition be an element in a temporal sequence? There is a fundamental mystery here, which is named but not explained by such terms as "instantiation" and "participation." It is only perhaps the pervasiveness and familiarity of the phenomenon that blinds us to its mysterious and paradoxical character.

Climacus is not of course concerned with this problem in its abstract, speculative form. It must be remembered that there are different senses of "eternity" for Climacus. There is first the "abstract eternity" of logical possibility. Here the eternal merely consists of universal possibilities, and the problem of participation is essentially the speculative question as to how particular objects are related to the universal "possibles." This question, insofar as Climacus deals with it at all, is answered by the concept of creation.

For an existing human being, however, who does not merely exist in the sense of plants and stones, eternity appears in a different quality, as does the problem of participation. An existing human being has the eternal within her already, and her task in existence is to reduplicate those universal possibilities in action. For a being who must make choices the universals are not merely abstract possibilities, but ideals. Thus eternity for an exister is value-impregnated, and the individual learns of the eternal in ethical and religious striving. She discovers that the true character of the eternal is ethical. Hence, for an exister, the process of participation is a self-conscious, active one, and the possibilities that she seeks to participate in by duplicating them in action are moral ideals.

It is this fundamentally moral character of eternity that must be kept in mind. Otherwise Climacus' paradox will appear to be a speculative difficulty grounded in the ontological difference between time and eternity. On this speculative line of thought the absolute paradox is that a particular object is simultaneously an eternal form without ceasing to be particular. This may be an element in Climacus' thought; at times he seems to push this forward as a roadblock to speculative thought. It may be that Climacus finds this speculative problem to be the best *analogue* within the province of speculation to the paradox in the Christian revelation. Hence he seizes on this Platonic language as a recognizable starting place for a speculator attempting to understand Christianity. Christ is the particular who is also the universal.

However, the primary meaning of the paradox is not speculative but moral. In all human moral experience temporality fails to perfectly realize the eternal. Man's moral strivings are at best only strivings. The absolute paradox is that a person who is a particular, temporal individual and who therefore outwardly resembles other temporal individuals is nevertheless the full, complete realization of the eternal moral reality that provides the standard for all the rest of existence. The realization is so perfect that one can no longer speak of a difference between the individual who realizes the standard and the standard itself. The individual is the standard. It is this assertion that Climacus regards as "the strangest possible proposal."

Many commentators have assumed that the paradox revolves around the ontological "contradiction" between God and man. How can a finite, particular entity be simultaneously the eternal reality that underlies everything finite? This is essentially the problem of how the creator could become a creature. But though this may be a roadblock for speculative thought (Climacus certainly does not claim that reason can finally comprehend or explain how God could become man), this is not the "contradiction" or incongruity that makes the paradox so hard to accept. The contradiction in the paradox is a "qualitative" contradiction wherein that which is absolutely unlike man (God) becomes man in order to abolish this unlikeness (IV, 214; p. 59). But in what does this absolute unlikeness of God and man consist? Surprisingly, the difference does not stem from the fact that man is finite and created. "But if the God is absolutely different from man, this cannot be grounded in what man owes the God, for in so far they are akin" (IV, 214; p. 58). Here Climacus seems to assert a type of "analogy of being." Insofar as man is a creature of God, he is like God, without of course erasing the distinction. Though they are not ontologically identical, in this respect God and man are not absolutely unlike each other either. The unlikeness between man and God is moral, and is to be explained as a result of man's free choice.

> [Their difference must therefore consist] in what man owes himself, or what he has himself deserved. But what can this difference be? Aye, what else but sin, since the difference, the absolute difference, is due to man himself (IV, 214; p. 58).

The paradoxicality of the paradox consists in the idea that a finite human being, who outwardly resembles other sinful human beings, could be the perfect realization of the eternal moral idea. This is illuminated by comparing this paradox with the Socratic paradox. We have seen that Socrates' life, as the exemplar of the highest level of human existence, is also a paradox in that it represents a synthesis of the temporal and eternal. Socrates, however, would have been the first to admit that his existence was not identical with the eternal itself. As such, the true "follower" of Socrates is the person who follows Socrates' example and relates himself existentially to the eternal. If he becomes a disciple of Socrates, he has eternally missed the boat.

As Climacus understands it, however, the Christ-paradox is different. Christ, though outwardly a mere individual like Socrates, is not just a partial realization of the eternal, he is a perfect realization of the eternal; he is identical with the eternal. His existence is a perfect "reduplication" of the eternal. Christ is the truth, the truth as a way, the eternal truth as existing.[18] Hence from the Christian point of view the person who wishes to commit himself to the eternal must become a follower of the historical Jesus Christ, who, contrary to human expectations and universal human experience, *is* the eternal.

The eternal as the basis of all value is that which makes meaningful choice possible. Eternity is thus the absolute that permeates the whole of existence and gives history meaning. From the viewpoint of immanence eternity is something man possesses eternally. Christianity claims, however, that the eternal has come into being at a definite point in time and as such is something to encounter in history (VII, 497; p. 506). Despite its historicity the Christ event remains the absolute, and thus becomes that which gives the individual's history significance by making meaningful choice possible. Climacus therefore calls it "the fulness of time" to signify the claim that it is a particular historical event, which nonetheless claims to be meaningful for all time and is in that sense "contemporary with every age."

It seems to me that this is the heart of Climacus' contention that the incarnation is a paradox. All human moral experience is the experience of man's struggle to temporally realize the eternal. That experience is a record of conflict and ultimately failure. The idea that a human being who is human like all other human beings could be fully eternal and fully temporal at the same time thus contradicts man's universal experience and all his reasonable expectations. If one were to claim that Jesus were the best man who ever lived, there would be no paradox, or at most the relative paradox that this man who was poor and obscure, lacked education, and so on, was nonetheless morally superior. But the claim that Jesus' human life infinitely and perfectly realized the ideal, simply *was* the ideal, lies in a completely different category.

Climacus freely admits, even emphasizes, that this claim runs contrary to man's universal experience and therefore to his reasonable expectations. Since it is something totally foreign to his experience, a human being cannot comprehend or understand how such a thing is possible. For man, eternity and temporality are experienced as incongruous qualities which he unsuccessfully attempts to synthesize. I argued earlier, however, that this proposal is not a logical contradiction, but "the strangest of all things," the "improbable." We can now see how this is possible.

We saw in our analysis of humor that "contradiction" to Climacus does not necessarily mean logical contradiction but qualitative contrast. The contradiction that is embodied in Christ is in fact identical with the contradiction we encountered in our analysis of humor. It is the fundamental incongruity between human striving and the eternal.[19] The humorist still rests within immanence; he uses his understanding of the conflict between the temporal and the eternal to "write off" existence as a "jest." Eternity lies behind him, so what does existence matter? The Christian, on the other hand, believes that what he himself experiences as "contradictory" has been fully realized in Christ. Christ is the union of these contradictory elements. Eternity *exists* and must be acquired in time. Therefore the incarnation as a past event about which I must make a decision becomes more than merely a past event. As the eternal it becomes the future possibility that has a claim on my life.

We can now understand the grounds for Climacus' claim that the incarnation is an "absolute" paradox, an event that appears paradoxical not merely to some human beings, but to "man as man". It appears paradoxical to all human beings because the "contradictory" qualities Christ claims to unite are the universal elements of existence, experienced by all human beings as conflicting. The paradox thus appears to be a paradox to all human existers and continues to be a paradox to every human exister so long as, and to the extent that, he does not manage to combine the qualities of eternity and temporality in his own existence.

The paradox of the incarnation is fundamentally grounded in the paradox of existence itself. It is for this reason that Climacus stresses that a deep understanding of existence is the prerequisite for a proper understanding of Christianity. Such an understanding does not make Christianity easy to understand, but it makes it easier to understand that Christianity cannot be understood. The individual who has ceased to exist and become "speculation" may indeed "explain" the paradox, but her explanation is rooted in her inability to understand the paradox, which is in turn rooted in her failure to understand existence. The "contradiction" between the eternal and the temporal is only understood by the individual who has energetically devoted herself to an existential realization of the eternal. Religiousness A, through its awareness of human guilt, is the presupposition for a proper understanding of Christianity. The person who has never attempted to temporally realize the eternal has a very mediocre idea of the difficulties in doing so and consequently may find it easy to "understand" the notion of a man who is also God. But the ease with which she understands such a thing is merely a function of her lack of existential depth. The exister who has not *completed* the task of existing herself never reaches the place where the incarnation becomes *truly* easy to understand. She therefore never makes the error of assuming that the incarnation is a theory or doctrine to be speculated on, but is immediately led to the proper relation of action. She can either believe that Jesus is

God and hence make Jesus the focal point of her life, or she can be offended at such a claim and hence repudiate the necessity for building her life around Christ. But in both cases the decision leads to changes in her existence.

Despite the universality and absoluteness of the paradox, I see nothing in this concept that undermines our earlier contention that the incarnation is not a formal, logical contradiction. However unlikely or impossible it may seem to man that an individual human being could be the perfect realization of the eternal, and no matter how difficult such a thing might be to understand, it is hard to see how someone could claim to know that such a thing is logically impossible. It may seem incredible, but it cannot be known to be nonsense. For in order to know that eternity and temporality were logically contradictory concepts, one would have to have a clear understanding of both concepts, hence of existence itself. But this is just what man as existing cannot achieve. To know that the paradox is logically impossible would require the same standpoint that would be necessary to resolve the paradox, i.e., an eternal viewpoint. It follows that the same considerations that make the paradox absolute and prevent its resolution by existers also suffice to prevent an exister from resolving the paradox by exposing it as a logical impossibility. Since the paradox is the boundary of reason, the only strictly logical conclusion that reason can draw about it is that the paradox is a mystery, something that reason cannot comprehend. To conclude from this that it is nonsense is just as rash as to claim to comprehend it and in both cases is grounded in a failure to respect the limits that existence itself places on thought. It is certainly possible for an exister to be a thinker, but he always remains an exister and never becomes "pure thought."

7. The Paradox: Against and/or Above Reason?

As we have analyzed it, the paradox is a fundamental mystery that is most properly described as above reason, since reason has no power to "resolve the knot" of the paradox either way, either positively or negatively. However, Climacus consistently describes faith in the paradox as a faith "against the understanding." It is fairly clear that Climacus wants to say both that there is no necessary conflict between reason and the paradox and that there is in fact a tension between reason and the paradox. Can these two claims be reconciled?

Before we can even investigate the matter, a remark must be made about what Climacus means by "reason." When he speaks of reason, Climacus speaks about a concrete human activity. He does not discuss the relation between the paradox and "logic" or "pure reason" understood as abstractions, since no such entities as "logic" and "pure reason" *exist*. Reason is first and foremost "human reason." Though Climacus often uses it as a noun, the root meaning comes from a verb. When used as a noun, "reason" refers to a dimension of human activity. It is existers who think, and their thinking reflects the funded experiences and attitudes of existence. We have already seen that for Climacus the "contradiction" contained in the paradox is relative to those elements of existence experienced by existers as conflicting. From the viewpoint of "logic," if such a perspective is assumed to be possible, there would not necessarily be any tension with the paradox. But for Climacus to gain such a perspective he would have to desert existence for eternity, so as to think *sub specie aeternitatis*, which is something that he claims an exister cannot do. Hence for better or worse "reason" for Climacus means concrete human thinking, human reasoning as it is shaped by the experiences and attitudes acquired in the course of existing.

To understand the relation between reason in this sense and the paradox, let us first examine the case of a "happy relation" between reason and the paradox. This happy relation exists in the individual who has the passion of faith, which is described as a condition in which reason and the paradox are on "good terms" with each other (IV, 220; p. 67). The formula for this relation is given several times: "The Reason sets itself aside and the Paradox bestows itself" (IV, 224; p. 73). One can already begin to see the ambiguity in Climacus' view of the relation of reason and the paradox. On the one hand, reason is "set aside." However, it must be noted that it is reason that sets *itself* aside. In relation to the paradox reason "cannot itself think it, could not even have itself discovered it, and when it is proclaimed, it cannot understand it, sensing merely that its downfall is threatened. In so far the Reason will have a lot of objections against it" (IV, 214-215; p. 59). However, Climacus notes that we have seen that "the Reason, in its paradoxical passion, wills its own downfall" (IV, 215; p. 59).

Both sides of this ambivalent relation stand in need of clarification. Both are explained by what we earlier called the imperialistic character of reason. When human beings think, their thought, like every other aspect of their existence, stems from a passion. In this case the passion is the desire to understand and explain what appears, to connect and to harmonize the world in a lawful and orderly manner. This is the passion that gives birth to science, and Climacus does not wish to denigrate it. It is on the contrary a "universal human quality." It is thus natural for a human being to attempt to understand whatever she encounters, and equally natural to react negatively to that which resists explanation. "In so far" reason will have a natural negative orientation to the paradox.

However, in our analysis of the paradox as a boundary or limit to reason we noticed the pervasiveness of the attempt to discover a boundary or limit to reason and we argued that the possibility of such a boundary is not inherently illogical. The thesis that there are no limits to reason, that all reality is essentially transparent to human thought, is not rationally self-evident, even though it may be the "natural" attitude of the concrete thinker. If in fact human thinking is influenced by sin, as Christianity asserts, this thesis may well be false, though "natural" to sinners. Climacus even interprets, as we have seen, the restlessness or imperialistic character of thought as at bottom a quest for such a limit, though "custom" or "habit" obscures this. For is not the continual testing of every boundary, the attempt to understand everything, equivalent to an attempt to discover an ultimate boundary, to find "something which thought cannot think"? But if the ultimate goal of reason is to discover the ultimate mystery and thereby to define its own limits, the paradox could *in a way* be said to be the fulfillment and not the destruction of reason.

Since reason is an activity carried on in passion, it is conceivable that other human passions might present an analogy to the ambivalent relation of reason and the paradox. This is in fact the case. Climacus says that "the highest pitch of every passion is to will its own downfall" (IV, 204; p. 46). The passion that he chooses as the best analogue to reason's relation to the paradox is the passion of love, which is also said to be paradoxical.

> Consider the analogy of love, though it is an imperfect picture. Self-love lies at the basis of love; but the paradoxical passion of self-love when at its highest wills precisely its own downfall. This is what love wants also, so these two powers understand each other in the passion of the moment, and this passion is precisely love (IV, 215; p. 59).

Climacus' meaning here is fairly clear. All human love begins as self-love, which he regards as universal. Consider the case of a man courting a woman. The lover who courts his fair love is, initially at least, selfishly motivated. He is enchanted by the girl, gets pleasure from her company, wishes to win her for his own sake. However, in attempting to win his lady, the lover begins to center his attention not on himself, but on her. If he truly becomes a lover, if his passion attains the highest pitch, he will soon forget himself and care only for the woman. This is in one sense the downfall of self-love, since his world now centers around the other person.

But in another sense it is the fulfillment of self-love, since it is by renouncing his own happiness that he becomes happy. Of course in a happy love-relation an analogous story could be told from the feminine perspective. The upshot is that self-love is submerged but not annihilated (IV, 215; p. 59).

For Climacus the same sort of relation holds between the paradox and reason (IV, 215; pp. 59-60). Self-love is to love as reason is to the paradox. Although the paradox is discontinuous with all that reason knows, expects, and understands, it is possible for reason and the paradox to come together in passion "in a mutual understanding of their unlikeness." It is possible for reason to recognize the discontinuous character of the paradox without judging it negatively, if reason can accept the thesis that there are limits to human understanding.

Of course not all love is happy love. It is possible for a selfish person to refuse to love because of his self-love. "He who in self-love shrinks from love can neither grasp it nor dare to venture it, since it is destruction" (IV, 215; p. 59). The lover who thus shrinks from love cuts himself off from true happiness. He fails to see that if self-love is to be fulfilled, it must be denied. In his unhappiness he may become bitter at love and at the loved one. His love may turn to hate. Such an unhappy love is in its deepest root passive, according to Climacus, even when it appears audacious and spiteful. It is fundamentally a *reaction* on the part of the "wounded individual."

Climacus calls this passion "misunderstood self-love" and says it, too, has its analogue in the relation between reason and the paradox. When reason imperialistically asserts its claim to universal dominance, it inevitably clashes with the paradox. This condition of unhappy love is termed offense, and the implication is that reason, by refusing to acknowledge its limits, fails genuinely to fulfill itself.

Climacus insists strenuously that offense is also a passive condition and that the offended person, when he denounces the paradox, actually confirms "the correctness of the Paradox" (IV, 217; p. 63). "All that it [the offended consciousness] has to say about the Paradox it has learned from the Paradox" (IV, 219; p. 66). The grounds for this assertion are as follows. The paradox is the event in which what is absolutely unlike man (God) became man. But since God as the absolutely unlike is knowable only in the paradox, it follows that the paradoxicalness of the paradox can be known only through the encounter with the paradox. In more concrete language this means that man's sinfulness, the moral failing that makes the paradox appear a paradox, is itself only discovered by the encounter with the God. In this encounter man learns what God is like and thus how unlike God he is. But it is this unlikeness that makes the paradox the most improbable of all things. Hence Climacus concludes that the improbability of the paradox is entailed by its actually being the paradox, and that it is by encountering the paradox that man discovers its improbability. In this way the "improbability" of the paradox is actually a sign of its genuiness (IV, 220; p. 67).

Reason would of course like to pose as the discoverer of the paradox's improbability. What happens here is that reason denounces the paradox as "the most improbable of all things," insisting that it cannot understand it. To this the paradox replies, "It is exactly as you say; the only wonder is that you regard it as an objection, but the truth in the mouth of a hypocrite is dearer to me than if it came from the lips of an angel or an apostle" (IV, 219; p. 65). The railings of the offended person against the paradox are an indirect proof that the paradox is indeed what it claims to be, the paradox.

This last quotation is particularly interesting and is worth exploring in greater detail. It is taken from Hamann, who was strongly influenced by Hume, particularly Hume's essay on miracles. The thrust of this essay is not that a miracle is logically impossible (which would be impossible to show about a purported matter of fact), but that it is unbelievable, because if one judges by mankind's universal experience, a miracle must be seen as "the most improbable of all things." Hence a miracle is always the most improbable explanation of an event. A natural explanation, no matter how far-fetched, is always more likely. Hume concludes that the Christian faith, which requires belief in miracles, not only "was at first attended with miracles but even at this day cannot be believed by an reasonable person without one."[20] Hamann knows that Hume may be mocking, but he says that what Hume says is nevertheless true. Faith is a miracle, and "truth in the mouth of a hypocrite is dearer to me than from an apostle."[21] For Climacus the paradox is *the* miracle, and he is happy with Hume's definition of a miracle: the most improbable of all things. The paradox can only be believed when a human being ceases to allow mankind's general experience and the resulting view of what is probable and reasonable to be the final determinant of belief.

Offense stems at bottom from what we might call the self-assertiveness of the man who insists that there are no limits to his understanding and that his standards of probability and reasonableness are the ultimate determinants of truth. It is therefore really a form of pride, which confirms our earlier claim that the paradoxicalness of the paradox is a function of man's moral distance from God. To the extent that man insists on his own self-sufficiency, he will not be able to accept an action of God that implies that man "lacks the truth" and hence that the truth must be given to him. Since man is fundamentally prideful (traditional theology has held that pride is the root of man's sinfulness), it is to be expected that concrete human reason will react negatively to the paradox. Offense is in that sense a "natural" reaction, and Climacus is therefore justified in speaking of faith as something that is *against* the understanding. It does conflict with man's prideful claim to be able at least in principle to understand everything. But the thesis that human understanding has no limits is in effect a claim that the human understanding is divine. Hence the prideful attitude of the offended consciousness is in effect an attempt to displace God and deify man. Though faith is "against" the understanding, it is the sinfulness of man that creates the tension. Since on the assumption that the paradox is true this sinfulness is a universal condition, Climacus is quite justified in saying that the paradox is against human reason. It goes against human reason as it naturally is. But Climacus himself shows that this natural condition is not the only possible one and that this negative relation is therefore not the only possible one if the paradox is a reality. There is also a possible happy relation between reason and the paradox, which is made possible when the individual encounters the paradox and receives the condition of faith from the God. In the encounter with the God man is offered the chance to learn his true condition and his limits. He is taught by the God that his condition is in error. The individual must himself learn this, however. (This is the analogy between the Socratic and Christian hypotheses, a fact that is, as we shall see later, of extreme importance.) If the individual, with the God's help, learns his true condition, then he can accept the condition of faith from the God and happily believe what he cannot understand, that the God has entered time so that he, a temporal being, can become eternal.

8. *Kierkegaard and Climacus on the Paradox*

As Kierkegaard is often labeled an irrationalist on the strength of Climacus' remarks on the paradox, it is worthwhile to note his own interpretation of Climacus. That interpretation agrees closely with the line of thought we have here advanced.

One of Kierkegaard's most significant comments on the *Postscript* occurs in a *Journal* entry concerning Hugo de St. Victor:

> Hugo de St. Victor states a correct thesis (Helfferich, *Mystik,* Vol. I, p. 368): "Faith is really not supported by the things which go beyond reason, by any reason, because reason does not comprehend what faith believes; but nevertheless there is something here by which reason becomes determined or is conditioned to honor the

faith which it still does not perfectly succeed in grasping."

This is what I have developed (for example, in *Concluding Postscript*) — that not every absurdity is the absurd or the paradox. The activity of reason is to distinguish the paradox negatively — but no more (*J. and P.* I, 7).

This entry contains all the characteristic Climacus theses: The paradox is fundamentally above reason, not understandable (and thus if reason does not recognize its limits, the paradox will conflict). Even in reason, however, there is a "something" (reason's fundamental need to discover its limits) that makes possible a happy marriage of reason and faith.

Later on in the same entry Kierkegaard gives a more systematic treatment of the concept of the paradox. The paradox is "the improbable or the absurd" (notice that these two concepts are equated — the absurd is not a logical contradiction). The paradox is not merely an event but a concept with definite boundaries. It is only superficiality to think that "all sorts of absurdities are equally at home in the absurd." The concept of the absurd is determined negatively as reason's limit, which means it is fundamentally beyond reason. The fact that the paradox is incomprehensible to reason does not give reason the power to condemn it:

> The *absurd*, the *paradox*, is composed in such a way that reason has no power at all to dissolve it in nonsense and prove that it is nonsense; no, it is a symbol, a riddle, a compounded riddle about which reason must say: I cannot solve it, it cannot be understood, but it does not thereby follow that it is nonsense (*J. and P.* I,7).

Kierkegaard here goes so far as to say that the believer, though never altering the paradox by claiming to comprehend it intellectually, nevertheless can positively see that the paradox is *not* nonsense.

> But, of course, if faith is completely abolished, the whole sphere is dropped, and then reason becomes conceited and perhaps concludes that, *ergo*, the paradox is nonsense. What concern there would be if in another realm the skilled class were extinct and then the unskilled found this thing and that to be nonsense — but in respect to the paradox faith is the skilled (*J. and P.* I,7).

The whole temptation to regard the paradox as nonsense comes about from having a "fantastic" concept of reason as "pure reason." Actual human reason has limits, which always must be known negatively. Such "negative concepts" actually provide the "highest principles of all thought" (VII, 185; p. 197).

This long entry on the theme of the paradox is confirmed by another entry nearly eight years earlier, in which Kierkegaard claims that he is in essential agreement with such philosophers as Leibniz, who claimed that Christianity is above, but not against, reason:

> What I usually express by saying that Christianity consists of paradox, philosophy in mediation, Leibniz expresses by distinguishing between what is above reason and what is against reason. Faith is above reason (*J. and P.* III, 3073).

Here Kierkegaard goes on to give some helpful insights into what he means by reason and faith. Leibniz means by reason a "linking together of truths" or "a conclusion from causes." This does not mean for Leibniz, the rationalist, what it would mean to an empiricist like Hume. Causal knowledge for Leibniz is a priori, if it is true knowledge. What makes the paradox a paradox is that it resists this a priori rational understanding. Since the paradox is not an "idea which has arisen in a human heart" but a transcendent act by God, it does not link up with man's a priori expectations. The paradox lacks continuity with human thought, whether that thought be man's recollection of the eternal or his conclusions about what is likely or probable which are derived from experience. "Faith therefore cannot be *proved, demonstrated, comprehended*, for the link which makes a linking together possible is missing, and what else does this say than that it is a paradox" (*J. and P.* III, 3073). The paradox is precisely what is discontinuous with human thought.

Several other entries could be cited, but I believe these are sufficient to show both that Kierkegaard's interpretation of Climacus is in line with our own and that he personally shares Climacus' view. The only difference is that at least in his later years Kierkegaard is personally committed to Christianity and thus he has that understanding of the paradox that the "skilled" person possesses, while Climacus is an external observer. It is no doubt this difference that accounts for the fact that in his own authorship Kierkegaard almost never uses the terms "paradox" and "the absurd." There is a type of resolution of the paradox in the life of faith, though not one gained by detached intellectual contemplation. It is a resolution that is made possible by commitment and action. As the individual through the relation to the paradox is herself transformed (as she *becomes* eternal), she naturally comes to see the paradox in a different light. It is for this reason that Kierkegaard says that for the believer the paradox is *not* the absurd (*J.*

and P. I, 8). The paradox remains the paradox, however, even for the believer, since so long as she exists temporally, her transformation is never complete or final. And the believer continues to understand that to the nonbeliever the paradox will be the absurd. The special relation of the believer to the paradox will be discussed more extensively in chapter 12.

9. *The Functions of the Paradox*

One fact that comes through clearly in all of Climacus' discussions of the paradox is that he considers its paradoxicalness an asset to Christianity, not a liability. In other words, though not a Christian himself, Climacus has some friendly advice for those who wish to speak for Christianity. His advice is that the paradoxicalness of Christianity should be emphasized, rather than minimized or, worse, eliminated.

The reason for this is that Climacus sees the paradox as doing a number of useful, in fact vital, services for Christianity. Examining these services or functions gives a good deal of insight as to why Climacus regards paradoxicalness in such a favorable light. There are four main functions, which we shall examine in more detail.

1. *The paradox preserves the transcendent character of Christianity.* Climacus sees that traditional Christianity has always proclaimed that its roots are in a divine revelation rather than general human experience or thought. Beginning with works like Kant's *Religion Within the Limits of Reason Alone,* liberal theologians had argued that the truth of Christianity was essentially discoverable apart from such a revelation, either through reason (Kant) or experience (Schleiermacher). Thus Kant argues that even if Christianity were founded by a special, divine revelation, faith in such a revelation is not essential, since the content of that revelation is accessible to reason.[22] Climacus thinks that if the Christian revelation in Christ is discontinuous with human reason and experience, this loss of transcendence can be prevented. He also thought it was important to do so, since if the content of Christianity is accessible to human reason, then Christianity does not differ essentially from paganism, which also assumed that "the truth is within man." What makes Christianity genuinely different, a true alternative to Greek thought and other religions, is the assumption that man lacks the truth (is a sinner) and that it must therefore be brought to him in a transcendent way.

It is for this reason he claims that anyone who tries to understand Christianity will inevitably distort it. Such a person confuses Christianity with "something which has arisen in the human heart" or with "the Idea of human nature"; he claims "all theology is anthropology" (VII, 505; pp. 513-514). Christianity, on the other hand, since it sees man as sinful, naturally goes against the expectations of human nature. Christianity wants to transform human nature, "to make all things new." "Christianity is not content to be an evolution inside the total determination of human nature, such a proposition is too little to offer God" (VII, 487; p. 496). In a marginal note to this section of the manuscript Kierkegaard added the following explanation: "The incarnation would in such a case have direct analogies in the incarnations of paganism, while the difference is: incarnation as a human invention and incarnation as stemming from God."[23]

2. *The paradox ensures the existential character of Christianity.* Climacus thinks there is an overwhelming temptation to transform Christianity into an intellectual set of doctrines to be assented to, reflected on, or perhaps even doubted. Christianity is an existence communication, however, though this does not, as noted earlier, entail that it has no intellectual content. The fact that this content is paradoxical in form and that it is the limit or boundary to reason should force the individual to see that the proper relation to assume toward it is not that of detached intellectual contemplation but existential commitment. The paradox should, like Kant's antimonies, serve as a "hint" to turn the individual from speculative to more practical issues. For why should the individual spend his time attempting to understand that which he cannot understand but only believe? An earlier draft of the *Postscript* makes the point clearly.

> One can not really assume that the essential eternal truth came into the world because it needed to be explained by a speculator; it goes better to assume that the eternal essential truth has come into the world because men needed it, and the reason why they needed it is certainly not to explain it, so that they could have something to do, but in order to exist in it. (*Papirer,* VI, B, 40-26).[24]

3. *The paradox preserves and strengthens human freedom and selfhood.* Because of the paradox the acceptance of Christianity on the part of the individual must be free acceptance. Becoming a Christian is a choice, and choice requires passion and hence subjectivity. This in part duplicates the second function, since it guarantees that the individual's appropriation of Christianity will be subjective and not merely objective. But there is also something new here; the paradox does not overpower a

person. It leaves her room to accept or reject the truth. This ensures that the subjectivity of the individual is not crushed but expanded when she becomes a Christian. The individual does not become less but more of a person. She can only appropriate the paradox in the passion of faith, but faith as a passion becomes the basis of a new existence, which always is rooted in passion of some kind.

This is expressed by Climacus in many places, but most effectively in the analogy of the fairy tale in which the king loves the peasant maiden, in chapter II of the *Fragments*. How can the king realize their union? Since he loves the maiden, he naturally desires her to grow and become more of a person. If, however, he appears before the woman in all his kingly glory, she will be overawed. It will not suit the king to force the woman to be his, nor even to dazzle her with riches and pleasures. Even if the girl by this means became happy, it would not make the king happy, since he would understand that her happiness was based upon a deception, her ignorance that apart from the king she would have been nothing, humanly speaking. How can the king make the maiden happy by his side? How can he give her "confidence enough never to remember what the king only wished to forget, that he was a king and she had been a humble maiden" (IV, 196; p. 33). Of course everyone knows the way out taken in the fairy tale; the king comes to woo the girl in the disguise of a peasant so as to ensure that she really loved him, that her love is freely given, and that she is aware that her love is freely given. If the girl becomes nothing, if she is overpowered by the king, such a free response is impossible.

Of course Climacus knows that his analogy is an imperfect one, since the difference between a king and a peasant is nothing compared to the difference between God and man. Nevertheless the lesson is clear enough. To make it possible for man freely to choose the truth, the truth came into existence in the form of an individual man. Such an incarnation is necessarily paradoxical, as, in a lesser and relative way, is the appearance of the king in a peasant's form. But it makes possible a free response on man's part.

The difficulty is that on the Christian view man really does owe everything to God. How is it then that:

> "he [the learner] becomes nothing and yet is not destroyed; that he owes him [the Teacher] everything and yet remains confident, that he understands the Truth and yet the Truth makes him free; that he grasps the guilt of his untruth and yet again his confidence is victorious in the Truth" (IV, 198; p. 38).

The answer is that the Truth lovingly stoops to the level of man, sorrowful because this lowliness may be misunderstood and become an offense to mankind, yet lovingly comprehending that there is no other way. If man loved God only when God revealed himself in power and glory, he would love only the power and glory, If a man loves "only the omnipotent miracle-worker" "and not him who humbled himself as your equal," he does not truly love God (IV, 201; pp. 41-42). It is by coming to man in this way that God discloses his character, which is pure selfless love, and thereby discloses to man how different from God he really is.

Climacus goes no further in this direction, but the reader who is interested in this theme would do well to look at the writings of Anti-Climacus in *Practice in Christianity (Training in Christianity)*. In the section entitled "From on High He Will Draw All Men Unto Himself" Anti-Climacus explains how Christ *draws* men to himself but never entices or allures them.[25] It follows that in the process of being drawn to Christ the individual becomes more of a self; his dependence on Christ makes him increasingly independent of his environment by increasing the inwardness or subjectivity that makes possible true action. In an earlier section of the book, "Blessed Is He Who is Not Offended by Me," Anti-Climacus gives a fuller and more concrete account of the concept of offense.[26] The incarnation, as an act of selfless love, precisely reveals God's character. It is for this reason that man, who is fundamentally selfish, cannot understand the act.

4. *The paradox guarantees human equality by reducing the intellectual differences among men to insignificance.* It is an article of faith to Climacus that the essential human task is equally achievable by all. If Christianity were an intellectual doctrine to understand, then those with intellectual gifts would have a decided advantage. Such a state of affairs would be monstrously inhumane and unjust on the part of God. The paradox, however, since it is incomprehensible, instantly collapses the distinction between those with a little more intelligence and education and those with a little less, since the fruit of reflection would only be to understand more profoundly what the simple man understands immediately, that Christianity cannot be comprehended.

> If Speculation explains the Paradox in such a way that it annuls it, and now intellectually knows that it is annulled, knows that the Paradox therefore is not the eternal essential truth's essential relation to an exister in the extremity of existing, but only an accidental relational condition to those with limited heads: then there is an essential difference between the speculator and the

simple, whereby the whole of existence from the bottom up is confused; God is offended by getting a group of hangers-on, a staff of clever heads, and humanity is injured because there is no equal relation to God for all people (VII, 191; pp. 203-204).

Thus the paradox preserves not only God's transcendence but man's humanness as well. For Climacus the paradoxical character of Christianity is a precious asset that Christians should fight to preserve.

[1] See pp. 24-27 for an analysis of Climacus' usage of these terms.

[2] The allusion here is to I Corinthians 2:9, a scriptural passage that Climacus and Kierkegaard frequently quote.

[3] See below, pp. 241, 266-270, for a fuller account of how this happens.

[4] See Kant's discussion of the antimony in *Critique of Practical Reason,* trans. by Lewis White Beck (Indianapolis: Bobbs-Merrill, 1956), p. 111. See also Kant's discussion of the paralogism of pure reason at B421 in *Critique of Pure Reason,* trans. by Norman Kemp Smith (New York: St. Martin's Press, 1965), p. 377, where Kant's point is equally valid for the antimony.

[5] See Hegel's *Philosophy of Nature,* translated by A. V. Miller (Oxford: Clarendon Press, 1970), pp. 17-22.

[6] See pp. 187-189.

[7] See pp. 225-232.

[8] Whether Hegel really rejected the principle of noncontradiction is of course controversial. Many commentators — rightly, in my opinion — argue that Hegel affirmed the principle to be valid but insignificant.

[9] Ludwig Wittgenstein, *Tractatus Logico-Philosophicus* (London: Routledge and Kegan Paul, 1963), p. 3.

[10] *Ibid.,* 6.54, p. 151.

[11] *Ibid.*

[12] *Ibid.,* 6.41, p. 145.

[13] Immanuel Kant, *Critique of Pure Reason,* A307—B364, p. 306; A568—B596, p. 486; A572—B600, p. 488; A575-577 — B603-605, pp. 490-491.

[14] *Ibid.,* A671—B699, p. 550.

[15] *Ibid.,* A426—B454, p. 396; A434—B462, p. 402.

[16] *Critique of Practical Reason,* pp. 111-112.

[17] *Critique of Pure Reason,* B-421, p. 377.

[18] See the discussion above of "truth as subjectivity," pp. 115-135

[19] See pp. 187-189.

[20] David Hume, *An Inquiry Concerning Human Understanding* (Indianapolis: Bobbs-Merrill, 1955), pp. 140-141.

[21] Niels Thulstrup in his note gives the source as Johann Georg Hamann, *Schriften,* ed. by F. Roth, 1821, p. 497. This remark is also found in *J. and P.* II, 1542.

[22] *Religion Within the Limits of Reason Alone,* pp. 122-123; 143-144.

[23] See Niels Thulstrups's "Commentary," vol. II of his edition of the *Afsluttende uvidenskabelig Efterskrift* (Copenhagen: Gyldendal, 1962), pp. 421-422.

[24] This passage is not found in the Hong edition of the *Journals and Papers.*

[25] XII, part II, 137-239; pp. 147-271.

[26] XII, part II, 73-134; pp. 75-144

Chapter XII

TRANSCENDENT RELIGION (2)
FAITH AND HISTORY

1. Introduction

In our lengthy analysis of the incarnation as a paradox we several times stumbled on the second aspect of this central Christian mystery: the believer's relation to the paradox. Not only is the entrance of the eternal into time a paradox; it is also a paradox that this should be the means whereby a temporal human being becomes eternal. The paradox reveals man's absolute unlikeness with God in sin, and then "wants to do away with the absolute unlikeness in absolute likeness" (IV, 214; p. 59).

Here, as in the last section, it is a great mistake to read Climacus as arguing for the truth of Christianity. His whole discussion still takes place within the compass of his hypothesis. In the last section we examined his analysis of the intellectual content of Christianity. It is an empathetic analysis in which Climacus tries to imagine how things look from the believer's standpoint. He therefore in many places speaks as if Christianity were true, and this has reflected itself in our exposition. However, the whole analysis should be read under the inscription, "*If* Christianity is true, this is how things are." Now we shall examine his account of the believer's (and unbeliever's) relation to Christianity. In the course of this Climacus tries to give a description of what might be called the logic of the decision to become a believer. What leads the believer to faith? In so doing Climacus again takes an empathetic point of view and often seems to speak as if Christianity were true. However, he is actually neither praising nor attacking the believer, but trying to describe the believer's situation as clearly as he can. One must always remember that his account of the believer's situation is still written from a detached and therefore nonbelieving standpoint.

It could well be argued that the question we shall address in this chapter is the central one in Climacus' whole authorship, "How can I become a Christian?" Though Climacus is not a believer, that does not preclude a personal interest in the question on his part. In fact, without such a personal interest Climacus' own account implies that he would not be able to understand Christianity (although such a personal interest is by no means equivalent to commitment). Climacus lived in a period like the present one, in which, despite the assumption that "we all are Christians," many believed that it was impossible for an educated, reflective person to be a Christian in the old-fashioned orthodox way. These attitudes were grounded not only in philosophical criticisms of religious belief in general and orthodox Christianity in particular, but also in the historical-critical attacks on the reliability of the Bible which those rational attacks gave birth to. Though Climacus does not argue that Christianity is true, he does show how a reflective Christian *might* respond to those attacks and preserve his faith.

These attacks come to focus for Climacus especially in Lessing's famous remark about the leap required to bridge the gap between the historical uncertainty surrounding the events Christianity is based on and the eternally significant decision that is demanded of the individual: *"Das, das is der garstige breite Graben, über den ich nicht kommen kann, so oft und ernstlich ich auch den sprung versucht habe."*[1] The ditch that must be leaped here really has two elements. There is first a metaphysical ditch. How can a particular historical event purport to be eternally significant for all historical ages? This ditch is simply the discontinuity of the paradox, and it is the root of philosophical criticisms of Christianity. The other element of the ditch is epistemological. How can the certainty of historical knowledge, which is at best probable, be a sufficient basis for a decision that has infinite importance? This is the historical challenge Climacus must analyze.

We have already seen his response to the first ditch and the resultant philosophical criticisms. Since Christianity is essentially a transcendent religion that "did not originate in any human heart" but, on the contrary, sees man as essentially unable to reach the essential truth about himself through natural reason alone, it is quite natural for Christianity to conflict with human speculative viewpoints. The paradox must be the historical event that is discontinuous with human experience and expectations. The surprising thing is that Christians have been bothered by the fact that Christianity contradicts immanent speculation and have even tried to alter their faith to make it more palatable. (This is the heart of Climacus' polemic against modernism and liberalism in theology.) Climacus himself thinks it is therefore necessary to secure Christianity's transcendence by means of the category of the paradox.

The question still remains as to how anyone could accept such a paradox. It would appear that Christianity's paradoxical character, however necessary, would make it difficult to believe it, and this is exactly what Climacus says. This is the root of the second ditch, the epistemological, historical one. How are these difficulties overcome by the believer? The easy answer is "by faith," but though this is Climacus' answer, by itself it does not answer the question, for one needs to know what faith is and how one gets it.

The object of faith for Climacus is the God-man, the entry of the God into history in the form of an individual person. Climacus regards the historicity of the incarnation as absolutely essential. If Jesus' life is merely a collection of stories or myths, or if Jesus is merely a creation of the early church (so that it is considered unimportant whether or not what the early Christians believed is literally true), then Christianity is essentially transformed into its opposite, and no "advance" on Socrates has been made at all. For in such a case Jesus' life would merely represent a possibility that man must be assumed to be able to know. What distinguishes Christianity, according to Climacus, is that man is assumed to really lack the truth, and therefore must acquire it in existence in a genuinely historical relation to the God as he actually appeared. "For the God's presence is not accidental in relation to his teaching, but the essential" (IV, 221-222; p. 68). "But for the disciple the outward figure (not its detail) [of the God-man] is not indifferent. It is what the disciple has seen and handled. . ." (IV, 229; p. 80). The beginning of eternity, though not merely historical, is historical in the ordinary sense. It is "the news of the day" (IV, 223; p. 71). It is the fact that Christianity requires belief that the God has actually come into existence that makes faith necessary (IV, 251; p. 109). On any other assumption we have a return to recollection. "The absolute fact is also an historical fact. Unless we are very careful to insist on this point our entire hypothesis is nullified" (IV, 262; p. 125). It should be clear from all this that Climacus' view of Christianity is utterly removed from that of many contemporary theologians, who say that the factual historicity of the incarnation is insignificant, preferring to talk instead about the meaning these "myths," "stories of faith," or "symbols" have for man today.

This firm insistence on historicity on the part of Climacus may seem embarrassing and old-fashioned. But Climacus is quite well aware that this is embarrassing, since it is precisely this element of Christianity that goes against human expectations by insulting man in denying him the self-sufficiency he thinks he possesses. In any case Climacus is not personally committing himself to the belief that such an event really happened; he is merely analyzing what is genuinely distinctive and therefore interesting about Christianity.

Should someone object that Climacus has no right to define Christianity for us, his reply would be twofold. First, Christianity has historically defined itself this way; Climacus is no theological innovator. He is simply reminding other people and himself of what the simplest catechisms and confessions of faith maintain. Second, he would not wish to get into a foolish quarrel over a name. If someone wants to call some other type of view "Christianity," then the other person ought at least to have the clarity to distinguish by some sort of qualifying adjective that view from the one Climacus is offering. In any case Climacus' view has historically been called Christianity, and it is at least worth considering, even if for no other reason than that it offers a genuine alternative to the Socratic viewpoint. It is a crime to pass off some contemporary "rationalized" version of Christianity as the old-fashioned historical brand, and thereby prevent people from even considering whether they wish to be Christians in the traditional sense.

Of course it must be stressed just as firmly that the faith of the Christian is not merely ordinary historical faith. It is not mere cognitive assent to the proposition that such and such an event really occurred, but a life-commitment to an historical individual. Such a commitment is logically tied to an historical event that claims to be of more than historical interest. Specifically, it is an event that claims to give meaning and value to all of history, and therefore it becomes the locus of eternity to the believer. It is not a "mere" fact, but that fact which to the believer possesses absolute significance.

Someone might here object that since Climacus wishes to talk about historic Christianity, his view is incomplete. The charge in this case is that many essential elements of the Christian faith are left out of Climacus' account, even with respect to the incarnation. He does not mention the resurrection, for example. This objection seems to me to miss the point of what Climacus is attempting to do. He is not a theologian attempting to give a full account of the content of Christian belief, but a thinker who has "abstracted" from Christianity what appears to him to be the decisive kernel that suffices to distinguish Christianity from all immanent religions and systems of thought. He then playfully presents his abstraction in the guise of an hypothesis he has invented. Such an invention could scarcely be supposed to contain the whole of Christian dogma. In any case the element Climacus has abstracted certainly seems to be a key one, since almost every element of Christian belief — be it creation, atonement, sanctification, resurrection, or whatever — focuses around Christ and his divinity. The earliest and simplest Christian creed appears to have been the simple assertion that "Jesus is Lord," so Climacus' abstraction is defensible.

2. Faith and Historical Evidence

On the title page of the *Fragments* Climacus poses three questions:

> Is an historical starting point possible for an eternal consciousness; how can such a starting-point have more than merely historical interest; is it possible to build an eternal happiness upon historical knowledge?

The answer to the first two questions is, "Yes, an historical starting point is possible if the eternal itself has entered history. This starting point could be more than merely of historical interest only if the event is more than a merely historical event."

The answer Climacus gives to the third of these questions is more difficult to discern. Niels Thulstrup, in his introduction to the *Fragments*, suggests that the answer is no, since "one cannot base an eternal happiness upon merely historical knowledge, for it can be based only upon faith."[2] If one takes "to build" (*bygge*) to mean "to logically base," this answer is surely correct, and I think it is the answer Climacus intended his reader to reach. However, such an answer is in another sense misleading, for though Climacus argues that faith cannot be logically grounded in historical knowledge, it is still in one respect built on historical evidence. In others words Climacus' view of the relation between historical knowledge and faith is complex, with both negative and positive aspects. We shall delineate this complexity by first looking at the negative aspects of the relation between faith and history and then at the positive aspects of the relation.

(1) Faith as Not Based on Historical Knowledge

From Climacus' point of view there is no direct or immediate transition from historical knowledge to faith. Despite an insistence on the historicity of the incarnation, Climacus insists equally firmly that the decision whether or not to believe the event really happened is not one for the historian to make scientifically, but one for the individual to make personally. The thrust of his argument is simply that historical knowledge is neither sufficient nor necessary to produce faith.

Climacus tries to show that historical knowledge is not a sufficient condition to produce faith in the individual by making a thought experiment. He has us imagine a contemporary of the God's appearance who zealously secures all possible knowledge about the individual who purports to be the God.

> Suppose there were a contemporary who had even reduced his sleep to a minimum in order to follow about this Teacher, whom he followed more closely than the pilot fish the shark; suppose he kept a hundred spies in his service who secretly watched this Teacher everywhere, and with which he himself conferred each evening, so that he knew the Teacher's movements to the least detail, knew what he had said and where he had been each hour of the day, because his zeal led him to attach importance even to the least trifle — would such a contemporary be the disciple? By no means (IV, 225; p. 74).

It seems that Climacus should really answer "Not necessarily," for though such behavior would be very odd for a disciple, and such a disciple might be an inferior sort of disciple, it is not impossible that he should be a believer. His behavior could even be a misguided expression of his faith, jumping to the conclusion that since Jesus (or whoever the object of faith was) was God, then everything that concerns Jesus must be of infinite importance to him. This would be analogous to those who seek after "fragments of the true cross" or other relics merely because they have some association with Jesus' life. However, Climacus' main point is secure. Historical evidence is certainly not sufficient to make a person a disciple.

One might still think that historical evidence would be a necessary condition for faith, even if insufficient. Climacus rejects this suggestion, too, or at least he suggests that only a very bare minimum of such knowledge might be necessary.

> Suppose there were a contemporary who had been living abroad and only returned home when the Teacher had only a day or two left of his life. If engagements had again prevented him from getting to see the Teacher, so that he was brought into touch with him only at the last moment, when he was about to yield his spirit — would this historical ignorance prevent him from becoming the disciple, when the Moment became for him decisive for eternity? (IV, 225-226; p. 74).

One might object here that even this person is not totally historically ignorant; he has been made aware of the God's actual historical existence. Also, one might think that if such a person did become a disciple, he would try, if possible, to gain more knowledge about the God's earthly life. Climacus might well concede both these points. It is hard to see how the necessity for such a minimum of historical knowledge can be avoided and why the disciple should not seek more if he can obtain it. Climacus' point is merely that the minimum of historical information that is absolutely necessary if faith is to be present is indeed minimal, so minimal that no one living in Christendom could be said to have been prevented from faith by a lack of historical knowledge.

> Even if the contemporary generation had left nothing behind them but these words: "We have believed that in such and such a year the God appeared among us in the humble figure of a servant, has lived and taught among us, and finally died" it would be more than enough. The contemporary generation would have done what was necessary (IV, 266; p. 130).

This statement has been frequently misunderstood. Climacus is not saying that this minimal core is all that is really significant in the biblical record of Christ's life. From the believer's point of view the content of the God's life on earth is tremendously significant, since it is to him a revelation of God's character, and it is also the record of his redemption and reconciliation to God. "But for the disciple the outward figure (not its detail) is not a matter of indifference. It is what the disciple has seen and handled" (IV, 229; p. 80). Climacus is merely saying that from a detached,

philosophical standpoint the "core" of historical knowledge he has cited
appears to be "more than enough" for faith to occur. He consistently
carries through his fiction of merely considering a hypothetical religion he
has "made up." So far as he can see, very little historical information would
be strictly necessary to make faith a real possibility.

He is trying to undercut the insidious view that the decision to become a
Christian is a learned question, in which the individual must await the
results of an interminable scholarly debate among historians. He argues
that from a detached viewpoint one can see that no conceivable result of
the scholarly debate over the historicity of Jesus' life would make faith
impossible, just as no conceivable result would make faith necessary. If
that is the case, the individual who is waiting for a scholarly resolution of
the question is simply evading the choice that she must personally make.

This is essentially the point behind Climacus' discussion of the "Bible
theory" in the *Postscript* as well. He has in mind by the "Bible theory" the
attempt to give a rational basis for faith by trying to demonstrate
objectively that the Bible provides a totally reliable, historical basis for the
faith. His procedure is the same. He first imagines that one has all possible
knowledge of the Bible's reliability.

> I assume, accordingly, that everything that any learned theologian in
> his happiest moment has ever wished to prove about the Bible has
> been successfully proved. These books and no others belong to the
> canon; they are authentic; are complete; their authors are
> trustworthy — one could say it is as if every letter was inspired (one
> cannot say more; for inspiration is an object of faith, is not
> quantitatively dialectical, is not to be reached by adding a sum).
> Furthermore there is no trace of contradiction in the holy books
> (VII, 17; p. 29).

Climacus claims that the result of this idyllic condition would be
insignificant. "Has then a person who did not have faith come a single step
nearer to its acquisition? No, not a single step" (VII, 18; p. 30).

The correctness of this conclusion may not appear so obvious to the
reader as it does to Climacus. It seems to me that all he is entitled to say
here is that from this scholarly result *alone* nothing follows with respect to
faith. We shall attempt to explore the basis of his reasoning later, when we
examine his view of the nature of historical evidence and how conclusions
are reached on the basis of such evidence.[3] But his thesis, that faith does
not result *directly* from scientific inquiry, is clear enough.

Nor of course does unbelief simply result from scientific inquiry:

> I assume the opposite, that the enemies have succeeded in proving what they desire about the Scriptures, with a certainty which goes beyond the most hot-headed wish of the most ill-tempered enemy —what then? Has the enemy thereby abolished Christianity? By no means. Has he harmed the believer? By no means, not in the least. Has he won the right of relieving himself of responsibility for not being a believer? By no means. Because the books are not written by these authors, are not authentic, are not *integri*, are not inspired (though this cannot be disproved, since it is an object of faith), it does not follow that these authors have not existed; and above all, it does not follow that Christ has not existed (VII, 19; p. 31).

Climacus seems to be saying here that *someone* wrote the books of the Bible at least; they represent the testimony of some individuals or groups, and the contemporary individual is still confronted with the challenge as to what he shall make of that witness.

Climacus' view at this point might at a superficial glance appear to conflict with the traditional Protestant view of the Bible as the inspired word of God, which serves as the final and sufficient rule of faith and practice. This is not the case, however. All he wishes to maintain is that the inspiration and authority of the Scriptures are matters that, if accepted, are accepted by faith. Inspiration cannot be either proved or disproved scientifically. The Scriptures cannot therefore provide an objective rational proof for Christianity that would make faith unnecessary, since they are themselves accepted by faith.

Climacus decisively rejects the idea that one can simply appeal to authority in religious matters and thereby evade rational reflection or "dialectics" with respect to belief. "The dialectical does not allow itself to be excluded" (VII, 14n; p. 26n). But the result of such inquiry is not that it is impossible for the believer to accept an authority as inspired. Such an inquiry cannot give a scientific, rational basis for such an authority, but it can lead to an honest recognition that the acceptance of inspiration itself requires an exercise of faith.

It is illuminating to compare Climacus here with evangelical Christians and fundamentalists who continue to uphold the authority of the Bible by maintaining that it is inerrant or infallible. Climacus in no way denies the evangelical the right to accept the Bible as an inspired authority. All that he asks of evangelicals is that they recognize their acceptance of this authority as an act of faith, rather than claiming that the authority of the Bible provides an objective, rational security that makes faith unnecessary. Climacus does seem to differ from some evangelicals on the question of the relation between inerrancy and inspiration. Many evangelicals regard inspiration and inerrancy as linked, even if not identical, while Climacus seems to believe that errant books could nonetheless be inspired.

It is interesting that some leading evangelical thinkers go a long way in the direction of Climacus' view.[4] They are willing to admit that a distinction can be drawn between inspiration and inerrancy and that the former concept does not strictly imply the latter. The most sophisticated defenses of inerrancy do not turn on the claim that inspired books must be inerrant. They make inerrancy a matter of faith as well, in the following fashion. It is not claimed that only an inerrant Bible could be inspired. Rather, it is argued that the Christian believes the Bible is as a matter of fact inerrant. The ground of this conviction is the believer's faith in Christ. The argument here is that the Christ of Scripture who is accepted by the Christian as God, from all that we know of him historically (apart from any assumption of inspiration), accepted the Bible (at least the Old Testament) as infallible. The person who in faith accepts the Christ presented in the Bible as God, and therefore submits to Christ's authority, ought also to accept in faith Christ's view of scriptural authority. On this line of reasoning the acceptance of inerrancy is not an attempt to evade the necessity of faith, but is itself an expression of faith. Regardless of the merits of such a view, it appears to be in principle quite compatible with Climacus' point of view. This is as it should be. As a philosopher Climacus retains a strict neutrality with respect to what the content of faith should be; what he is trying to show is that faith does not follow directly from objective, rational argument.

(2) Faith as Built on Historical Evidence

We have already claimed that Climacus' view of faith's relation to history is complex. Though he insists that faith is not based on historical evidence in the sense that it follow directly or immediately from the evidence as a matter of knowledge, he also says that historical evidence can lead to faith. In that sense one can answer the question on the title page of the *Fragments*, "Can an eternal happiness be built on historical knowledge?" with a "yes" as well as a "no". This positive relation between historical evidence and faith in Climacus' view is often unnoticed, since Climacus, probably for polemical reasons, emphasizes the negative relation. But the positive relation is important, and Climacus admits it, albeit in a somewhat grudging way.

The positive relation of faith to historical evidence is a consequence of Climacus' insistence that the content of Christianity concerns a genuinely historical event. We have encountered this positive relation already in our consideration of the negative relation. In looking at the thesis that historical evidence is not a necessary condition for faith, we found it necessary to weaken the claim to the thesis that only a bare minimum of historical evidence is necessary to faith. Since the object of belief is an actual historical event, it follows that belief in it must be precipitated by some kind of positive challenge or witness. The potential disciple must find out about the God's appearance in some way, through either firsthand observation or historical testimony.

However, the positive relation goes deeper than this need for some kind of minimal historical information. Climacus is aware that the God needs somehow to signal his presence to men. If the God's life simply resembled that of an ordinary man in every respect, no one would   notice his existence at all.

> But the God did not assume the form of a servant to make a mockery of men; hence his purpose cannot be to pass through the world in such a manner that not a single human being got to know it. He will therefore no doubt provide some way of gaining understanding about himself, though every accommodation to provide an understanding does not essentially help the one who does not receive the condition; which is why he [the God] yields to the necessity only unwillingly, and also why such a sign when given is as capable of repelling the learner as of drawing him nearer (IV, 222; p. 69).

It appears to me that Climacus is even more unwilling to admit this fact than the God is to give the sign. His whole polemical bent is directed against those who make faith unnecessary (and impossible) by claiming that Jesus' divinity can be rationally demonstrated. Yet, however grudgingly, he admits that were there nothing historically unusual about Christ, nothing in the historical account that could serve as a clue to the truth by pointing to Jesus' divinity, faith would be impossible as well.

The problem is that in stressing the fact that there is no direct or immediate transition from historical knowledge to faith in Christ, Climacus threatens to sever the link between them completely, in which case faith in Christ appears to be totally arbitrary. Why not believe that my neighbor Sam is God, or any number of millions of people, or even dogs or cats? Strictly speaking, one could not prove that any of them was or was not divine either. This would seem to imply that faith in their divinity is possible. Perhaps it is possible logically, but I do not think it is really. I am not denying, nor would Climacus want to deny, that it is possible to believe that someone other than Jesus is God. But it does seem incredible to say that a person should be able to believe that *anyone* is God. In such a case the person chosen as "god" would be arbitrarily chosen, and the consciousness of this arbitrariness would preclude genuine faith. Anybody claiming to be God who wishes to be believed must have some set of distinguishing characteristics that point toward the truth of his divinity. Such characteristics would be historical evidence in the sense that they support the claims made, though of course whether an individual could *recognize* those characteristics as supportive might depend on her own condition and abilities.

It is quite true that the conclusion that Jesus (or someone else) is God cannot be deduced from an historical account of his life. Faith therefore does not follow directly or immediately from historical evidence. But it is not true that the historical account and the conclusion that Jesus is God are totally logically unrelated either. There must be elements in the historical narrative that point to Jesus' divinity and that therefore help to make faith possible. The historical account and the conclusions the individual draws in faith can be seen to fit or cohere with each other. I personally do not see any justification for Climacus' claim that the God yields to this necessity only unwillingly, though an unwillingness to grant certain kinds of evidence is conceivable. Such "signs" in no way make faith unnecessary or impossible. In fact, it is clear that without such an "accommodation" faith would also be impossible.

What sorts of things could function as "signs" of this sort? Climacus mentions himself the lofty lifestyle of the God, who is sketched as one "who has no possessions and desires none" (IV, 222; p. 69). The God is not concerned about food, shelter, or domestic security, but seeks only "the love of the disciple" (IV, 222; p. 70). Other sorts of signs, which Scripture and the Christian church have traditionally urged, are of course the performance of miracles, the changed lives of those who encountered Jesus, and direct or indirect claims of divinity on Jesus' part. These are all discussed by Climacus' Christian counterpart Anti-Climacus in *Practice in Christianity*.[5] His discussion is in line with that of Climacus. Neither Climacus nor Anti-Climacus denies the necessity of some such things, but they both stress the insufficiency of such historical evidence to produce faith. Their point may be readily conceded here, since no matter how many signs are given, the necessity for faith remains. It is always possible to interpret the evidence in some other way, and the nature of the evidence and what is being evidenced is such that, as Climacus says, the individual may well be repelled rather than attracted. Thus a person may prefer to believe that an historical account is fabricated rather than believe in miracles; or the fact that an account contains miracles may be taken as evidence for its falsity rather than a confirmation of supernatural claims. But it does not seem to me that this destroys the significance of the positive pointers for the person who *does* respond in faith, since without them his faith would be a blind and arbitrary act. The pointers would even be significant to the unbeliever, since they at least make faith a live possibility that he must reject. Without such pointers it is hard to see how the unbeliever could be held responsible for his rejection.

Climacus, in his assessment of the historical witness, admits that this witness plays a positive role. In his account of the "disciple at second hand" he maintains the necessity of such a witness. "The successor believes *by means of* (this expresses the occasional) the testimony of the contemporary by virtue of the condition he himself receives from the God" (IV, 266; p. 131). What this seems to say is that some historical evidence is necessary to make faith possible, though it does not cause faith to become a reality. Thus Climacus can hold on to his thesis that the decisive element that determines whether a person actually becomes a believer does not lie in the evidence but in how the individual views that evidence and responds to it.

Without contradicting this, I think one could go still further on the basis of Climacus' own assertion about the necessity of a sign and maintain not only that *some* kind of historical account is needed to make faith possible, but that a particular kind of historical account is needed to make faith a viable possibility. Perhaps this must be softened somewhat, since I do not deny that God *could* use a very weak or faulty historical witness to produce faith. The normal situation would still seem to be that the historical account that provides the "occasion" for faith is an account that positively witnesses to, and coheres with, the conclusions faith must draw.

I am not sure that this is totally consistent with Climacus' comments on the "bare minimum" of historical witness necessary for faith, however, as well as with his lofty dismissal of the significance of critical battles over the authenticity of Scripture. For although faith might always be logically possible, it does not seem that it would be really possible to a reflective, educated person if, for example, overwhelming evidence were produced that the whole of Christianity were a late invention.

What is of real value in Climacus' view is untouched by this criticism, even if the criticism has merit. For what he has shown is that it is not necessary for the defender of Christianity to prove its truth, nor for its opponents to prove its falsity, in order for a decision to be made by the individual. The decisive factor in one's decision about Christianity is personal and subjective, not scientific and objective. The individual cannot and should not wait for the learned world to resolve the controversies before making a decision, because it can be shown that the matter is not one that can ever be scientifically resolved. I do not think, however, that this implies, as Climacus seems to think, that the individual should be indifferent to the historical evidence that bears on his decision and the learned controversies that surround this evidence. But all the Christian and the non-Christian should hope to get from the scholar in the way of support is an assurance that her decision is based on a credible interpretation of the evidence; she should not look for proof.

It seems to me that the Christian has nothing to fear from this sort of historical-critical inquiry. The authenticity and historicity of the Christian records, though far from indisputable, is also far from indefensible. Thus the Christian does possess a genuine historical witness about which a decision must be made. Though faith is necessary to believe, the Christian may maintain with some right that those who say that the truth of Christianity is impossible are expressing *their* own personal faith, which colors the way they read the evidence. For a truly uncommitted eye it is clear that a great deal of what passes for scientific, critical-historical investigation of the New Testament actually begs the significant questions the individual must decide by assuming that miracles do not or cannot happen, that the notion of a single individual being God is impossible, etc., which in turn implies that the documents must be later inventions, not written by contemporaries. These reactions are exactly what Christianity should expect from human beings, according to Climacus, but they in no way should allow the individual to escape from the necessity for decision by shoving the decision over onto a "neutral" scientific discipline, which actually is shot through with personal commitments.

3. *The Nature of Faith*

So far we have attempted to sketch out the relation between faith and historical evidence, both positively and negatively, in such a way as to show how faith is possible. Now we must attempt to look at the nature of faith and see how faith may become actual according to Climacus' account. Climacus gives a very clear and careful analysis of what he means by faith or belief (*tro*). He distinguishes between faith in the ordinary sense, which is an aspect in all historical knowing, and faith in the "eminent sense," which is the distinctive kind of faith required by Christianity. This latter kind of faith includes within it the ordinary kind, so the analysis of faith in general is significant for Christianity as well.

(1) Faith in the Ordinary Sense

The necessity for faith with respect to historical knowledge stems from the character of historical events. Climacus shares the dominant view of twentieth-century philosophy that no natural events are logically necessary. "Nothing which comes into existence does so by a logical ground, but everything by a cause" (IV, 239; p. 93). The contingency of natural events follows from the fact that they have "come into existence" and therefore have suffered change. What is necessary, on the other hand, cannot change; it necessarily is always what it is (IV, 237; p. 91). If an event is in itself not necessary, it is impossible to demonstrate its necessity. Climacus therefore agrees with Hume that "matters of fact" are not subject to logical demonstration.

What is true of nature in general is even truer of human history. Human existence is "historical in the stricter sense"; in contrast to nature it has a "dialectic with respect to time." What Climacus means here is that it is only human beings who are conscious of themselves as temporal beings. They not only live in time, but their awareness of time is itself a part of their life. In this awareness the "now" comes into being, which provides a distinction between past and future. This is the distinction discussed earlier between time and temporality. The distinction between past, present, and future presupposes a being who is not merely in time, but conscious of time. Such a consciousness makes history in the strict sense possible, since it enables the individual to unify her life. By understanding what she has been (past), she chooses (present) what she shall become (future). In this way her past, present, and future form a unity, and her life becomes a history. The same understanding of purposive action as temporally qualified enables one to view the history of the race as genuine history.

History is doubly contingent because it involves a "coming into existence within a coming into existence." Human beings not only exist as part of nature and thus partake of nature's contingency; they themselves are the authors of free acts, which are therefore doubly contingent. Man as a natural being is endowed not only with actuality but possibilities, and these possibilities add a new difficulty for the knower. This means that the fact that an action is historical doubly entails that it is logically nondemonstrable; it can never be truly regarded as necessary.

It is true that "what has happened has happened and cannot be undone" (IV, 240; p. 95). In one sense the past is therefore unchangeable. But it is a mistake to conclude from this that a past event is necessary, since as a past event it retains its character as having come into existence.

Even if what is past cannot now be changed, it does not follow that the past could not have been different. This fact that a past event is one that could have been otherwise introduces uncertainty, which is a difficulty for the historian. The fact that everything that has come into existence is uncertain means that the apprehension of the historical will always contain an element of wonder. One can always ask, "Why are things like this rather than like that?" and wonder that the world has been the way it has been, just as one wonders how it will be. Thus the historian and the philosopher, to the extent that the philosopher deals with existence, must express this wonder, which is quite in accord with Plato's and Aristotle's dictum that philosophy begins in wonder. To pretend to show the necessity of the actual and thereby remove the wonder, as Climacus claimed Hegel had done, is to falsify the character of the historical.

To this outline of the nature of the historical Climacus adds some epistemological reflections. He follows the majority of classical philosophers in holding that "immediate sensation ... cannot deceive" (IV, 244; p. 100). Error can be avoided if the individual merely restricts himself to what he immediately perceives. When an individual makes an existential judgment, however, such as "this star exists," he goes beyond immediate sensation. *Immediately* he is only aware of the star as present to him, as *there*. (Climacus does not commit himself as to whether such an immediate impression is objective or subjective, but I think he would say that such a distinction is not present in immediate experience, only arising upon reflection.) As soon as the individual make a judgment that the star actually exists as part of the natural order, and therefore that the star has come into existence, he has gone beyond what is immediately sensed, "for the *coming into existence* cannot be sensed immediately, but only the immediate presence" (IV, 244; p. 100). Of course what is true of stars is even more true of the historical.

These remarks provide the key to understanding the nature of historical knowledge, according to Climacus. The uncertainty of the historical demands a mode of knowing that can resolve this uncertainty.

> Now faith[6] has precisely the required character, for in the certainty of faith there is continually present as revoked an uncertainty, which corresponds in every way to the uncertainty of coming into existence. Faith thus believes what it does not see; it does not believe that the star is there, for that it sees, but it believes that the star has come into existence (IV, 245; p. 101).

Like Hume, Climacus argues that the logical uncertainty that pertains to all existential matters, but especially history, is ultimately resolved by belief, though as we shall see, he does not completely share Hume's view of the character and origin of belief.

Climacus' position here is easily misunderstood. He is not denying that beliefs can be supported by evidence or that historians can make investigations to discern the truth. His claim that all historical knowledge requires belief should not be understood as a claim that such judgments are arbitrary. All he is claiming is that when all the evidence is amassed and the investigating is finished, logical doubt is always possible. Uncertainty remains, and this uncertainty must be negated by the individual if he is to come to a decision. Of course, normally the individual is hardly conscious of this uncertainty or his negation of it, since the beliefs he already has rule out certain possibilities. But these already-acquired beliefs are nonetheless commitments.

All of this is illuminated by Climacus' discussion of skepticism. He sees, correctly, that ancient skepticism was grounded in an attitude of the will.

> The Greek skeptic did not deny the validity of sensation or immediate knowledge, but, he says, error has an entirely different ground; it comes from the conclusions that I draw. If I can only refrain from drawing conclusions, I will never be deceived (IV, 246; p. 102).

The Greek skeptic willed to maintain this attitude so as to preserve his peace of mind. The nonskeptic, in a similar way, refuses to doubt and instead wills to believe. This does not imply that everyone should be a skeptic; it simply implies that skepticism is overcome not by logic but by commitment. William James points out that "believe truth" and "shun error" are not identical maxims. The one who seeks truth runs the risk of error; one may, by refraining from all judgment, avoid error — except the error of failing to achieve the truth.[7] The question of skepticism turns on a value judgment. Which do you value most: finding truth or avoiding error? To the skeptic who asks, "How do you know you are not wrong?" the believers (all who are not skeptics) answer, "I don't, but that is the risk one must take, and I am willing to take it."

> When faith resolves to believe it then runs the risk of an error, but it nevertheless believes. There is no other way to believe; if one wishes to avoid risk, it is as if one wanted to know with certainty that he can swim before going into the water (IV, 247n; p. 103n).

From this one can see that with regard to existential knowledge Climacus is in agreement with those contemporary philosophers who have rejected foundationalism, the epistemological theory that knowledge can be developed with absolute certainty from absolutely certain bases. Climacus agrees that knowledge of historical matters is grounded at least in part in personal commitments which cannot be given an objective basis, but which help to provide bases for those judgments we term objective.

What is the nature of this personal commitment, which is of course just another word for faith or belief in "the ordinary sense"? Climacus says that belief is "an act of freedom, an expression of will" (IV, 247; p. 103). This should not be taken as necessarily implying conscious deliberation on the part of the individual, since we have already seen, as in the case of the star, that many beliefs are more or less automatic and spontaneous. Climacus' psychology is sufficiently complex to recognize that individuals are not transparent to themselves and that they are not therefore clearly conscious of all their desires and acts of willing. It is possible for faith to be exercised so immediately and spontaneously that the individual is hardly conscious of having made a choice. This may even be the most frequent state, just as the individual makes many other sorts of choices without thinking about them. Such choices are grounded in part in past choices which have established patterns or habits. In a similar way many choices the individual makes with respect to her beliefs are the results of her established belief patterns.

Such belief patterns, which guide or control new beliefs, I shall call "plausibility structures." An individual is not necessarily aware of her own plausibility structure in its entirety, though she is capable of becoming aware of any part of it, especially if it is challenged by some new claim. The "faith" of most people is embodied in such a plausibility structure, which they are hardly aware of, but even if an individual believes something in a completely spontaneous way, it is still possible for her in retrospect to become aware of the alternatives to her belief, which she therefore discovers herself to have negated. In such a case her belief becomes a conscious choice, as of course may be the case when a belief is first acquired.

If belief is grounded in will, than it is also grounded in passion. We have seen that for Climacus existential choice is not an exercise in arbitrariness but is made possible by valuing, by passion. The sorts of passion that make possible ordinary belief can be very varied in character; nevertheless, belief as a whole can be illuminated by comparing it with its opposite passion, doubt. Climacus does not see doubt and belief as similar cognitive attitudes that differ only in degree of certitude.

> Belief is the opposite of doubt. Belief and doubt are not two types of knowledge, determinable in continuity with one another, for neither of them is an act of knowing; they are opposite passions. Belief is a sense for coming into existence, and doubt is a protest against every conclusion that transcends immediate sensation and immediate knowledge (IV, 248; p. 105).

From this one can see that Climacus agrees with Newman's claim that belief is an all-or-nothing affair that is not a matter of degree.[8] This does not mean that the passion of faith cannot be very different in its quality. It is possible to believe fearfully and for belief to be present in a wavering and intermittent way, mixed with doubt. But belief itself is an action, a resolution of uncertainty. There is a sense in which it is either there or it is not, just as an action is either performed or not performed, though it may be performed in different ways. To the degree that belief is present, the cognitive uncertainty of a situation is resolved. The individual has acted. To the extent that a person *believes* something, what she believes is for her certain. She may be quite aware of how uncertain her belief might appear from an uncommitted stance, but it is precisely that uncertainty which she fought through and resolved in forming her belief. Therefore, the logical inconclusiveness surrounding a belief does not make the believer *qua* believer uncertain (IV, 248; p. 104). To claim that the believer in Jesus, for example, cannot be certain in the light of the fact that there are other possible ways of construing the facts, is to misunderstand the nature of belief by confusing it with cognition. (The person who asks, "How can you believe since ..." is really asking how the belief was formed; he wants an account of how the uncertainty was resolved.)

As we have seen, belief in this sense is a factor in all historical knowledge. Because of this Climacus sometimes speaks as if there were no such thing as historical knowledge, as if faith and knowledge were two mutually exclusive domains. At other times, however, he does speak of historical knowledge. Strictly speaking he is here inconsistent and is using the term "knowledge" in an inconsistent way; this is not without implications, as we shall see, for Climacus' analysis of Christian faith. However, I think one can see why he talks in these two different ways. For Climacus historical knowledge is not knowledge, since it is made possible by a personal commitment or faith. However, there is a thing that is generally called historical knowledge, and Climacus sometimes employs this terminology. We shall examine the relation between faith and knowledge more closely in the final chapter.

In what is generally called historical knowledge, Climacus argues that faith is pervasively present, not only in the final conclusions drawn but all along the way. Faith is present in the sorting of evidence, for example, and most of all in the set of expectations as to what is probable or improbable, possible or impossible, which guides the historian as well as the ordinary person in weighing the evidence. As William James would say, some hypotheses are live and tempting, while others are simply dead. This set of expectations, which I earlier called a plausibility structure, is itself composed in part of beliefs, though attitudes are included as well. As noted before, although these commitments are commitments, the individual is not necessarily completely aware of all of them.

There is nothing distinctively Christian or even religious about such faith; Climacus thinks it is a general human passion. However, the Christian kind of faith, despite its distinctiveness, is also faith in the ordinary sense, since the object of the Christian's faith is genuinely historical (IV, 250; p. 108). Thus everything said about faith in the ordinary sense applies to Christian faith. These epistemological reflections are a kind of front-line defense against the attempt to abolish faith by replacing it with knowledge. In effect Climacus is claiming, "One cannot even dispense with faith with respect to ordinary historical matters. How then is it possible to do so with respect to an event which surpasses human understanding, the God's entrance into time?" Other important characteristics of Christian faith come into view here as well. These include the idea that faith is a decisive passion that gives the individual certainty. It is also important to see that faith does not have to be self-consciously reflective; this helps make intelligible Climacus' claim that it is quite possible for the simple and uneducated person to be a Christian. What is required is faith, not a reflective understanding of faith's nature.

(2) Faith in the Eminent Sense

Faith in the eminent sense is not so much a different kind of faith as it is a special subclass of ordinary faith, since, as we have already seen, eminent faith is also faith in the ordinary sense. Nevertheless, the special kind of faith demanded by Christianity is genuinely unique.

This eminent faith can be briefly defined as the passion that has as its object the historical entrance of the God into history. To believe in this event one must surmount not only the uncertainty that attaches itself to all historical events, but the special difficulties arising from the fact that the historical event in question is one that human reason cannot comprehend. The qualitative difference between God and man, due to sin, is such that man cannot understand how an individual human being could be God or how God could become an individual human being. It is the "strangest of all things," "the most improbable thing imaginable," and is therefore the absolute paradox. Such a paradox goes against the expectations of the human understanding, which in its pride assumes that the absolute truth is an immanent possession and that whatever is beyond human comprehension is nonsense.

This relation between the paradox and reason, which we discussed in the last chapter, can be sharpened, I think, by developing the recently introduced concept of a plausibility structure. All human decisions as to historical beliefs, all historical reflection and weighing of evidence, is done in the context of a network of prior commitments. This enables the individual to judge an event as probable or improbable, evidence as hard or soft. The hardness of the evidence and likelihood of an event are independent factors. Implausible stories require strong and reliable evidence, which often takes the form of trustworthy testimony. Very common and likely events, however, may be accepted on the basis of rather flimsy testimony. Both the probability of an event and the reliability of testimony are evaluated on the basis of a plausibility structure. In a sense all previous beliefs are part of one's plausibility structure. We evaluate new candidates for belief partly on the basis of their consistency with other beliefs. A great deal of evidence would be required to make me give up my belief that Abraham Lincoln was a real person, because giving up that belief would contradict so many other things I believe firmly. But in addition to our other particular beliefs, there are more basic commitments in the plausibility structure, beliefs about what sort of events are likely or unlikely, what sorts of testimony are trustworthy. These basic commitments are not arbitrary; they represent the funded experience of the race, which the individual appropriates in appropriating his specific culture, as well as the individual's own personal experience. Yet these basic "control beliefs" are not in the final analysis rationally demonstrable. It is logically possible for events to contradict our firm expectations. This does not ordinarily prevent us from acting; we assume the sun will rise tomorrow. But it is important to note, as Wittgenstein does, that "the chain of reasons has an end."[9]

We can now restate Climacus' view of the absolute paradox. The plausibility structure of every human being is limited by his own condition and the condition of the race. If, as Christianity says, the race is sinful, then man has no experience of the absolute love that is God's nature, and no understanding therefore of how such a thing as an incarnation is possible. Besides, human beings in their sinfulness have an attitude of prideful self-sufficiency. Therefore the concrete plausibility structure that is actually operative in deciding what is reasonable and unreasonable in every person as he naturally is apart from faith cannot but judge the incarnation as "the most unlikely event imaginable." The event is totally discontinuous with the whole of human experience and contradicts the central attitude that shapes concrete human thinking.

How, then, can such a thing be believed? Climacus says it is only possible by a miracle, the miracle of faith. Faith is not a mere human achievement, since it is, humanly speaking, an impossibility. No individual can achieve the state of faith merely by his own efforts, which is what lies behind Climacus' statement that faith in the eminent sense is not an act of will (IV, 227; p. 77). He does not mean to deny that faith involves a decision, but to assert that the decision is not one a person can make by himself. Climacus says that faith is "the condition" that makes belief possible, and he claims that this condition is a gift to the believer from God.

The individual who is to believe in the incarnation must become a new person. The old sinful self, with its sin-permeated plausibility structure and way of thinking, must be destroyed, and a new self created. We have seen already that for Climacus the self is an achievement made possible by passion. From the Christian point of view man cannot truly become a self by himself; he must allow his old self to die and become a new self through the passion of faith that God makes possible. We can clearly see now why faith in the eminent sense is never merely intellectual. It is a passion that transforms the individual's whole existence. The Christian does indeed believe something; he is committed to the fact of God's entrance into history. But the very nature of this fact is such that it cannot be believed *only* intellectually. It requires not only a change of thought but a radical change of character. As the absolute paradox that clashes with man's natural way of thinking, the incarnation can only be believed by the person who has died and been reborn, the individual who has been gripped by the life-transforming passion of faith. The individual who exists in virtue of this passion that the God has made possible cannot think of going "beyond" faith. For his very existence is made possible by faith. He cannot therefore regard the God's appearance as merely a doctrine to be assented to intellectually; the God is not merely a Socratic teacher who vanishes into insignificance. Rather, the God is the one to whom the individual owes his life. The individual's attitude toward the God must in such a case be that of a disciple, a follower.

Climacus does not, of course, in the run of his experiment explore the details of the process whereby an individual is reborn. As a nonbeliever he could hardly be expected to be familiar with these details. He nevertheless sketches out in an abstract way the sort of change that must take place and how it might occur. The individual is "saved from slavery" and "redeemed from captivity" (IV, 187; p. 21). To make this possible the Teacher must somehow himself make an "atonement," "taking away the wrath which hung over the deservingly guilty" (IV, 187; p. 21). In other words, the transition to the new existence is a liberating transition in which the individual gains the possibility for true action. To gain this liberation the guilt and responsibility that is the result of the individual's sin must be taken care of by God.

The fact that faith cannot be attained merely by intellectual reflection and is never merely the result of historical evidence Climacus sees as a strength. For it places all human beings who are faced with the choice on an equal footing. If Christianity were an intellectual doctrine amenable to rational understanding, more intelligent people would have an advantage. If it were an ordinary historical fact, those with more evidence, contemporary eyewitnesses and so on, would have an advantage. Christianity's paradoxical character erases the differences between the more or less intelligent and between the immediate contemporary of the incarnation and the member of a later generation. The difficulty in gaining faith is the same in every age; every disciple receives the condition from the God in a firsthand way. This is an expression of the deep humanism we have seen in Climacus before, a humanism that demands equality before God for all men.

> Would God establish a covenant with some people in such manner that their covenant with him established a difference between them and all other men which cries to heaven [for justice]? ... Would God permit time the power of deciding to whom he would grant his favor? (IV, 268; p. 134)

Climacus says that on the view he has sketched salvation is "equally difficult for every human being in every time and place," since no person can achieve faith himself, yet it is also "equally easy," since the God grants the condition to everyone who will receive it.

Actually this principle of equality presents Climacus with a grave difficulty. If salvation is really dependent upon an historical revelation, then the equality would not seem to extend to those who have not heard about the historical events because of the time and place of their birth. Indeed, in the *Postscript* Climacus expressly affirms that if Christianity is true, then countless numbers are excluded from blessedness "not by their own fault but by the accident that Christianity has not yet been preached to them" (VII, 508; p. 516). This appears to contradict the view of the *Fragments*.

So far as I can see, Climacus gives no real answer to this contradiction. One can only speculate as to possible responses he could make. He could fall back on a doctrine of election, but that seems inconsistent with the *Fragments* and highly unlikely. More probably he would attempt to dismiss the question as a speculative one with no relevance to an exister who *has* been confronted with Christianity. In other words, he might claim that he is writing only for those who do know about the God's appearance and that people in such a situation have no right to speculate as to how God deals with individuals in a totally different situation. This seems to me to entail, however, that one must admit that the person who has not gained an historical faith in Christ is not *necessarily* excluded from blessedness.

This suggestion actually comports well with Climacus' claim that historical information about the God's appearance is not necessary for faith. He has already gone far in that direction by his insistence that one cannot specify any particular amount of historical information to be necessary to salvation. The man who only encountered Jesus at the last minute of his life could be transformed as well as the man who had exhaustive knowledge of Jesus' life. What Climacus might do is to assert that in the case of an individual who has not heard about the God's historical appearance at all, faith appears in the hope and expectation of God's action. The individual who is existing in the categories of religiousness A and therefore understands his inability to deal with the problem of his guilt might not know *what* God has done, but perhaps he could believe that God has done *something*. The pagan would in this case be analogous to the Old Testament saint whom Christians view as justified by Christ, even though they had no knowledge of Christ's historical appearance. To avoid a reversion to a religion of immanence, this addition to Climacus' view would have to include an assumption that God in some transcendent way reveals himself and his character to the pious individual, thereby imparting the consciousness of sin that makes faith possible. Otherwise faith becomes a merely human act. But this assumption is not an impossible one for Climacus to make, since the Christian believes that this was the case in the Old Testament. The fact that God is supremely active in Christ does not entail that he cannot transcendently reveal himself in other specific ways in history.

4. *Faith and Sin-Consciousness*

We have already asserted that faith is God's gift to man. But if faith is not something that man can achieve on his own, but can only be received from God, can the individual do anything to gain faith? At this point it would be natural, in one sense, for Climacus to opt for a doctrine of election and predestination. From such a perspective man can truly do nothing to gain salvation. It is totally the work of a sovereign God, who elects to give to some individuals the gift of eternal life.

Such a theory of predestination is totally alien to Climacus, however, who continually emphasizes the reality and significance of human choice. Such a mode of salvation would be to Climacus analogous to the mighty king compelling the peasant maiden to become his queen. Such an action would not make the king happy, because he knows that love that is not freely given is not true love. The king wants the maiden to become more of a person by responding to him in freedom. He does not wish to reduce her to nothing by taking away her power of choice altogether. In a similar way Climacus stresses that God in Christ makes salvation possible for all but at the same time he makes it possible for individuals to reject this salvation. It is only in this way that salvation is really possible, because only in this way can man truly become what God intends him to be: a self who has freely chosen God.

How can Climacus say that faith is a gift of God and at the same time allow for the possibility of human choice? The answer lies in a consideration of the consciousness of sin. The individual's natural state is one in which he regards himself as already possessing the truth and regards the paradox as nonsense. If he is to be brought to the point of accepting the paradox, he must somehow be made to realize that he lacks the truth, that his condition is fundamentally one of untruth. If he realized that was his condition, he might well expect the truth to be something that is discontinuous with his experience and that surpasses his ability to comprehend. Such a recognition would be a recognition of the limits of his reason, and we have seen in chapter 11 that such a recognition is both reason's downfall and reason's fulfillment. The consciousness of sin might therefore be described as the condition for the condition, the recognition that makes faith possible for the individual. This is exactly what Climacus says. Sin is "a decisive expression for religious existence .... it is not a moment within something else, within another order of things, but is itself the beginning of the religious order of things" (VII, 227; p. 239).

This conviction that the gateway to Christianity is the consciousness of sin is one of the most pervasive convictions of Kierkegaard as well, to which many *Journal* entries witness.[10] And in the "Moral" of *Practice in Christianity* Anti-Climacus puts it as clearly as possible in answering the question as to how the individual can be brought to the place of faith in Christ:

> 'But when the Christian life is something so terrible and frightful, how in the world can a person get the idea of accepting Christianity?' Quite simply, and, if you want that too, quite in a Lutheran way: only the consciousness of sin can, if I may dare say so, force (from the other side the force is grace) one into this horror. And in that very instant the Christian life transforms itself and is sheer mildness, grace, love, compassion (XII, 64-65; p. 70).

How does the individual acquire the consciousness of sin? At first glance it seems that the individual still has no choice in the matter, since Climacus holds that the consciousness of sin is, like faith, made possible by a revelation. Sin lies outside the boundaries of immanence. This does not mean that man is not previously capable of understanding himself as guilty before God in a decisive way. The decisive element in religiousness A is a realization of such a guilt-consciousness. Climacus distinguishes, however, between guilt-consciousness and sin-consciousness (VII, 509; p. 517). Guilt-consciousness alone cannot propel an individual to faith; only sin-consciousness, which is made possible by the God's entry into time, can do this. When the individual receives a true revelation of God's character, then he fully understands the extent to which he is separated from God. By an encounter with Christ the individual is brought to understand his guilt in a new way, as sin. The difference is not merely quantitative but qualititative. The person who understands himself as guilty still believes he ought to be able to repair the damage himself. The entrance of God into time reveals to the individual his sinfulness, his complete inability to repair the damage, by showing him that he totally lacks the truth.

One might think that a person's inability to overcome his sinfulness would mean that he was not morally responsible for his condition. Climacus argues that this is not necessarily the case. If a choice is a choice in reality and not simply in imagination, it cannot always be undone or its consequences prevented. The individual who made the choice is still responsible for it, however, and for its consequences, despite his inability to remedy them. Aristotle is called in to support this viewpoint:

> "The vicious and the virtuous have not indeed power over their

moral condition, but at first they had the power to become either the one or the other, just as one who throws a stone has power over it until he has thrown it, but not afterwards" (IV, 186-187n; p. 21n).

Man could have chosen bondage or freedom, but having chosen bondage, he cannot undo the choice and free himself. This is the heart of the Christian view.

The consciousness of sin is therefore the condition that makes it possible for the individual to believe in Christ, and we have seen that this consciousness is not attainable by the individual alone:

> If man is to receive any true knowledge about the Unknown [the God] he must get to know that it is different from him, absolutely different from him. The Reason cannot possibly get to know this by itself...It will therefore have to obtain this knowledge from the God,...(IV, 214; p. 57).

Climacus does not, however, veer at this point toward election and predestination. For although a revelation is necessary to make sin-consciousness *possible,* such a revelation by no means makes such a consciousness necessary. The individual must choose to recognize the truth that is offered to him about his condition. Sin-consciousness is therefore something that, though made possible by the God's revelation, the individual must learn for himself. The following passage is extremely important to understand this key point:

> If the Teacher [the God] is to be an occasion by means of which the learner is reminded, he cannot assist the learner to recall that he really knows the Truth; for the learner is in untruth. The Teacher can then become for him the occasion to remember that he is in untruth. But in this consciousness the learner is excluded from the Truth even more decisively than before, when he lived in ignorance that he was in untruth . . . . The learner, in thus being thrust back upon himself, . . . discovers his untruth, with respect to which act of consciousness the Socratic principle holds, that the Teacher is merely an occasion whoever he may be, even if he is a God; for my own untruth is something I can discover only by myself (IV, 184; p. 17).

Climacus adds significantly that this is the only point in his hypothetical alternative (Christianity) that is analogous to the Socratic position, which emphasized man's ability to save himself.

Some have thought that there is an inconsistency in Climacus' thinking here. Can my error be something I must discover by myself and also something I can only know with God's help? It seems to me that these two assertions are quite compatible and that together they explain how salvation can be something man must freely choose and yet at the same time be something man cannot achieve merely by his own efforts. It is quite consistent to hold that only by God's revelation can a person become aware of his true condition, yet at the same time hold that the person may refuse to accept this awareness offered to him by the God. The divine revelation is a necessary but not a sufficient condition for the consciousness of sin to arise. The individual must therefore "learn" this for himself, even though God makes it possible. In that sense the one who teaches me my sinfulness is, with respect to this item, a Socratic teacher who occasions a deeper self-knowledge, "even if such a teacher were the God." This "even" is a typical piece of Climacus' humor, since he argues later that such an awareness is *only* made possible by the God.

From the fact that the individual can himself learn, with God's help, that he is a sinner, it does not follow that the individual can save himself. For what the individual discovers is precisely that he lacks the truth and cannot save himself. In this manner Climacus' account protects both Christianity's transcendence and human freedom. Salvation is completely the work of God, since all that man can discover by his own effort is that he is in error, and even this discovery is made possible by God. Yet the individual's choice to accept or not to accept God's revelation of his sinfulness determines whether he can choose to accept the gift of faith that God offers in Christ.

5. *The Leap*

The actual decision to become a believer Climacus calls "the leap." This expression, taken from Lessing, has been much misunderstood. In popular presentations the Kierkegaardian leap is presented as a "blind leap" or a "leap into the dark," which are expressions that Climacus never uses. The leap is neither blind nor arbitrary, since Climacus insists that the individual must have a clear idea of what he is leaping to (Christianity precisely defined by means of God's transcendent entrance into history) and why he might choose to leap (the consciousness of sin).

The leap is simply Climacus' metaphorical way of emphasizing that the decision to become a Christian is a choice, a free personal decision. Every choice is for Climacus a "leap," a decisive resolution of the self made possible by passion. In dealing with salvation Climacus echoes what Vigilius Haufniensis, the pseudonymous author of *The Concept of Anxiety*, says in dealing with sin, which is that *every* free action contains an element of the mysterious. Psychology can explain the conditions that make an act possible, but one cannot explain the necessity of a free act without abolishing its character as a free act.[11] For that reason one cannot give a definitive explanation of why some people choose to become Christians and others do not, why some people are willing to accept the consciousness of sin and others are not. But this is a general characteristic of free choices. Climacus wants to insist that the choice to become a Christian is always a personal chioce for which the individual is responsible, but he by no means thereby suggests that the choice is arbitrary.

He also makes it clear that ultimately the reasons people do *not* leap are as personal and subjective as the factors that make faith possible. It might appear that Climacus approves of Lessing's horror of the gap between historical evidence and the eternal decision that must be based on that evidence. Actually he is showing that the reasons Lessing did not leap, if indeed he did not, had nothing to do with the historical data but had everything to do with Lessing.

> Perhaps the word *Sprung* [leap] is merely a stylistic phrase, and perhaps this is why the metaphor is expanded for the imagination by adding the predicate *breit* [wide], as if the least leap did not have the characteristic of making the ditch infinitely wide, as if it were not equally difficult for one who cannot leap *at all* whether the chasm is wide or narrow, as if it were not the dialectical passionate abhorrence for the leap which makes the chasm so infinitely wide . . . (VII, 79: p. 90).

The difficulties in becoming a Christian are not rational difficulties pertaining to the integrity of the documents or reliability of the historical accounts. The difficulties are subjective and must therefore be overcome not by objective evidence, but by developing the proper kind of subjectivity.

> Conceding that Christianity is historically true—in case all the historians of the world were to unite in investigating for the sake of attaining certainty—it is still impossible to attain in that way more than an approximation. Historically, there are therefore no objections to make; but the difficulty is a different one; it comes when the subjective passion has to be put together with something historical,

and the task is not to give up the subjective passion (VII, 502; p. 511).

No psychological formula can be given for how one gains the ability to decide to become a Christian, and in any case this decision is not one the individual can will apart from an encounter with the God. However, one can say something about the proper way to prepare oneself to become a Christian, and this is what Climacus has done in the *Postscript.* The proper introduction to becoming a Christian is "deepening oneself in existence" (VII, 488; p. 497). The person who already understands his guilt before God is the person who is ready to be informed that his guilt is really sin. In this way Climacus thinks he has shown that Christianity is an existential communication that the Hegelians have wronged by transforming it into a doctrine to be speculated about. Christianity purports to be the answer to the problems of existence. Whether this is true or false, one can at least say that it can be understood properly only in relation to existence, by one who understands the nature of existence. In this way both the intellectualist perversion of Christianity and the comfortable illusion that people are born Christians in Christendom are exposed.

The relationship between Christian existence and human existence in general is expressed by Climacus in a characteristically paradoxical way: "There is nothing new in Christianity in such a manner that it has not apparently been present in the world before, and yet all is new" (VII, 470; p. 480). By this Climacus means that Christianity is not a mere aesthetic novelty, but the means of existing that proposes to transform and fulfill— paradoxically by negating them—all the universal elements of human existence. Christianity thus presents itself as the fulfillment of the quest for the self, for the truth as subjectivity, which was the major theme of Climacus' analysis of the ethical and religious life. To the Christian the statement that truth is subjectivity resolves itself into the two statements: Man is in untruth, but Christ is the truth. To the person who wishes to become a Christian Climacus therefore recommends an in-depth course in existence. It is precisely when man has pressed existence to the limits, as Climacus thought was done in religiousness A, that the individual is ready for a confrontation with that which surpasses human limitations. In this way the pathos of religiousness A is taken up into Christianity. Christianity is the religious pathos that has been in the world before; it is in that sense the fulfillment of all mankind's religious striving. But it is the old that has become new.

6. Can Faith Be Understood?

There is a curious paradox in Climacus' account of faith. On the one hand he insists that faith is not something that can be understood. On the other hand the whole literature of Climacus seems designed to help us to understand faith. Climacus helps us not only to understand faith in the sense that he shows that it cannot be understood, but to make this "incomprehensible" faith clear. He even, *if* one takes one perspective on what he says, shows that faith appears to have a certain logic or reasonableness about it. That perspective is of course the perspective of faith itself.

One might conclude from this that the incomprehensibility of Christianity is only due to lack of faith and that the presence of faith should make possible a type of understanding of Christianity. This is supported by the consideration that the paradoxicalness of the paradox is due to sin. To the extent that a sinful person is transformed, it would seem that Christianity would no longer appear paradoxical. Of course to the extent that the transformation is incomplete (as it will be in existence), the understanding will only be partial, and the individual will always remember that the God's appearance was to him a paradox prior to, and apart from, the transformation brought about by faith in the paradox. Nevertheless it would seem that Climacus should be willing to admit that the Christian can, as Paul says, at least see now "in part" or "through a glass darkly."

Climacus does in fact seem to say something like this. He considers the question as to whether his hypothesis (Christianity) is understandable by making an analogy with birth. Becoming a Christian is being reborn. Can birth be understood? It depends upon who is trying to understand it.

> The thing of being born, is it thinkable? Yes, why not? But who is it who is supposed to think it, one who is born, or one who is not born? This latter is an absurdity which no one could ever have imagined; . . . The same must also hold in the case of the new birth (IV, 189; pp. 24-25).

Faith is the passion that reconstructs an individual's whole self, and it is reasonable that her thinking would be restructured as well. Her old plausibility structure, with its sinfully informed attitudes and experience, is replaced, at least in a partial and gradual way, by a new one which is informed by the new life that the God gives. This idea that faith is a reconstitution of the person Climacus expresses by calling faith a new or "higher" immediacy, an "immediacy after reflection," which must be distinguished from the older, aesthetic immediacy. There seems no reason to deny that this new life will make possible new ways of thinking as well. Thus Climacus seems to agree with the classical Augustinian position that faith leads to understanding.

Climacus also seems to deny this, however. In many places and in many ways he rejects and even pours contempt on the claim to have achieved a "higher understanding."

> One gives up, as he says, the understanding in order to believe—but then he acquires a higher understanding, such a higher understanding that by virtue of it he comports himself as an incomparably clever seer, etc. But it is always dubious to want to have a profit or apparent profit out of one's religiousness (VII, 492; p. 501).

I do not believe that Climacus means by this polemic to deny that the believer gains a type or kind of understanding through faith, but his polemic shows the need to carefully define the nature of that understanding. A close look at Climacus' polemics against "a higher understanding" shows that he has two targets in mind. The first is those who claim to have gone "beyond faith to understanding." This is the familiar learned perversion of Christianity that we have met countless times before. If we recognize that the new understanding of the Christian is an understanding made possible by the passion of faith, it can easily be seen that the understanding cannot replace the faith without ceasing to exist. Hence Climacus' attack on this "understanding" that is supposed to be superior to faith is consistent with recognizing a type of understanding that faith brings into existence and maintains.

The second target of Climacus' polemic is the "awakened" individual, who in his thinking is actually irrational, but who is always claiming to possess a "higher understanding." This sort of person "who can not make any progress along the narrow path of science and learning and thinking, leaps away and becomes absolutely awakened" (VII, 492; p. 501). It is precisely this sort of irrational leap that many take Climacus' leap to be. Climacus' comments about this sort of position make it very clear that he is no friend of such antics. It is certainly possible for an individual to possess a simple, unreflective faith. But the person who feels the need to think about his faith ought to be unflinchingly honest and exact, according to Climacus. He should be able to present every objection as well as anyone and to reject the easy way out of the awakened individual, who meets every objection by claiming that he possesses some kind of "higher understanding" (VII, 495; p. 504).

Climacus' point, however, is that in the process of thinking through these objections, the believer is confirmed in his faith. For the content of his faith is that which contradicts the understanding (with its distorted plausibility structure) as it naturally is. If his faith were not such that it was the object of offense to the one who lacks faith, then there would be something wrong with it. The believer can understand the objections that will be raised by the unbeliever, since he was himself (and perhaps to some extent still is) an unbeliever. Thus even the individual with faith continues to define his belief as "against the understanding," since he remembers how Christianity appeared to him before he became a believer, and to some extent he still possesses the old type of understanding himself. He is in any case confronted by an unbelieving world that still operates with the natural man's standard of reasonableness. The believer then retains the interpretation of faith that the unbeliever offers as a continually negated possibility. But it is a possibility he rejects with an understanding of why he rejects it.

The problem with the awakened individual is that he wishes to be recognized by the *world* as having a higher understanding, or he complains over his lack of recognition. But such an attitude is impossible for the believer, since he understands that those who lack faith cannot and will not regard his thinking as reasonable. Hence he cannot expect recognition from unbelievers or blame them for failing to extend such recognition. Even if the believer does possess a higher type of understanding, he will not parade it in public or attempt to gain a reputation for cleverness by it. For he knows that what he sees cannot be seen by others, unless of course they also share his faith.

So I conclude that faith should make possible a type of understanding, though still with a certain degree of uneasiness. If Johannes Climacus, polemical soul that he was, could comment on such a notion, he might well denounce it as the sort of "glimpsing" he found ridiculous. I cannot see, however, that he would have good grounds for doing so, since with the qualifications I have made such an understanding seems fully consistent with his basic principles. The key is to distinguish the type of understanding made possible by faith from the type that presumes to make faith unnecessary.

Whatever Climacus would think, I have a feeling that Kierkegaard would agree with this idea. Kierkegaard says that the believer understands that Christianity is to the unbeliever the absurd and can therefore talk quite calmly about Christianity as the absurd, but "at the same time it naturally follows that for the believer it is not the absurd. " (*J. and P.* I, 8).

In another journal entry he says that only those who are competent about a matter can truly make a judgment about it. Those who are "unskilled" may say that something is nonsense, but their judgment makes no difference. With respect to the paradox, however, it is the people who possess faith who are the skilled (*J. and P.* I, 7). This agrees with Anti-Climacus' description of faith in *The Sickness Unto Death* as the healthy passion "which resolves contradictions" (XI, 152; p. 173). But perhaps it is asking too much to expect such an understanding of faith from Johannes Climacus, who understands what Christianity is but not what it is to be a Christian.

[1] "That, that is the nasty, wide ditch, which I cannot cross, however often and earnestly I have attempted the leap."

[2] P. lxxxiii.

[3] See pp. 260-270.

[4] The type of argument that follows can be traced back to B.B. Warfield and beyond. See his *The Inspiration and Authority of the Bible* (Philadelphia: Presbyterian and Reformed Publishing Co., 1948). More contemporary statements can be found in J.I. Packer, *'Fundamentalism' and the Word of God* (London: Inter-Varsity, 1958) and in Clark H. Pinnock, *Biblical Revelation* (Chicago: Moody Press, 1971).

[5] See, for example, XII, 25-27, 90-93, 124-126; pp. 29-31, 96-99, 132-135.

[6] Danish *Troen,* which can be translated "faith" or "belief." In what follows I shall use "faith" and "belief" as synonyms.

[7] William James, "The Will to Believe" in *The Will to Believe and other Essays in Popular Philosophy* (New York: Dover, 1956), p. 18.

[8] See H.H. Price's clear reconstruction of Newman's position as developed in *The Grammar of Assent* in *Belief* (New York, Humanities Press, 1969) pp. 130-156.

[9] Ludwig Wittgenstein, *Philosophical Investigations,* 3rd ed. (New York: Macmillan, 1958), entry 326, p. 106e.

[10] See for example *J. and P.* IV, 4006, 4011, 4012, 4018, 4042, and 4043.

    se *The Concept of Anxiety* (IV, 294; p. 19).

Chapter XIII

CONCLUSIONS:
OBJECTIVITY AND SUBJECTIVITY
IN HUMAN EXISTENCE

1. The Inner and the Outer

One theme that permeates the whole of the Kierkegaardian authorship is "the inner and the outer" or "the subjective and the objective." *Either-Or*, the first of the pseudonymous books, begins with this theme:

> Perhaps at times, dear reader, a little doubt has come up for you about the correctness of the familiar philosophical thesis, that the outward is the inner, and the inner the outward (I, v; p. 3).

In this opening sentence Victor Eremita, the pseudonymous author, takes aim at the Hegelian principle that what is "inward," "subjective," or "spiritual" must express itself in what is "outward," "objective," or "actual." Eremita thinks there often is a discrepancy or incommensurability between these two, and *Either-Or* attempts to show how much more a person's inner life can possess than his outer life may show, both in the aesthetic and ethical realms.

This theme of the outer and the inner or the subjective and the objective is, I think, the dominant theme of Climacus also. His major point is also

281

similar to Eremita's: to highlight the incommensurability of the inner and the outward and emphasize the significance of inwardness. Climacus says his major thesis is that "subjectivity, inwardness is the truth." Whether one looks at Climacus' analysis of the aesthetic life, truth, communication, the ethical life, the religious life, or Christianity, the stress is always on the significance of subjective passion. In the aesthetic life passion embraces and realizes itself in the imagination. Communication must be "indirect" so as to make possible a subjective response from the hearer. The ethical task is not to transform society but to become a self by the cultivation of moral passion. The religious life is a "hidden inwardness" that centers on the passions of suffering and guilt. Christian faith is a personal passion that does not stem from objective historical learning. From Climacus' point of view even scientific and historical thinking, insofar as they concern existence, are rooted in passion.

This seems to me to be a tremendously fruitful and insightful way to think about these areas. What Climacus does is to view every aspect of human existence from the first-person-present perspective—the perspective of an exister. He forcefully calls to our attention the fact that imagining, learning, communicating, morally committing oneself, worshipping, and believing are all personal activities, and that therefore one's ability to carry them out depends upon becoming a true person or self. An individual's personal interests and capacities condition what she can know and how she lives. Therefore the person who ignores the questions "How can I become a self?" and "What kind of self should I become?" is absent-minded and comical, no matter how significant her life may be in an outward respect.

What makes it possible for the individual even to ask these questions is precisely the incommensurability between the subjective and the objective dimensions that Climacus highlights. Climacus sees a human self as more than a product of environment and heredity. The individual's potential for self-consciousness, his grasping of possibilities or awareness of "the eternal," gives his existence a meaning and significance that transcends what the outward observer may detect. The individual has the capability of reflecting upon, and passionately uniting himself with, what is eternally significant. Or, to speak from a Christian perspective, man is offered this potentiality through an historical revelation.

It is interesting to note that the significance of subjectivity was not foreign to Hegel, and Climacus is in some ways unfair to Hegel on this point. Hegel's philosophy contains a full account of the necessity of the individual separating himself from his culture and environment. To become spirit the life of immediacy must be broken, and it is broken by subjective development. The individual is capable of negating the outward environment through his inner consciousness of the eternal. Where then do Climacus and Hegel really differ?

The difference is that while Hegel recognizes the significance of inwardness, it is only as a "transcended moment." To fully realize himself the individual must express his "subjective truth" in an objective way. A good illustration of this is Hegel's moral philosophy. Hegel recognizes that true morality requires the individual to do more than merely "immediately" accept the mores of his society. The moral individual, like Socrates, must subject the practices of his society to the critical scrutiny of his own rational consciousness. In his rational consciousness the individual is "higher" than society. This is the inner personal morality exemplified in a thinker like Kant. However, Hegel says that the eternally valid ideals discovered in this way cannot remain merely personal and subjective. They cannot remain "mere ideals," they must find expression in actuality. This is realized in a social context, so that for Hegel the highest expression of morality becomes the political life man lives in and through the state. Thus the inner personal morality (*Moralität*) is transcended in a social ethic (*Sittlichkeit*).

What does Climacus find objectionable about this? It is not, I think, the fact that Hegel thinks inwardness demands outward expression that offends Climacus. It is the assumption that inwardness can be expressed *exhaustively* and *definitively*. Hegel, like Climacus, sees subjectivity as "negativity." But for Hegel this negativity must be resolved in a higher positivity. What Climacus resists is the final moment in the Hegelian dialectic: the synthesizing or harmonizing moment. Existence is unfinished; hence, as long as an individual exists, he never transcends subjectivity. He must remain "negative," continually negating the established order so as to continue to grow and to make existential advances. The tension between the inner passion and its outward realization must remain. In the final analysis Climacus thinks that Hegel's realization of "objectivity" is of a piece with his claim to provide a system. "System" connotes finality, closure; existence is a constant striving. Therefore existence cannot be a system for an exister. For the same reason subjectivity cannot finally and exhaustively express itself in the outer and social realm for Climacus.

In maintaining this sense of the irreducibility of the individual to "systems," social structures, or even social movements, Climacus fulfills the role ascribed to Kierkegaard in a recent book: the humanistic thinker.[1] This genuinely humanistic thought of "the individual" that permeates all of Kierkegaard's authorship is a permanent protest against collectivism, mass society, and all the other dehumanizing forces that threaten man today. Now and in the foreseeable future the individual's dignity and meaning in the contemporary industrialized world will continue to be under attack.

Therefore, as a protest and as a corrective, this emphasis on subjectivity seems to me to have permanent validity. However, in his protest against the claim that subjectivity can exhaustively and definitively express itself in objectivity, Climacus tends to forget or suppress something that is true in the Hegelian perspective, something that he could recognize and does at times recognize without compromising his basic insights: Subjectivity demands outward expression. This tendency to minimize the objective expression of subjectivity seems to me to permeate almost the whole of Climacus' discussion. In maintaining that inwardness cannot be expressed *finally* in outwardness one must remember that true inwardness does strive for outward expression. The "hidden inwardness" that makes absolutely no outward difference in a person's life is a false inwardness. This is something that Kierkegaard himself came to see. In some of his later writings he pours contempt on Climacus' concept of "hidden inwardness."[2]

It is quite true, I think, that "becoming a self" is man's highest task.[3] Hence the primary achievement a person can have is the acquisition of subjectivity, for it is subjectivity that makes possible family life, political and social life, art, and science. The right kind of subjectivity is the key to the betterment of all these facts of life. What Climacus fails to see, or at least fails to give sufficient notice to, is that even though subjectivity is not reducible to these outer "relative" activities, it is only recognizable through these outer expressions. Genuine subjectivity demands this expression precisely because man's inner and outer life are not two separate regions. The human self is a unity, and when the self acts in relation to its social context, its actions are permeated by inwardness. Inwardness is in turn influenced by, and is acquired in the context of, these outer relations. The relation between subjectivity and objectivity is more "dialectical" than Climacus suggests.

Such a comment as this would hardly bother Climacus. As a humorist he writes for his own reasons and may well be quite content to be a one-sided "corrective." But it seems to me he could learn something on this point if he wished from his creator, Kierkegaard. In the first chapter of *Works of Love* Kierkegaard strikes exactly the right balance between subjectivity and objectivity in his title: "Love's Hidden Life and Its Recognizability by Its Fruits." Love, a subjective passion, has a hidden life and a hidden source, ultimately God himself. Love itself cannot be directly perceived; it must be believed in (IX, 19; p. 32). But true love demands expression, and hence love can be recognized through action in "the works of love" (IX, 14; p. 28). It is true than an incommensurability between the inner and the outer remains. Thus works of charity can be performed in an unloving way, and acts that appear outwardly to be unloving can be a true expression of love. And no merely human outward act is a perfect expression of love. The tension between the inner and the outer remains as long as one is in existence. But genuine love nevertheless demands outward expression.

I am not sure Kierkegaard himself fully appreciated the implications of this. In *Works of Love* he stresses that Christian love is "neighbor love," which is rooted in the command to regard every human being as equally lovable in that he is equally God's creature. Kierkegaard notes that outward social inequalities, in which rank, prestige, and money are the key factors, make this difficult. It is natural to give more attention, respect, and concern to the rich and powerful, less to the poor and the dirty. Kierkegaard says that the true Christian response to this situation is inwardly to rise above these worldly differences. The Christian is *not* to seek their abolition, but he is to regard them as temptations that seek to make him unloving and that he must "rise above" (IX, 73; pp. 82-83). The latter seems true enough, but the former does not seem to me fully to recognize the implications of the principle that love expresses itself in *works* of love. If man's outer social conditions are such that love is hampered or destroyed and my neighbor is tempted to becoming unloving, what could be more loving than to seek to change those conditions? Of course these changes must also be sought in a loving manner, and of course they will not succeed perfectly. There will always exist worldly differences that the Christian must rise above. But that does not remove the obligation to seek change where it is possible.

This point is expressed to some extent by Kierkegaard in the final phase of his life, the attack on the established church and "Christendom." There Kierkegaard seems to recognize that inwardness demands outward expression. His own attack was such an outer "deed," and in the attack he emphasizes the significance of such Christian ideas as voluntary poverty and even celibacy. He also gives prominent attention to the impact on the church's spiritual character of its social position as an arm of the state. Even here, however, Kierkegaard seems to fail to grasp the possibility of a positive expression for inwardness in man's outer life. His attack was totally negative; he accused the church of Denmark of criminally falsifying Christianity, and he challenged his contemporaries to stop their participation in public worship. However, he refused to consider any possible action to reform or remedy the evils he saw. He even refused to meet with those interested in such action.

Johannes Climacus' failure to emphasize the need for an outer expression of subjectivity can be clearly seen with respect to the issue of baptism, an interesting subject even if not especially important to non-Christians. The Danish church, being Lutheran, practiced and continues to practice infant baptism. Climacus thought that this practice, at least as it was currently understood, lay at the root of the illusion of "Christendom." Becoming a Christian, which Climacus saw as an act of boldness and courage that presupposed a mature understanding of existence, was something accomplished at the age of fourteen days; the new birth was confused with birth. This changed Christianity from a strenuous existential achievement to something that happened more or less automatically. One would think that Climacus would oppose such a practice, or at the very least that he would oppose the current theological understanding of baptism as the entrance into Christianity. Surprisingly, however, this is not the case. Though he says that baptism without an act of personal appropriation on the part of the individual is merely an expression of the possibility that the individual will become a Christian (and the nonbaptized child brought up Christianly has the same possibility) (VII, 523; p. 532), he does not call for any change in current customs.

The justification he gives is a rather strange one. In part he says that baptism is justified as a pious gesture on the part of parents. But his main argument rests on the claim that infant baptism makes it *harder* to become a Christian (VII, 331; p. 341). The reasoning behind this is that a person baptized as an infant naturally assumes he is a Christian. To really become a Christian he therefore must first dispel this illusion. *"Therefore it is easier to become a Christian when I am not a Christian, than to become a Christian when I am one already"* (VII, 317; p. 327). Since Climacus wants to show how difficult it is to become a Christian, he is for anything that increases the difficulty! It is hard not to feel at this point that Climacus the humorist is pulling the reader's leg.

In a more serious vein Climacus says that infant baptism is defensible because it makes the decision to become a Christian a purely inward one, with no external sign to mark the transition. This is good because inwardness and outwardness are said to vary conversely: "The less outwardness, the more inwardness, when it [the inwardness] is truly there" (VII, 331; p. 341). For the same reasons Climacus seems to feel that love that remains hidden and inward is superior to love that is outwardly expressed (VII, 359; p. 370). This principle seems to me to be simply false. Man's inner consciousness is not an atom that can be isolated from his outward activities. It is precisely the source of those activities. It is impossible to see them as divorced, as Climacus seems to at this point.

I should like to briefly look at the implications of this divorce of subjectivity and objectivity for three of Climacus' analyses of existence-forms. These are, respectively, the ethical life, the natural religious life, and the Christian life of faith.

2. The Ethical Life

We analyzed Climacus' ethic as a soul-making ethic and contrasted it with a society-transforming ethic. At that time we argued strenuously that Climacus' thesis that the primary ethical task is soul-making, or becoming a self, did not preclude a concern for outward action to alleviate human suffering and misery. It seems to me that when the connection between the inner and the outer is conceived properly, one must say more than that soul-making is not inconsistent with such outer action. The task of becoming a self demands such action, since true inwardness demands expression in action and is actually formed in the process of trying to express itself while understanding its failure to do so fully or perfectly. Though Climacus has rightly seen that the self is not a collection of social functions, the concrete self is a social being who participates in a multitude of social relations. Insofar as one becomes a self in truth, these relations cannot help but be affected. There is a kernel of truth in the criticism, which is usually made in a facile way that shows no understanding of Climacus' view, that Climacus' concept of the self is too individualistic. Being involved with others does not have to be a retreat into the crowd; it is an essential part of the ethical task itself.

3. The Natural Religious Life

In analyzing the religious life we saw that for Climacus the formula that defines the religious life is "To maintain an absolute relation to the absolute and a relative relation to the relative." With this formula I have no complaint. What I find difficult to accept is the way Climacus conceives the relation between the absolute and the relative. Climacus seems to see this relation only in negative terms; one must resign the relative for the sake of the absolute. This is a vital reminder if the absolute is to be truly absolute. However, Climacus does not consider how an absolute commitment that includes this willingness to resign the relative might nevertheless positively affect one's relative commitments.

To be fair one must admit that Climacus does say that the absolute commitment does express itself in the relative ends. However, this expression is in no way distinctive. Climacus does allow for a "double-movement," such as is envisioned in *Fear and Trembling* and *Repetition*. That is, the religious individual, having learned that he can do nothing without God, does go on to learn that with God he can do something. But the "something" the individual does with God seems in no way a distinctive or particular kind of "something." The individual's religiousness remains a "hidden inwardness" that does not betray itself by any outward sign except the individual's humoristic awareness of his deficiencies, which is another negative manifestation of subjectivity. The individual's hidden inwardness is an invisible reality (VII, 412; p. 424). When Climacus tries to think of a possible outward expression, he considers only the cloister, which is criticized only on the grounds that it is an attempt at displaying one's religiousness in an outward fashion (VII, 359; p. 370).

There is, curiously, one exception to this. In a note Climacus admits that though the religious man "appears to be like everyone else," this must not be understood as implying that he could be a "thief or a robber" (VII, 434n; pp. 446-447n). Why is this so unless the absolute commitment does express itself in a particular way in the relative circumstances of life? If the absolute commitment can make a difference in the way an individual lives his outward life, it surely would not be limited merely to making the religious individual a law-abiding citizen. Why would such a commitment, grounded as it is in guilt and repentance, not express itself in renewed moral striving?

Climacus would rightly insist at this point that even an exceptionally loving and self-sacrificing lifestyle will still fail to be a definitive expression of the truly religious individual's passion. The individual's actions would still fall short of the ideal, thus making it necessary to return to suffering and guilt as the decisive expressions of religiousness. But if this guilt is rightly apprehended in repentance, should it not continually make a difference in the individual's outer life? It is true that such outer actions can always be imitated by someone who wishes to appear to be religious but lacks true inwardness. But what concern is that to the religious individual? All that this entails is that the expression of religiousness in action is never final and definitive. Consequently the *recognition* of inwardness in action is never direct, but always requires faith. Even the saintliest life is most saintly when it is accompanied by a humoristic modesty and a continual understanding of guilt and the need for renewed repentance. Hence no one can be sure as to who is a saint. But it seems to me that the quality of life in society today is not so great that a truly religious individual who is striving to express an absolute commitment would outwardly "look like everybody else" in her relative life. Her outward life may fail to perfectly express her inward commitment, but that outer expression is nevertheless significant to her as a test of the genuineness of her subjectivity.

4. Christian Existence

Within the sphere of Christian existence the relation between subjectivity and objectivity appears in several different contexts. It can be seen in the relation between the intellectual content of Christian faith and its existential realization in action. It also comes to the fore in the relation between the objective historical account of the incarnation, which occasions faith, and the subjective passion of faith itself. In both of these contexts Climacus has made an energetic attempt to argue that it is subjectivity that is decisive. Though the objective dimension is not eliminated, its significance is reduced almost to the vanishing point.

Climacus asserts that Christianity is "subjectivity," an "existence-communication." He does not wish to allow the question of what Christianity is to become a learned question, dependent upon the results of scholarly inquiry into historical documents. Yet he himself admits that it is possible and even necessary to ask what Christianity is in an objective manner. But, as Climacus sees perfectly clearly, Christianity is an historical religion, and it is difficult to see how one can ask what Christianity is without paying attention to its objective manifestations in history.

It seems to me that Climacus himself gives the key to resolving this problem. The key is recognizing that subjectivity and objectivity are not distinct realms of being. There is no such thing as "pure" objectivity. Subjectivity always demands objective content and expression. Subjectivity inter-penetrates objectivity. In order for the individual to objectively determine what Christianity is without making the question an infinitely prolonged, learned one, his objectivity must be permeated by the right kind of subjectivity. The question as to what Christianity is must be asked by "one who in the direction of existence and in the interest of existing asks about it" (VII, 323; p. 333). When a person asks about Christianity from this perspective, the issues are transformed from learned questions, which presume the individual has an infinite amount of time and leisure, to existential questions. The individual's subjective passion will enable him to overcome the logical uncertainties and arrive at personal certainty. But this passion of the individual is still directed towards an objective content.

Climacus makes an energetic and provocative attempt to distinguish

Christian subjectivity—faith—from all other kinds of subjectivity, without reference to objective content. He therefore criticizes those who say that "only a certain kind of appropriation of the Christian teaching makes one a Christian," because the appropriation in this case must still mention the content of the teaching to distinguish itself from other kinds of inwardness. He wants the inwardness to be in itself distinguishable from any other kind (VII, 530; p. 538).

However, he himself says that this inwardness demands a certain content; its object is the absolute paradox of the incarnation. And I do not think that he himself has succeeded in describing that inwardness without mentioning the content. If subjective passions are intentional, in the phenomenologist's sense of always focusing on some objective content, then form and content, subject and object, cannot ultimately be identified apart from each other. One cannot describe the inwardness without mentioning the content, which is a teaching after all, even though a teaching of a different sort than certain others, a teaching that essentially concerns existence. If it is true that Christian subjectivity is so distinctive as to require a distinctive content, it is equally true that the content of Christianity is so distinctive as to require a distinctive sort of subjectivity. The strength of Climacus' account is not the minimizing of objective content, but the insight that the decisive factor in appropriating that content is subjective.

A similar point could be made about the role of historical evidence in producing faith. I agree with Climacus' argument that the decisive factor in the decision to become a Christian is the quality and nature of the individual's subjectivity. No historical evidence or argument could establish that Christ was living in such a way as to preclude any logical uncertainty. Yet it seems to me bizarre to maintain that the believer or potential believer has no concern for the quality of the testimony he is considering or believing.

How can he consider the objective evidence without making the decision an objective, learned one, which can never be finally resolved? The answer is the same as to the question about what Christianity objectively is. It lies in again seeing objectivity and subjectivity, not as mutually discrete realms, but as inter-penetrating. It is the believer's concern for an eternal happiness and consciousness of sin that allows him to draw conclusions that are for him certain.

What must be emphasized at this point is that the believer's procedure does not entail that his resolutions are intellectually dishonest. If Climacus is right in his analysis of existence and existential knowledge, all such resolutions are ultimately dependent on the quality and nature of the individual's passion, the nonbeliever's as well as the believer's. And since the questions concern existence, the individual does not have the luxury of suspending judgment. Logically, doubt is always possible or even rationally defensible. Logical uncertainties do get themselves resolved through a personal framework that is brought to bear on the data. This does not mean that the individual cannot honestly attempt to respect the data. But it does mean that the "neutral" scholarly route to the resolution of these questions is an illusion. For example, it seems to me that a great many of the conclusions reached by biblical and religious scholars concerning the records that are Christianity's foundation, both positive conclusions as well as negative ones, are shot through with personal commitments. This is only harmful when those conclusions are passed off as "objective results," which the individual can without further ado appropriate, instead of being recognized as rooted in faith.

Climacus sees that the historical evidence for Christianity is perfectly adequate—to the person who approaches it with the right sort of personal concern. But it seems to me that he is wrong in implying that the believer will be indifferent to that evidence. The believer is not indifferent to doubts over the historicity of her faith, but she resolves those doubts with the help of the subjective perspective from which she evaluates the evidence. From that perspective, however, she can exercise an honest concern for truth. She knows that evidence is not infinitely pliable; it has a "hardness" to it that demands respect. But the believer is in fact confident that her subjectivity provides the key that enables her to interpret the evidence properly without undue twisting or distortion.

In the final analysis this point about the interpenetration of subjectivity and objectivity does not seem to me to be antithetical to Climacus' thought. It is rather a consistent carrying through of his own principle that every aspect of human existence is an expression of passion. If Climacus is right, then this is a thought that the reader would profit from pursuing— with true passion.

My primary purpose in this book has not been to pass professorial judgments about where Climacus is right and where he should be corrected. It has rather been to help the reader understand a significant section of the Kierkegaardian authorship. In any case, if Climacus is right, the conclusions an individual will draw about his books will largely depend upon what kind of individual he is. The quality of passion that informs a person's life, be it aesthetic, ethical, religious, or Christian passion, will shape the way he reads. It is of course possible that Climacus' authorship will serve as the occasion for the transformation of the individual's passion by increasing his self-understanding. My concluding hope is that the reader will be challenged to continue his own thinking and wrestling; I have certainly not tried to make the reader a "parroter" or "rote-reciter," to use some of Climacus' favorite terms, either of myself or of Climacus. And I cannot resist the further hope that some of this thinking and wrestling, permeated by the right kind of passion, will bear fruit, not merely in a clearer understanding of Kierkegaard, but in a clearer understanding of the individual's own life.

[1] See Johannes Sløk, *Kierkegaard: Humanismen's Tænker* (Copenhagen, Hans Reitzel, 1978).

[2] The Christian pseudonym Anti-Climacus attacks "hidden inwardness" in *Practice in Christianity* (XII, 85, 196-202; pp. 90, 209-215). The articles in *The Fatherland* and *The Instant (Attack upon Christendom)* make it plain that in his last period Kierkegaard was committed to the idea that Christianity requires public confession and actions.

[3] This is a formal statement like "The primary intellectual task is to gain truth," which must of course be filled in with material content. Thus it is not inconsistent with the Christian's claim that man's highest task is to glorify God. This would be the material Christian concept of what it means for a human being to be a true self.

SELECTED BIBLIOGRAPHY

The following is a list of books that deal either with Kierkegaard or with related issues and are referred to at some point in the text; it includes the English edition of those works of Kierkegaard that are cited. The latter are listed for the convenience of the reader who only has access to these editions or is familiar with them. However, the reader should note that these editions are being superseded by volumes of *Kierkegaard's Writings* as they appear from Princeton University Press. These new translations carry in the margins the pagination of the first Danish edition of Kierkegaard's *Collected Works*. Since I also cite that Danish edition, readers should have no trouble locating passages.

This list is not an attempt at a bibliography on Kierkegaard. A fairly complete multilanguage bibliography of works prior to 1956 can be found in Jens Himmelstrup, *Søren Kierkegaard: International Bibliografi* (Copenhagen: Nyt Nordisk Forlag, 1962). An English bibliography that supplements Himmelstrup for some works prior to 1956 and then brings it up to 1970 can be found at the end of Josiah Thompson, ed., *Kierkegaard* (Garden City, N.Y.: Doubleday, 1972).

OLDER ENGLISH EDITIONS OF BOOKS
BY KIERKEGAARD

Attack Upon "Christendom," trans. by Walter Lowrie (Princeton: Princeton University Press,. 1968).

Christian Discourses, trans. by Walter Lowrie (Princeton: Princeton University Press, 1971).

Concluding Unscientific Postscript, trans. by David F. Swenson and Walter Lowrie (Princeton: Princeton University Press, 1968).

The Concept of Dread [*The Concept of Anxiety*], trans. by Walter Lowrie (Princeton: Princeton University Press, 1969).

Edifying Discourses, 2 vols., trans. by David F. Swenson and Lillian Marvin Swenson (Minneapolis: Augsburg Publishing House, 1962).

Either/Or, vol. I, trans. by David F. Swenson and Lillian Marvin Swenson (Princeton: Princeton University Press, 1971).

Either/Or, vol. II, trans. by Walter Lowrie (Princeton: Princeton University Press, 1974).

Fear and Trembling [with *The Sickness Unto Death*], trans. by Walter Lowrie (Princeton: Princeton University Press, 1973).

Johannes Climacus or *De Omnibus Dubitandum Est,* trans. by T. H. Croxall (Stanford: Stanford University Press, 1958).

Philosophical Fragments, trans. by David F. Swenson, rev. by Howard Hong (Princeton: Princeton University Press, 1974).

The Point of View for My Work as an Author: A Report to History, trans. by Walter Lowrie (New York: Harper & Row, 1962).

Purity of Heart Is to Will One Thing, trans. by Douglas V. Steere (New York, Harper & Row, 1956).

Repetition, trans. by Walter Lowrie (New York: Harper & Row, 1964).

The Sickness Unto Death [with *Fear and Trembling*], trans. by Walter Lowrie (Princeton: Princeton University Press, 1973).

Stages on Life's Way, trans. by Walter Lowrie (New York: Schocken Books, 1969).

Training in Christianity [Practice in Christianity], trans. by Walter Lowrie (Princeton: Princeton University Press, 1971).

Works of Love, trans. by Howard and Edna Hong (New York: Harper & Row, 1964).

OTHER BOOKS

Albert Camus, *The Myth of Sisyphus and Other Essays* (New York: Alfred Knopf, 1955).

John Dewey, *The Quest for Certainty* (New York: G. P. Putnam's Sons, 1929).

Ludwig Feuerbach, *The Essence of Christianity* (New York: Harper & Row, 1957).

Viktor Frankl, *Man's Search for Meaning* (New York: Washington Square Press, 1963).

G. W. F. Hegel, *G. W. F. Hegel on Art, Religion, and Philosophy,* ed. by J. Glenn Gray (New York: Harper & Row, 1970).

———, *Phenomenology of Spirit,* trans. by A. V. Miller (Oxford: Oxford University Press, 1977).

———, *Philosophy of Nature,* trans. by A. V. Miller (Oxford: Clarendon Press, 1970).

David Hume, *An Inquiry Concerning Human Understanding* (Indianapolis: Bobbs-Merrill, 1955).

William James, *The Will to Believe and Other Essays in Popular Philosophy* (New York: Dover Publications, 1956).

W. T. Jones, *Kant to Wittgenstein and Sartre,* 2nd ed. (New York: Harcourt, Brace, 1969).

Immanuel Kant, *Critique of Practical Reason,* trans. by Lewis White Beck, (Indianapolis: Bobbs-Merrill, 1956).

————, *Critique of Pure Reason,* trans. by Norman Kemp Smith (New York: St. Martin's Press, 1965).

————, *Groundwork of the Metaphysic of Morals,* trans. by H. J. Paton (New York: Harper & Row, 1964).

————, *Religion Within the Limits of Reason Alone,* trans. by Theodore M. Greene and Hoyt H. Hudson (New York: Harper & Row, 1960).

C. S. Lewis, *The Abolition of Man* (New York: Macmillan, 1947)

————, *The Last Battle* (New York: Macmillan, 1970).

Louis Mackey, *Kierkegaard: A Kind of Poet* (Philadelphia: University of Pennsylvania Press, 1971).

Gregor Malantschuk, *Kierkegaard's Thought* (Princeton: Princeton University Press, 1971).

George Mavrodes, *Belief in God* (New York: Random House, 1970).

H. P. Owen, *The Moral Argument for Christian Theism* (London: Allen and Unwin, 1965).

J. I. Packer, *'Fundamentalism' and the Word of God* (London: Inter-Varsity, 1958).

H. J. Paton, *The Modern Predicament* (London: Allen and Unwin; New York: Macmillan, 1955).

Clark H. Pinnock, *Biblical Revelation* (Chicago: Moody Press, 1971).

H. H. Price, *Belief* (New York: Humanities Press, 1969).

Bertrand Russell, *The Problems of Philosophy* (Oxford: Oxford University Press, 1946).

Jean-Paul Sartre, *Existentialism and Human Emotions* (New York: Philosophical Library, 1957).

Adam Schaff, *Marxism and the Human Individual* (New York: McGraw-Hill, 1970).

Johannes Sløk, *Kierkegaard--Humanismens Tænker* (Copenhagen: Hans Reitzel, 1978).

David F. Strauss, *The Life of Jesus, Critically Examined,* ed. by Peter Hodgson, trans. by George Eliot (Philadelphia: Fortress Press, 1973).

Mark Taylor, *Kierkegaard's Pseudonymous Authorship: A Study of Time and the Self* (Princeton: Princeton University Press, 1975).

Josiah Thompson, *Kierkegaard* (New York: Alfred Knopf, 1973).

Niels Thulstrup, *Afsluttende uvidenskabelig Efterskrift* (Copenhagen: Gyldendal, 1962).

Robert Tucker, ed., *The Marx-Engels Reader* (New York: W. W. Norton, 1978).

B. B. Warfield, *The Inspiration and Authority of the Bible* (Philadelphia: Presbyterian and Reformed Publishing Co., 1948).

Ludwig Wittgenstein, *Philosophical Investigations,* 3rd ed. (New York: Macmillan, 1958).

———, *Tractatus Logico-Philosophicus* (London: Routledge and Kegan Paul, 1963).

Nicholas Wolterstorff, *Reason Within the Bounds of Religion,* (Grand Rapids: Wm. B. Eerdmans, 1976).

INDEX

Terms which occur pervasively, such as "ethical" and "religious," have generally been omitted. Please consult the detailed Table of Contents for further help.

S

T

U

WESTMAR COLLEGE LIBRARY